I want to commend both a person and a book to you. First, Phil Newton is a pastor whose ministry I have long respected and a brother whose company I have always enjoyed. And he is still pouring himself into pastors and churches. He is a humble, godly, gifted, steady, servant of the Lord, deserving of the tribute that his books give to his faithful labors. Second, the book itself, *Fulfill Your Ministry: Essays in Honor of Phil A. Newton,* provides pastors, those preparing to be pastors, and church members alike an edifying outline of what the minister and the ministry should be. Each of its chapters supplies enriching truth for reflection and encouragement to those who are, or aspire to be, ministers of the Word, as well as to those who labor alongside them, support them, and sit under their ministry. I am thankful for God's servant Phil Newton, and thankful for this book, which is meant to acknowledge him, and to help those who pastor and preach in the churches.

Ligon Duncan, BA, MDiv, MA, PhD (Edin)
Chancellor and CEO, Reformed Theological Seminary
John E. Richards Professor of Systematic and Historical Theology
A Mind for Truth. A Heart for God®

In a world where too often we hear stories of evangelical leaders who have faltered, fallen, and failed; I am so grateful to commend a book in honor of a dear brother, Phil Newton. Dr. Newton is a godly, humble, gifted, wise, kind, Christian gentleman and pastor. This book so helpfully highlights the sort of commitments, ministry, and priorities that should drive the Under-shepherds of God's church. In addition, this book rightly honors a man who has a track record of faithful ministry for decades. We need models like that just like young Timothy had in the Apostle Paul. We need men who are closer every day to finishing well saying to us, "I have fought the good fight, I have finished the race,

I have kept the faith" so that we may too keep the faith. This book will encourage us all to do just that!

Nate Akin
Executive Director, Pillar Network

Phil Newton has been a mentor to so many pastors (including me) for so long, it is right for his passion for healthy pastoral ministry to be celebrated in a festschrift. I was richly blessed by each chapter in this rich volume; each one made me more zealous than ever for the glory of Christ in my ministry as a pastor. The contributors each mentioned Phil Newton's impact on them personally, but they especially honored him by their skillful contributions to this book. Both pastors and churchgoers alike will be helped immensely by this work.

May God use this book to strengthen churches all over the world!

Dr. Andy Davis
Pastor, First Baptist Church
Durham, NC

Phil Newton is well-deserving of a festschrift, and a collection of essays on pastoral ministry is precisely the right way to honor a man who has given himself for decades to such faithful ministry and continues to serve as a pastor to pastors. This is a great cast of authors, some very well known and some not, but each one carrying on this faithful legacy, several of them men mentored by Phil. This book will be a great help and encouragement for those aspiring to pastoral ministry as well as those already engaged in this noble task.

Ray Van Neste
Dean, School of Theology & Missions
Professor of Biblical Studies
Vice President, University Ministries
Union University

FULFILL YOUR MINISTRY: ESSAYS IN HONOR OF PHIL A. NEWTON

Roger D. Duke and
Matthew W. Moore, Editors

Fulfill Your Ministry: Essays in Honor of Phil A. Newton

© 2025 Roger D. Duke and Matthew W. Moore, Editors

Cover Design: Dustin Benge

ISBN: 978-1-955295-57-4

COURIER PUBLISHING

100 Manly Street
Greenville, South Carolina 29601

PRINTED IN THE UNITED STATES OF AMERICA

Contents

Foreword...7
Daniel L. Akin

Preface..9
Roger D. Duke & Matthew W. Moore

Introduction 13
Jeff Robinson

THE PERSON

1. Justification: Does It Make a Difference in Our Lives?..........41
   Thomas R. Schreiner

2. Pray with Humility and Hope:
   Lessons from Hezekiah's Prayer in Isaiah 37:16–20 53
   Mark Catlin

3. Pastors, Love Your Wives:
   An Exposition of Ephesians 5:25–33 73
   Todd Wilson

THE PASTOR

4. Layering in Pastoral Ministry:
   The Need for Repeating and Reminding..................................87
   Drew Harris

5. The Essential Role of Pastoral Leadership in Biblical
   Church Discipline 101
   David Lawrence

6. Worship that Leads to Missions...115
   Jim Carnes

7. Pastoral Ministry in Dying Churches 129
    Brian Croft

8. The Spiritual Formation of Ministerial Trainees..................145
    Matthew W. Moore

9. Pastoring by the Book:
    The Centrality of Scripture in Gathered Worship 161
    Chris Spano

THE PREACHER

10. Pastoral Preaching...177
    Rich Shadden

11. The Roots of South Woods:
    Ten-Thousand Fruits of Biblical Exposition 191
    J. Matthew Sliger

12. Prizing and Proclaiming:
    The Preeminence of Christ in the Canon 203
    Jordan Thomas

13. Preaching Christ from the Old Testament 225
    Mitch Kimbrell

14. John A. Broadus and Phil A. Newton —
    Both Cut from Aristotle's Rhetorical Cloth 241
    Roger D. Duke

15. Dogma and Declamation:
    Orthodoxy as Hermeneutical Principle in Preaching 259
    Tom J. Nettles

    Appendix of Appreciation for Dr. Phil Newton 279

Foreword

Daniel L. Akin

The call of a pastor is a high and holy calling. Men who aspire to this weighty assignment should be—they must be—called of God and biblically qualified. Numerous texts address God's expectations for His minister, but five in particular stand out: 1) Acts 20:17–38; 2) 1 Timothy 3:1–7; 3) 2 Timothy 3:16–4:5; 4) Titus 1:5–9; and 5) 1 Peter 5:1–4. When one examines these important biblical passages, a four-fold job description takes shape. God's minister serves as 1) pastor, 2) theologian, 3) evangelist and 4) missionary. Most pastors will excel in one or even several of these areas. It is rare that one will excel in all four.

The man that this book and its essays honor is that unique minister who faithfully checks all four boxes just noted. Phil A. Newton faithfully served as pastor of South Woods Baptist Church in Memphis, TN for 35 years (1987–2022). During those years he served as a loving shepherd to the flock entrusted to his care. A faithful expositor and careful theologian, he fed his flock the infallible and inerrant Word of God week after week for 35 years. As an aside, Dr. Newton has ministered to the larger body of Christ through his writings. He has authored or contributed to 14 books and over 60 articles through ministries like 9 Marks, The Gospel Coalition, and others. *40 Questions About Pastoral Ministry* and *Shepherding the Pastor* is essential reading for every leader in the Lord's Church.

Phil Newton also has the heart of an evangelist and missionary. Along with Brian Croft, he authored *Conduct Gospel-Centered Funerals: Applying the Gospel at the Unique Challenges of Death*. I was so blessed and impressed by this work I jumped at the opportunity to write its foreword. The book is simply a reflection of the heart of a man who continually sets forth the gospel of Jesus Christ and, on behalf of his Savior, pleads with sinners to "be reconciled to God." Whether from the pulpit or in private conversations, in the spirit of Spurgeon, Phil strives to be a faithful "soulwinner."

His missionary heart is also evident. Phil has traveled and ministered in Albania, Brazil, Canada, China, Colombia, France, Greece, Italy, Jamaica, Kenya, Portugal, Russia, Scotland, Switzerland, Turkey, Turks and Caicos, and Ukraine, sharing the gospel with the lost and encouraging fellow believers to love and serve Christ. Today (April 2024), Phil serves the Pillar Network as director of pastoral care and mentor. Pillar networks with and plants new churches. The missionary mandate of our Savior continues to flow through the veins of this man of God. I should add, Dr. Newton is also a member of the faculty of Southeastern Baptist Theological Seminary in Wake Forest, NC. He teaches Pastoral Theology, something God has well equipped him to do.

I dearly love and respect Phil Newton. He is my brother, friend, mentor and role model. Few men have encouraged me more than him. The Bible says give honor to whom honor is due. Phil Newton is worthy of honor. This book is a small but valuable contribution to that end.

Daniel L. Akin
President, SEBTS

Preface

Roger D. Duke & Matthew W. Moore

When Roger Duke, co-editor of this volume, first approached me (Matt) about editing and contributing to a festschrift honoring Phil Newton, I hesitated. It was not just because of my lack of confidence to spell or define "festschrift" correctly. My hesitation arose from my esteemed view of Phil; I certainly did not feel worthy enough to co-lead such a project.

Rewind. Phil was the primary instrument God used to move me toward doctoral work over a decade ago. Having planted a church, I was in a season of refinement concerning my own intimacy with the Lord and concerning my unsettled ecclesiology. Phil, along with the rest of South Woods Baptist Church, ministered to my family and helped restore my spirit so I would be prepared to serve the church well in the future. Phil so personally expressed confidence in God's ability to use someone like me, a measure of faith that became jeopardized in my life and ministry at the time.

Fast-forward. I agreed to join Roger because of Phil's role in my life, and the plan came together quickly with a list of contributors that know and love Phil. Their glad and edifying contributions come with the tenderness of relationships built on the gospel of Jesus Christ, as readers will see in the pages ahead. This volume aims to honor Phil and his influence on so many others while also providing rich personal, theological, ecclesiological, and practical encouragement to pastors.

Phil models what the Scripture portrays as a faithful and perseverant husband, friend, pastor, preacher, scholar, and mentor. For decades, Phil faithfully shepherded the saints at South Woods Baptist Church, loved and led his wife and children well, poured into the lives of his students, and mentored countless interns, always urging us in word and deed to fulfill the ministry to which we have been called. The apostle Paul, after reviewing the difficulty that lay ahead for ministers of the gospel, urged Timothy, "Fulfill your ministry" (2 Tim 4:5). The title *Fulfill Your Ministry* is more than a theme; it encapsulates the heartbeat of Phil's life and ministry. Even still, as Phil continues mentoring and caring for pastors today, he exemplifies a type of pastoral ministry derived from the Good Shepherd.

The contributors to this work emerge from the broad scope of Phil's influence. Long-time peers in ministry, such as Jim Carnes, Brian Croft, Roger Duke, Tom Nettles, and Tom Schreiner offer instruction concerning mission, revitalization, preaching, and doctrine. The list of mentees and interns testifies to Phil's influence on an array of pastoral matters. Todd Wilson exalts the importance of the pastor's marriage. Drew Harris and I relay what we have observed Phil do so well in training church members and future pastors. Mitch Kimbrell, Rich Shadden, Matt Sliger, and Chris Spano give gleaned insights on preaching and leading corporate church gatherings. Yet another group, Memphis co-laborers Mark Catlin, David Lawrence, and Jordan Thomas run the gamut of issues, including personal prayer, church discipline, and Christology. Each of these brothers have been challenged and enriched by Phil's influence. Now, they pass on that blessing for the readers' benefit.

In the years we have all known Phil, he has embraced the call to "fulfill your ministry" and championed that call to pastors everywhere. May this volume of essays stand as a lasting tribute to a life of continual service to Christ and His church.

Roger D. Duke

Matthew W. Moore, Editors

April 2025

Introduction

Tolle Scribe: The Pastor as a Writer-Theologian

By Jeff Robinson

I love writing, and I hate writing—it just depends on the day. As one of my friends, also a writer, puts it, some days the internal muse is singing and some days he calls in sick.

Indeed.

There are days when I can, in the span of a couple of hours, spin out 1,000 words that need little editing, that flow easily together like the waters of a gentle creek in mid-summer, and I can do it without breaking a sweat.

There are other days when I sit and watch the infernal cursor blink, and it seems to taunt me like that bully back in second grade. I write a paragraph, read it, fix it, read it, then delete it. I go get water, check the box scores, read a news story, browse biographies on Amazon, see if anybody liked my latest breaking-news Facebook post (Let's be honest here), text my wife—anything to avoid the task of writing, even as the deadline ticks down like a doomsday clock. Nuclear war is upon me, but I can't find the launch codes.

Eventually, I try again to stitch together a series of coherent, compelling words and phrases and clauses. But like a pitcher who gives up ten runs in the first inning, I just don't have it that day. I leave the writing game in frustration, vowing tomorrow will be different, and perhaps it will. The muse will sing, the cursor will pulse with life and give birth to words and those words will link up like boxcars behind a locomotive, creating an article or chapter.

My uneasy love relationship with writing dates all the way back to 1983, my sophomore year in high school, when I joined my high school's newspaper staff as a sports scribe. Though I had dreams of playing second base for the Cincinnati Reds, it was growing all too clear that my God-imbued gift set did not include hitting a curve ball 400 feet. Writing about baseball and other things, just maybe, was the thing for which He'd built me.

After high school I attended the University of Georgia and graduated from UGA's highly esteemed journalism school. For many years afterward, I worked as an ink-stained wretch in the newspaper business, laboring for both large daily papers and hometown weeklies. I wrote sports, news, and features—kind of a deluxe utility player. I interviewed George Jones and George W. Bush. I profiled top UGA Dawgs and a TOPGUN U.S. Navy pilot. I covered NASCAR races and the race riots following the Rodney King incident in 1991.

When I surrendered to ministry in the mid-1990s (a fortuitous providence since the newspaper business was soon to sink like the Titanic after it slammed broadside into a globe-sized iceberg called the worldwide web), I didn't need to become a pastor who writes; I was a writer whom God would need to form into a pastor, reverse for most of my many pastor friends who also write.

To do that, I began to read: C. S. Lewis and R. C. Sproul, John MacArthur and John Piper, Martin Luther and Martyn Lloyd-Jones, Phil Ryken and, yes, a writing pastor from Memphis whom I had yet to meet named Phil Newton.

God's providence made it clear that part of my ministry would be writing about theology and church history and pastoral ministry and Christian living, all great things, all involving the unpredictable, occasionally cooperative gift of writing. But pastors who are writers, including my dear friend Phil Newton, have helped shape me as a pastor through their writing.

Why should a pastor write more than his weekly sermons? For one thing, he has the ultimate illustration in the book he's called to exposit every Lord's Day.

An Ultra-Brief Theology of Writing

Our God is a speaking, writing God. He wrote 66 books of history, poetry, wisdom literature, prophecy, parables, fantasy (The dragon, Apollyon, and other stars of John's Apocalypse inspired Tolkien and Lewis), case law, commandments, epistles, and more.

He communicated in nouns and pronouns, definite and indefinite articles, adjectives and adverbs, verbs and prepositions, conjunctions and interjections. God wrote about darkness and light, heaven and hell, joy and affliction, this world and the world to come. He raised up Spirit-led writers and inspired them to pen mini and major biographies of figures like Moses, David, Queen Esther, Job, Ruth, Elijah, and, of course, Jesus Christ; and He inspired preachers like Paul and Peter to write letters that were profound theological treatises and guides for Christian living. Ronald Reagan was the great communicator, but God is the Master Communicator.

And God gifts many of his under-shepherds to write articles, memoirs, letters, and books that are not Spirit inspired, but nonetheless become instruments in his hands to help God's people understand the Bible better. After all, that's the bottom line and is the fundamental mission, yes calling, of every faithful pastor.

Pastor, if you can write, then, to paraphrase the Latin phrase that lit ablaze the pen of the most important pastor-theologian-writer of the early church, *tolle scribe*—take up and write. God has given pastors a local congregation, but across the ages He has also equipped scores of them to deploy the written word through memoirs, letters, articles, edited and published sermons, and books to impact the lives of millions beyond their local venue of ministry. Let's call them (and you) pastor-theologian-writers.

Church History and Writing Pastors

Paul may have been the first pastor-theologian who wrote regularly. His epistles bulge with sound theology, redemptive history, hortatory, biblical application, and godly wisdom—all under the inspiration of the Holy Spirit. And there were dozens of figures in the early church whom God used to produce important works of theology, helping the church sort orthodoxy from heresy on issues surrounding the divinity and humanity of Christ as well as the Trinity—Irenaeus of Lyons, Athanasius, Justin Martyr, among scores of others.

For evangelicals, the most important of these early pastor-theologians whose written words changed history was St. Augustine of Hippo.

Augustine of Hippo: Testimony, Polemics, and Historical Method

Augustine of Hippo (AD 354-430) is one of the most impactful writing pastors of the early church. The great church father contributed varied works, the most famous being his darkness to light testimony in the *Confessions* and his massive apologetic for the Christian faith which also helps believers live as citizens of this world in *City of God*.

But Augustine left behind far more than those two well-known volumes. The Augustinian corpus is diverse in terms of subject matter. He wrote a profound defense of the Trinity and upheld the necessity of sovereign grace in polemical works against the soteriological errors of Pelagius.

Augustine's writing is clear, punchy, and filled with memorable phrases, most famously writing in his *Confessions*, "You have made us for yourself, O Lord, and our heart is restless until it finds its rest in you."

Augustine's soteriological sons, the Reformers, used their significant communication skills to produce some of the richest and most nutritious spiritual food for hungry Christian souls in the history of the church.

Reformation Exemplars: Luther and Calvin

Around 1440 in Germany, the goldsmith Johannes Gutenberg invented the movable-type printing press, which started the printing revolution. The printing press was one of the most earth-shaking pieces of technology in human history, its potential illustrated powerfully in the spiritual reformation that began to stir just a few years later in Europe.

The printed page was the weapon of choice in the Reformers' war against the superstition, immorality, and false doctrine of the Roman Catholic Church. Martin Luther (1483-1546) fired the first major volley with his challenge to the church at Wittenburg in the publication and dissemination of his 95 *Theses*.

Luther's pen and the printing press allied to produce dozens of more important works such as *Bondage of the Will* (published 1525), his polemic against Erasmus' view of free will, a *Commentary on Galatians* (1535), which influenced many other noteworthy writing pastors such as John Bunyan, and other polemical works such as *On the Babylonian Captivity of the Church* (1520) and *A Treatise on Christian Liberty* (1520), among numerous others. Luther also published smaller and larger catechisms, commentaries on other biblical books, hymns, and volumes of his sermons.

Luther's writing dripped with language of the day, as he excoriated the papacy and the superstitions of the Roman Church, speaking of "Romish dogs" and "papish asses" (aka donkeys in the 16th century). To see the verbal muscle and raw emotion of his writings, look no further than Luther's words that recount his wrestling with the phrase "the righteousness of God" in Paul's writing and subsequent discovery of the liberating truth of the imputation of Christ's righteousness in Romans 1:17: "I beat importunately upon Paul at that place, most ardently desiring to know what Paul wanted. At last, by the mercy of God, meditating day and night, I gave heed to the context of the words…. That place in Paul was for me truly the gate to paradise."[1]

His writing output was voluminous, encompassing dozens of volumes, similar to that of John Calvin.

It's no exaggeration to say John Calvin (1509-1564) invented systematic theology as we know it. His *Institutes of the Christian Religion* (numerous editions, definitively published in 1559) remains one of the most influential works of Christian doctrine ever written as it articulated Reformed Doctrine and its application simply, clearly, and thoroughly.

While Calvin preached for his congregation in Geneva, he produced a staggering number of written works, including at least 47 books on the Bible which encompasses expository commentaries on most books of the Bible. He also produced a polemical work on predestination, *Concerning the Eternal Predestination of God* (1552),

---

1   John Dillenberger, ed., *Martin Luther: Selections from His Writings* (Garden City, NY: Doubleday, 1961), xvii.

as a product of his debate with Dutch Roman Catholic Theologian Albert Pighius. The Genevan reformer also published a number of works on ecclesiastical issues such as church discipline and the Lord's Supper, and also wrote hundreds of letters to his many friends and Reformation church planters across Europe, particularly in France.

Many readers are shocked at the clarity and simplicity, the pastoral tone and devotional quality of Calvin's writings, particularly in the *Institutes* and in his Bible commentaries. Here's a sampling from the *Institutes* as Calvin discusses the truthfulness of God's Word and the power of the Word as inspired by God through men:

> Therefore, illumined by [the Spirit's] power, we believe neither by our own nor anyone else's judgment that Scripture is from God; but above human judgment we affirm with utter certainty (just as if we were gazing upon the majesty of God himself) that it has flowed to us from the very mouth of God by the ministry of men.[2]

Calvin's heirs, the Puritans, were pastors, theologians, and writers *par excellence*.

The Puritans: Words and Words and Words, but Good Words

To say the Puritans were a people of the Word and words is a little like saying Jonathan Edwards was bright or weather at the North Pole is inhospitable. They preached and preached and preached. They wrote and wrote and wrote. Leland Ryken humorously described the Puritans' tendency to preach and write with a tsunami of words:

---

2 John Calvin, *Institutes of the Christian Religion*, John T. McNeil, trans. Ford Lewis Battles, 2 vols. (Philadelphia, PA: Westminster Press, 1960), I.vii.5.

Prolixity, the vice of being long-winded and verbose, was one of the Puritans' most salient traits. Many Puritans lacked the type of self-criticism that let them know when enough had been said. They certainly failed to realize the power of things unstated and only suggested … . The Puritan glut of words is evident in their style of writing.[3]

Richard Baxter, looking back over his life, pondered that notion as if he'd read Ryken's critique: "And concerning almost all my writings I must confess that my own judgment is that fewer well studied and polished had been better."[4]

Puritan-written volumes now available through publishers such as Banner of Truth and Reformation Heritage number in the hundreds and for that 21st century pastors should be profoundly grateful. And, while some of the Puritans may have written as if to filibuster until Jesus returns, many among them penned works that constitute some of the richest and most spiritually beneficial theological and practical works ever written.

John Owen (1616-1683) and Jonathan Edwards (1703-1758) were perhaps the most scholarly and learned among Puritan pastors, and they produced works that have stood the test of time as standard reading for Reformed pastors: Owen's *The Death of Death in the Death of Christ, On the Mortification of Sin, Communion with God,* and numerous other titles and sermons within his 16-volume works as published by Banner of Truth.[5] Edwards' works number in the dozens and include many doctrinal sermons, plus well-known theological and practical

---

3   Leland Ryken, *Worldly Saints: The Puritans as They Really Were* (Grand Rapids: Zondervan, 2010), 193.

4   Ibid.

5   Crossway is currently republishing scholarly editions of Owen's works one at a time. I strongly recommend these editions because they include some helps in deciphering Owen, who, as Peter said of Paul, his written some things that are hard to understand.

volumes such as the *Religious Affections, The Freedom of the Will, A Surprising Narrative, and Charity and Its Fruits.*

Here, we need to place something like a warning label on the works of Owen and Edwards. Their writing tends toward the verbal excesses Ryken previously described and reading some of their works can be like sledding on pavement—not the starting place for a reader new to the Puritans. Still, their writings are worth the work for those who are more advanced in the knowledge of Bible, doctrine, and church history.

But there is much fruit to be had from reading the Puritans, many out of the box.

John Bunyan (1628-1688) is probably the best-known author among Puritan pastors. His *Pilgrim's Progress* (1678) has been estimated to have sold more copies than any other book in history save the King James Bible. His allegorical works such as *Pilgrim's Progress* and *The Holy War* (1682) employ fantasy elements to show the trials and temptations of the Christian life and the reality of spiritual warfare in the life of every believer.

Bunyan also wrote a powerful work detailing his conversion to Christ and the ensuing inner war for assurance in *Grace Abounding to the Chief of Sinners* (1666). Bunyan wrote several doctrinal treatises and a personal favorite (though lesser known) on perseverance of the saints, *The Heavenly Footman* (1698).

The beauty of Bunyan's works is this: the author wrote them while imprisoned in the Bedford jail for preaching the gospel in a church not licensed by government. Writes John Piper of Bunyan:

> The smell of affliction was on most of what Bunyan wrote. In fact, I suspect that one of the reasons the Puritans are still being read today with so much profit is that their entire experience, unlike ours, was one of persecution and suffering. To our chipper culture, this may seem somber at times, but the day

you hear you have cancer, or that your child is blind, or that a mob is coming, you turn away from the light books to the weighty ones that were written on the precipice of eternity where the fragrance of heaven and the stench of hell are both in the air.[6]

Pastor, you never know what vitality an article or book you write may possess far after you have retired from this life to glory. Bunyan, an uneducated tinker (fixer of broken pots), speaks powerfully and perennially today, though he's been dead for more than 300 years.

Besides Bunyan, Thomas Watson (1616-1686) may have been the most skilled preacher and writer among Puritan pastors. Charles Spurgeon, a tireless lover and promoter of Puritan literature, said as much in his "Brief Memoir of Thomas Watson" that introduces the Banner of Truth reprint of Watson's *A Body of Divinity* (1692), an exposition of the Westminster Assembly's Shorter Catechism. Watson's *Body* was the first Puritan work to roll off Banner's presses in 1958:

> Thomas Watson's *Body of Practical Divinity* is one of the most precious of the peerless works of the Puritans; and those best acquainted with it prize it most. Watson was one of the most concise, racy, illustrative, and suggestive of those eminent divines who made the Puritan age the Augustan period of evangelical literature. There is a happy union of sound doctrine, heart-searching experience and practical wisdom throughout all his works, and his *Body of Divinity* is, beyond all the rest, useful to the student and the minister.[7]

---

6   John Piper, *27 Servants of Sovereign Joy: Faithful, Flawed, and Fruitful* (Wheaton, IL: Crossway, 2022), 172.

7   Thomas Watson, *A Body of Divinity* (Carlisle, PA: Banner of Truth, 2000), vii.

Watson, who was ejected from his church alongside more than 2,000 other non-conformist pastors in 1662 for violating the Clarendon Code, published numerous other doctrinal works and collections of sermons, including *The Ten Commandments* (1686), and *The Beatitudes* (1660). Watson is unparalleled among the Puritans in his ability to paint dramatic pictures with words and to turn memorable phrases about sublime doctrines. Reading Watson is easy and pleasurable, like a massage for the heart and mind. In describing communion, he wrote: "In the Word preached, the saints hear Christ's voice; in the sacrament they have his kiss."[8]

As one brief sample, here's one way among several Watson encourages believers to live to God's glory:

> It brings glory to God, when the world sees a Christian has that within him that can make him cheerful in the worst times; that can enable him, with the nightingale, to sing with a thorn in his breast. The people of God have ground for cheerfulness. They are justified and adopted, and this creates inward peace; it makes music within, whatever storms are without.[9]

And one more, Watson on faith: "Faith knows there are no impossibilities with God, and will trust him where it cannot trace him."[10]

Like Watson, John Newton and Samuel Rutherford were, first and foremost, pastors, but they were pastors whose pens flowed with light.

---

8   Thomas Watson, *The Beatitudes* (Carlisle, PA: Banner of Truth, 2000), 251.

9   Watson, *Body of Divinity*, 14.

10   Ibid.

Pastoral Letters That Dripped Doctrinal Honey: Newton and Rutherford

Most people know John Newton (1725–1807) as author of the most famous hymn in recent church history, *Amazing Grace*. But Newton has one of the most scintillating testimonies of God's grace ever written. Newton was born in London to a godly mother and an atheistic father, a debauched sailor who worked to transport slaves to England from West Africa. Newton's mother died when he was young, and John followed in his father's profession. Mercifully, God saved Newton out of those sinful labors (through a Jonah-level storm at sea) and called him to pastor for many years at Olney.

Newton served as pastor of two churches, remaining at Olney from 1764 to 1779 before accepting a call to St. Mary's Woolnoth in London, where the self-described "old African blasphemer" remained for 27 years. Newton wrote hymns and theological treatises, but he is best known for many volumes of letters he wrote to church members, fellow pastors, and government leaders around London. His works are available in a beautiful four-volume set from Banner (recently re-typeset and re-edited), and much of his work appears in the form of letters.

A number of his letters were published in one volume, *Cardiphonia or the Utterance of the Heart in the Course of Real Correspondence* (1780). The letters are a brilliant blend of doctrine, biblical instruction, wise counsel, application, encouragement, and personal engagement.

Newton possessed many deep friendships with fellow pastors, including John Ryland Jr., with whom he exchanged many letters.[11]

---

11 These excellent letters show the profundity of their friendship and were published in 2009 by Banner of Truth in one volume, *Wise Counsel: John Newton's Letters to John Ryland Jr.*

In one letter, he warns a young pastor who has recently surrendered to a call to ministry, was recently married, and evidently is being well paid for his first church position:

> A parish is an awful millstone indeed to those who see nothing valuable in the flock but the fleece... . His grace is sufficient for you; but undoubtedly such a scene of prosperity as seems to lie before you is full of snares, and calls for a double effort of watchfulness and prayer. Your situation will fix many eyes upon you, and Satan will doubtless watch you and examine every corner of the hedge around you, to see if he can find a gap by which to enter.[12]

In a letter to another newly ordained man, Newton deals him a dose of realism to dispel overly sentimental expectations about the call to ministry:

> You have, doubtless, often anticipated in your mind the nature of the service to which you are now called and made it the subject of much consideration and prayer. But a distant view of the ministry is generally very different from what it is found to be when we are actually engaged in it. The young soldier, who has never seen an enemy, may form some general notions of what is before him; but his ideas will be much more lively and diversified when he comes upon the field of battle. If the Lord was to show us the whole beforehand, who that has a due sense of his own insufficiency and weakness would venture to engage?[13]

Prior to Newton's ministry, Samuel Rutherford (1600-1661), served in a similar local church ministry in Scotland. Rutherford was a longtime pastor who served as one of the Scottish commissioners

---

12   John Newton, *The Works of John Newton, Vol. 1* (Carlisle, PA: Banner of Truth, 2015), 477-78.

13   Ibid, 104.

to the Westminster Assembly. Andrew Bonar selected letters from Rutherford and provided a biographical sketch for the volume which has been in continuous print since its first appearance in 1664. Similar to Newton's letters, Rutherford wrote clearly and pithily, encouraging parishioners, ministry friends, and government leaders in their walk with the Lord.

In a letter to "a Christian gentlewoman on the death of her daughter," dated April 23, 1628, Rutherford wrote (evidently following a personal visit to her home):

> Ye know that the weightiest end of the cross of Christ that is laid upon you lieth upon your strong Savior…. While ye prodigally spend time in mourning for her, ye are speedily posting after her. Run your race with patience. Let God have His own; and ask of Him, instead of your daughter which He hath taken from you, the daughter of faith, which is patience; and in patience possess your soul. Lift up your head: ye do not know how near your redemption doth draw, thus recommending you to the Lord, who is able to establish you.[14]

Newton was a letter writer to fellow pastors and church members, but two 19th century pastors were lions for the cause of orthodoxy at a time when Protestant liberalism and new evangelical theologies were contending for the hearts and minds of evangelicals.

Spurgeon and Ryle: Confronting the Spirit of the Age

The best writers are those who allow something of their personality to bleed through in their prose, distinguishing them from other writers. The big personalities of John Charles "J. C." Ryle (1816–1900) and Charles Haddon Spurgeon (1834-1992), perhaps more

---

14   Andrew Bonar, ed., *Letters of Samuel Rutherford* (Carlisle, PA: Banner of Truth, 2012), 36.

than any other well-known Reformed pastor-writers, ring clear in their written works. The writings of Ryle and Spurgeon pulse with life.

Spurgeon was brilliant at making his voice heard in his writing, same as in his preaching. Why do millions still read Spurgeon's books, sermons, and various writings 132 years after his death? In part, it's because of the way in which he couples conviction with joy, which was so much a part of his personality and ministry.

"His writings ripple with mirth," writes Michael Reeves in the preface to Alex DiPrima's new biography of Spurgeon.

> "… he was not frivolous but joyfully earnest. He was also a bighearted man of deep affections. Still today, his printed sermons and lectures throb with passion. He was a deeply kind and tender man. He was no pushover but a lion of conviction and courage. While joyful and resolute, he was not a triumphalist. Indeed, he struggled acutely with much pain and depression And yet he never comes across (in his writings and sermons) as gloomy. And perhaps this is what draws people: they see in Spurgeon a man who was so gloriously and unusually *alive*."[15]

Spurgeon published more than 140 books in his nearly five decades of ministry at Metropolitan Tabernacle/New Park Street, most on theological topics and practical issues of Christian living; straight doctrine and straight living went hand-in-hand for Spurgeon.[16]

One of Spurgeon's great delights was the *Sword & Trowel* magazine, a monthly publication which Spurgeon founded in 1865 and continued until his death. The *S&T* contained hard-hitting articles on theology, interaction with current and cultural events,

---

15 Alex DiPrima, *Spurgeon: A Life* (Grand Rapids: Reformation Heritage, 2024), 6.

16 For an excellence, in-depth discussion of Spurgeon's writing and publishing activities, see chapter 11 in Tom Nettles, *Living by Revealed Truth: The Life and Pastoral Theology of Charles Haddon Spurgeon*.

book reviews, sermons, and more. Perhaps the great highlight of the *Sword & Trowel's* history under Spurgeon was his articles on the "Downgrade Controversy" in which he locked horns with liberal theology that had slithered into churches of the British Baptist Union. Spurgeon wrote revealing letters and articles monthly toward the end of his life, exposing the dangerous doctrines and pleading for a return to orthodoxy.

Spurgeon wrote about the controversy first through a series of anonymous letters. But in August of 1887, Spurgeon joined the battle, through an article under his byline titled, "Another Word on the Downgrade." Spurgeon did not mince words in assailing the liberalism that was manufactured in German academies and exported to England and beyond:

> The case is mournful. Certain ministers are making infidels. Avowed atheists are not a tenth as dangerous as those preachers who scatter doubt and stab at faith… Germany was made unbelieving by her preachers, and England is following in her tracks.[17]

J. C. Ryle was similarly courageous in confronting the worrisome theologies of that day. John Piper calls Ryle an embodiment of "masculine Christianity," which Piper defines, in part as:

> "Theology and church mission marked by overarching godly male leadership in the spirit of Christ, with an ethos of tenderhearted strength, and contritcourage, and risk-taking decisiveness, and readiness to sacrifice for the sake of leading, protecting and providing for the community … ."[18]

---

17   C. H. Spurgeon, "Another Word on the Downgrade," *The Sword & Trowel*, August 1887.

18   For the full definition, see John Piper, *27 Servants of Sovereign Joy: Faithful, Flawed, and Fruitful* (Wheaton, IL: Crossway, 2022), 906.

Ryle was ordained in 1841 as the first bishop of Liverpool. He was an Anglican contemporary to Spurgeon in London, whose best-known book was and is, *Holiness: Its Nature, Hindrances, Difficulties, and Roots*, engaging the passive spirituality of the rising Holiness movement, an approach to Christian spirituality that first appeared in his day. *Holiness* is typical of Ryle's writing and has much in common with Spurgeon's prose: bold, courageous, plain-spoken on issues, bristling with memorable illustrations, and strong, communicated through memorably worded phrases and clauses. A prime example:

> The true Christian is called to be a soldier and must behave as such from the day of his conversion to the day of his death. He is not meant to live a life of religious ease, indolence, and security. He must never imagine for a moment that he can sleep and doze along the way to heaven, like one travelling in an easy carriage. If he takes his standard of Christianity from the children of this world, he may be content with such notions; but he will find no countenance for them in the Word of God. If the Bible is the rule of faith and practice, he will find his course laid down very plainly in this matter. He must "fight."[19]

Ryle wrote many more works, including several collections of articles, as well as an excellent series of *Expository Thoughts on the Gospels*. Piper was spot on in his characterization of Ryle, and this bleeds through in his works. He did not mince words in exposing heresy or upholding orthodoxy and was, like Spurgeon, a man of the Bible down to his marrow. What Spurgeon famously said of Bunyan was certainly true of the "Prince of Preachers" and his contemporary, the bishop Ryle: cut him anywhere, and he bleeds Bible.

---

19 J. C. Ryle, *Holiness: Its Nature, Hindrances, Difficulties, and Roots* (Moscown, ID: Charles Nolan, 2001), 63.

In the 20th century, Martyn Lloyd-Jones and James Montgomery Boice preached and wrote such that their books and commentaries remain standard resources for 21st century pastors.

Lloyd Jones and Boice: Sermons that Become Commentaries

"The Doctor," Martyn Lloyd-Jones (1899-1981), who pastored Westminster Chapel for 30 years until 1968, capitalized on his prodigious preaching and conference address output to produce an impressive corpus of works that remain staples in the libraries of Reformed pastors across the globe. MLJ's sermons were often edited so they could be more easily read than heard. This is true in his 14 volumes on Romans and in his eight volumes on Ephesians, among others.

Lloyd-Jones' written works range from expositions of Bible books to books on revival, the Puritans, culture, church issues, evangelicalism, among other vital topics. More often than not, his books were sermons or conference addresses adapted for reading, so they reflected MLJ's straight-forward, no-nonsense use of language.

James Montgomery Boice (1938-2000), who served as senior pastor of Tenth Presbyterian Church in Philadelphia from 1968 until his death from liver cancer in 2000, was similar to Lloyd-Jones. Boice also turned sermons into Bible commentaries and wrote numerous books on topics ranging from biblical inerrancy (Boice was deeply involved in the defense of biblical inerrancy in the late 1970s) to the culture.

My favorite Boice work is an underrated systematic theology published in 1986, *Foundations of the Christian Faith: A Comprehensive & Readable Theology* (IVP Academic). The beauty of Boice's work was that he wrote in a way that made his works accessible to all Christians. He made theology, church history, and Christian living plain, and, like a skilled teacher, illustrates truths well and always sought to answer the question, "So what?" For Boice, application always follows exposition.

In the 21st century, writing pastors have been central to a new Reformation that has seen the embrace of Reformed Theology among a new generation

Sproul, Piper, and MacArthur: Voices of a New Reformation

The March 12, 2009 issue of *TIME magazine* named "The New Calvinism" as one of "10 Ideas Changing the World Right Now." That proclamation was astounding, but, for many younger evangelicals it was profoundly true, as the doctrines of grace had been revealed as the plain teaching of Scripture, turning their lives upside down for Christ.

Collin Hansen exegeted *TIME's* trend in his 2008 book which gave the movement a name: *Young, Restless, Reformed: A Journalist's Journey with the New Calvinists* (Crossway). The *TIME* article names John Piper, Albert Mohler, and "the pugnacious Mark Driscoll" as among the leading conduits of a revival of Reformed teaching. Other major players could've been added, which Hansen mentions in his book, primary among them being R. C. Sproul and John MacArthur. Piper, Sproul, and MacArthur (as well as Driscoll, who was discredited due to leadership sins) were pastors who wrote blogs, articles, and books.

Sproul's genius was in taking complex issues of theology, philosophy, and church history and writing about them in a style that made sublime but murky ideas easily understandable to laypeople. Sproul wrote some of the most important books that influenced thousands in the YRR movement, including *The Holiness of God, Chosen by God,* and *What Is Reformed Theology?* Sproul sought to bring about a resurgence in interest in theology through his Ligonier Ministries' teaching videos, but also through his articles and books. He founded Ligonier in the early 1970s and founded a monthly devotional magazine, Tabletalk, with the same intent. Sproul wrote on the holiness of God with vigor, hoping a robust recovery of that doctrine would draw many Christians to take a closer look at the teachings of the Protestant Reformation and, above all, their Bibles.

Wrote Sproul biographer and Ligonier teaching fellow Stephen J. Nichols:

> R. C. hoped back then that the rediscovery of the centrality of the holiness of God would lead a new Reformation. He longed for that. R. C. never studied the past like one would visit a museum. The past was not historical curiosity. For him the past served to catapult him to the future. He studied the Reformation and awakenings of the past because he longed to see a new Reformation and a new awakening.[20]

Piper was equally important in the lives of many who embraced Reformed Theology in the late-90s and early-2000s. This reawakening came through his sermons, particularly at conferences such as the annual Desiring God Conference in Piper's home of Minneapolis, and the now-defunct biannual T4G conference in Louisville. Equally important have been Piper's articles and books, particularly *Desiring God: Meditations of a Christian Hedonist* (Crossway, 2011), *A Hunger for God* (Crossway, 2013), and *Don't Waste Your Life* (Crossway, 2003).

---

20   Stephen J. Nichols, *R. C. Sproul: A Life* (Wheaton, IL: Crossway, 2021), 272.

Piper's works have channeled the ethos and God-glory saturated theology of Puritan Jonathan Edwards for a new generation. My favorite Piper works are his massive work, *Providence*, and the equally voluminous *27 Servants of Sovereign Joy*, which profiles 27 great Christian leaders from the early church until now. Like Sproul, Piper makes theology and church history accessible for regular Christians, a tremendous gift. Like Spurgeon and Ryle, Piper's prose crackles with life and as influenced thousands of young, restless, and Reformed believers over the past 30 years.

Here's a sample from the introduction of *27 Servants*:

> God ordains that we gaze on his glory, dimly mirrored in the ministry of his flawed servants. He intends for us to consider their lives and peer through the imperfections of their faith and behold the beauty of their God … . The history of the world is a field strewn with broken stones, which are sacred altars designed to waken worship in the hearts of those who will take the time to read and remember … . The aim of providence in the history of the world is the worship of the people of God. Ten thousand stories of grace and truth are meant to be remembered for the refinement of faith and the sustaining of hope and the guidance of love.[21]

MacArthur also contributed many excellent commentaries and books to the YRR movement, including *The Gospel According to Jesus: What Is Authentic Faith* (Zondervan, 2009), a muscular biblical response to the Lordship controversy, and an equally stout rejoinder to unprincipled pragmatism in *Ashamed of the Gospel: When the Church Becomes Like the World* (Crossway, 2018). Another important book in this recovery of "Big God Theology" was *Knowing God* by J. I. Packer, an Anglican theologian whose works continue to

---

21   Piper, *27 Servants*, 27-28.

serve laypeople and ministry leaders profoundly. A current pastor who is also an excellent model of the pastor-theologian-writer I have in mind with this essay is Joel Beeke, who has written everything from a four-volume Reformed systematic theology to the best book I've ever read on how a pastor should handle his critics. Don't miss Packer or Beeke, brother pastor.

Bottom line: As in the first Protestant Reformation, the impact of writing pastors on this new reformation among younger evangelical pastors and laypeople has been seismic.

Phil Newton and the Writing Pastor Model

For many years, I was privileged to serve as a senior editor for The Gospel Coalition. When Collin Hansen interviewed me for the job, he asked me to name pastors I would bring on board to write for TGC; Phil's name was the first one off my lips. And for my entire tenure there, Phil was my go-to pastor on issues facing local church leaders.

Phil Newton is a quintessential model of the pastor-theologian-writer. All who know Phil know him as a pastor's pastor—and his articles and books are an important legacy of that descriptor. Phil has wed his decades of ministry experience and his academic achievements to a highly capable pen to write books and articles on everything from elders in the local congregation to how to preach a funeral sermon.

A quick search of his articles there reveals a diverse and incredibly helpful corpus of articles: "How to Criticize Your Pastor (Well)," "The 8 Stages of a Long Pastoral Ministry," "What Should We Preach During a Crisis?," "How Deacons Are Essential for a Healthy Church," "What's Wrong with Saying 'God Called Me to Ministry'?" and "Should You Pastor a Church You Would Never

Attend?" This is a small sampling among dozens of Phil's articles. Phil is my favorite living writer on local church leadership and related ministry issues. There's no one better.

What does this mean for other pastors? In a letter to his friend Arthur Greeves, C. S. Lewis wrote, "When you are fed up with life, start writing: Ink is the cure for all human ills, as I have found out long ago."[22] Writing can be good for you (especially when the muse is singing—see the intro above). Here are a few practical points to ponder:

1. You may be a writer and don't (yet) know it.

You preach every week, so if you more or less manuscript your sermons, you are writing the equivalent of a book chapter weekly. Lloyd-Jones, Boice, Spurgeon, and myriad others took sermons and turned them into articles. God's timeless truth is evergreen and always relevant, so can you take that sermon on the sovereignty of God and turn it into a 1,000-word piece on how trusting a sovereign God can dispel anxiety in the believer? Or, a sermon on 1 Timothy 3:1-7 into an article outlining the things a church should look for in its search for a lead pastor. The possibilities are endless. Lloyd-Jones used his Friday night theology lectures to assemble a systematic theology that was published in three volumes, *Great Doctrines of the Bible*, still available from Crossway. Might you contribute such a work?

2. You don't have to have command of language like C. S. Lewis or a mind that's omnicompetent like Albert Mohler to be a successful writer.

It certainly helps, but few of us fall into that category, including the author of his essay. Lewis, a supremely gifted writer, gives wise

---

22 Corey Latta, *C. S. Lewis and the Art of Writing: What the Essayist, Novelist, Literary Critic, Apologist, Memoirist, Theologian Teaches Us Life and Craft of Writing* (Eugene, OR: Cascade Books, 2016), 1.

counsel here: "We must use the talent we have, not the talents we don't have."[23]

My friend and former pastor, Tom Schreiner, writes beautifully, not because he employs many big words, but because his writing is simple, clear, and elegant. Like Sproul, Schreiner is a genius at making the Bible and theology clear, putting it on a level that is accessible to a Christian at every stage of maturity from the new believer to the Bible scholar. That's a rare gift. If you have it, use it.

3. If you don't want to write for publication, write for yourself and for your congregation.

During my years in pastoral ministry, I was often asked questions on issues I had not yet worked through and some I'd never even given much thought. I learned to say, "I don't know" and to be content with that answer. I would also usually say, "I don't know about that because I haven't written about it." I tend to process things verbally, which means I talk through it with a conversation partner, or I write about it. Pastor, you should do the same. Learn by writing out your thoughts. Consider putting a pastor's blog on your church website as another means of teaching, encouraging, and edifying your church. That might be a good place to start. If nothing else, it has potential to do you a world of good.

4. Fill your mind with good books by authors who write well.

I often tell my students, "You have to read well to write well." That is axiomatic. The best writers have minds filled with good ideas, usually gleaned from somewhere else. They know something

---

23 C. S. Lewis, *On Writing (and Writers): A Miscellany of Advice and Opinions* (New York: HarperOne, 2022), ix.

about history and culture and the world as God has created it. They know all this through reading good books. Good writers will put good words and good thoughts and good sentences into your head and, after reading for a long time, you'll be able to express these ideas in your own words, through your own personality, such that they become ideas expressed uniquely by you.

As I've written elsewhere, read widely, read both fiction and non-fiction, and read daily. Read for both head and heart. By God's grace, I've been a voracious reader since childhood. I grew up on a farm in rural Georgia with nothing much to do besides read *World Book Encyclopedia* (the Google of my youth) with its many volumes and engaging all the biographies and history books my father was reading.

My favorite genre is biography, and I've read everything from bios on John Calvin and George Whitefield to Calvin Coolidge and George Jones, from the inventor of blimps to a band bio of Led Zeppelin, Henry VIII and Henry Aaron.

Good biographies have the double benefit of teaching about the subject and his or her historical context. People, their life and times, utterly fascinate me. Read old books and new books, dead authors and living authors. Read things you enjoy. In that category, I sometimes read books on baseball history and biographies of my favorite rock stars from the '70s and '80s—now older, and usually wiser, sometimes even born again (like Alice Cooper and Foreigner's legendary lead singer, Lou Gramm) to a living hope in Christ.

Conclusion

Writing pastors are a gift to God's church as the selected witnesses here demonstrate. Books have the potential to change lives. Most pastors preach each Lord's Day to the same congregation, whether it is less than 100 or just under 10,000. Books and articles allow the writing pastor to reach a broader audience with the things of God.

Thirty years ago, during the first months of my growing hunger for theology, church history, and the things of God, I read Packer's *Knowing God*, Timothy George's *Theology of the Reformers*, C. S. Lewis' *Mere Christianity*. While struggling to determine whether I should remain a Baptist (I did and still do) after embracing Reformed Theology, I read works by Tom Nettles, *Baptists and the Bible* and *By His Grace and For His Glory*.

Carefully reading these books gave me a far deeper understanding of the Bible, theology, and church history. These books gave me a deeper understanding of God and His gospel, and they drew me closer to the Lord. These books completely altered the trajectory of my life and took me from secular journalism and, in part, led me to embrace a call to full-time vocational ministry. The written word possesses that power. So, brother pastor, *tolle scribe*, take up and write.

THE PERSON

Chapter one

Justification: Does It Make a Difference in Our Lives?

Thomas R. Schreiner

Introduction

I am privileged to write an essay in honor of Phil Newton who has served so faithfully as a pastor for years and years. Phil did not seek fame or notoriety; he functions as an example to us all as a pastor who loved and shepherded his people. How we need more pastors like Phil who serve faithfully, biblically, and humbly. Paul says to honor Epaphroditus for his ministry and love (Phil 2:29), and it is my joy to honor Phil with this small offering. My hope is this essay will give some indication how the doctrine of justification is practical for everyday living.

Justification by grace alone through faith alone is one of the distinctives of evangelicalism and particularly of the Reformation. Sometimes it is objected that justification is a cold doctrine, that it does not warm our hearts or feed our souls; thus, it does not change our lives. Justification's importance is doubted by some since it does not fit in their purview with life in the Spirit and the call to live in a way that pleases God.[1] My purpose in this essay is not to define

---

1   Cf. Albert Schweitzer, *The Quest of the Historical Jesus: A Critical Study of Its Progress from Reimarus to Wrede*, translated by W. Montgomery (New York: Macmillan, 1968), 225.

justification by faith alone. I have done this elsewhere.[2] Here I want to explain why the doctrine matters by explaining that it makes a significant difference in our everyday lives. Often those who have questions about the practical benefit of justification by faith focus on what we *do* instead of *how* we *think* and *feel*. I am not dismissing what we do in the least and will return to that matter at the conclusion of this essay. However, it is short-sighted to think only about what we do, for what we think and feel influences what we do. We are not just machines who perform tasks. What we think and feel about ourselves often fills the horizon of our lives. We often fail to do what we should because of how we are feeling. Our behavior and actions flow out of our thinking and our emotions. Thus, I want to consider some of the practical benefits of justification.

My purpose is not to exposit a particular text on justification by faith. The focus will be especially on what justification means in our lives, so I will be briefer on explanation and longer on application. Five benefits of justification will be featured here: 1) justification produces praise—so our souls are filled with joy; 2) justification brings assurance—we know God smiles on us; 3) justification removes guilt—we know God loves us and accepts us; 4) justification makes us realistic about our lives—we still struggle with sin; 5) justification unleashes love—faith produces love in our hearts for God and others. Some of these are closely related, but it is helpful to turn the diamond different ways so that we see its various facets.

Justification Produces Praise

Justification by faith alone means we are right with God by faith and not by our works. Paul declares in both Galatians 3:2 and 5 that

---

2   Thomas R. Schreiner, *Faith Alone. The Doctrine of Justification: What the Reformers Taught … and Why It Matters* (Grand Rapids: Zondervan, 2015).

we are justified by faith instead of by doing the works of the law. Our works cannot save us since we are sinners, and God demands perfection (Rom 1:18–3:20; Gal 3:10). Since we are saved not by our works but by faith in Christ, our redemption brings glory exclusively to God. We aren't saved because our faith is great but because our faith is in almighty God who sent his Son to atone for our sins (cf. Rom 4:17–25). As Jonah said in his prayer when he was rescued from the great fish, "Salvation belongs to the LORD" (Jonah 2:9).[3] God has secured our salvation through the cross and resurrection of Jesus Christ. Romans 3:24–26 teaches that God redeemed us through the death of Christ, a bloody death that appeased and satisfied God's righteous anger. Since justification is God's work and not ours, since we have done nothing to earn God's favor, we respond in praise.

Many of our hymns and songs celebrate justification. Hymns such as *Amazing Grace*, perhaps the most beloved song among believers, express our gratefulness. The hymn is beloved for good reason; when we *realize and feel* that God has poured out his grace on us entirely apart from our works, his grace stuns and amazes us. We are filled with praise and thanks. We say from our hearts thank the Lord, thank the Lord, for all his love. We give thanks with gratefulness to the Holy One of Israel for delivering us from our own foolishness and rebellion. Some criticize justification by faith alone because they think it leads us to be passive. Such criticism can only be valid if we take grace for granted. But when we are astonished by the wonder of our salvation, when we are full of praise and joy, we live different lives.

When we are filled with joy because we are right with God, we are happy in God. True joy can't be hidden. True joy in God is contagious. Such joy in God touches those with whom we have

---

3   All citations are from the CSB.

contact, pointing them to the gospel of grace, pointing them to the love of God in Christ Jesus our Lord. When we truly feel that we are right with God based on his grace, we are filled with "inexpressible and glorious joy" (1 Pet 1:8).

Joy, of course, expresses itself differently in different personalities. A quiet person has an unobtrusive joy, while an extroverted person's joy manifests itself in a more outgoing way. Thus, joy should not be confused with a particular personality type. On the other hand, whatever one's personality, there is true and genuine joy. It is fascinating how many people miss this in considering the practical benefit of justification. They fail to consider the radiance and excitement that fills our lives when we know the gospel.

Such joy isn't natural to us. It comes through the gospel. It comes from knowing and experiencing the free grace of God. That is why Luther taught us that we must relearn the gospel every day and Satan tries to turn us away from this truth. Luther remarks,

> Every day I experience only too well how insistently the devil assails this core [the truth of justification] in an effort to wipe it out. And although tired 'saints' consider it unnecessary to keep at this matter—they imagine that they know it inside and out and have learned all there is to know—still I know how wrong they are, and that they know absolutely nothing about the importance of this point. If this one teaching stands in its purity, then Christendom will also remain pure and good, undivided and unseparated; for this alone, and nothing else, makes and maintains Christendom.[4]

For Luther the doctrine isn't merely an intellectual belief but one that we put into practice in the rough and tumble of our everyday lives; putting it into practice isn't easy.

---

4   Martin Luther, *Selected Psalms III* (vol. 14 of *Luther's Works*, ed. Jaroslav Pelikan; St. Louis: Concordia, 1958), 36–37.

Justification by faith is alien to the way we think and the way we live, and that is why Luther captures so powerfully how difficult it is to live by this truth. Luther again opined:

> Particularly when you hear an immature and unripe saint trumpet that he knows very well that we must be saved through the grace of God, without our own works, and then pretend that this a snap for him, well, then have no doubt that he has no idea of what he is talking about and probably will never find out. For this is not an art that can be completely learned or of which anyone could boast that he is a master. It is an art that will always have us as pupils while it remains the master. All those who do understand and practice it do not boast that they can do everything. On the contrary, they sense it like a wonderful taste or odor that they greatly desire and pursue; and they are amazed that they cannot grasp it or comprehend as they would like. They hunger, thirst, and yearn for it more and more; and they never tire of hearing about it.[5]

Luther rightly discerns the difficulty of learning what justification means amid life's trials. We lapse back naturally and easily into works-righteousness. It is second nature to us to feel like we must earn something so that we can prove our worth and significance. Furthermore, everything we do in life is based on works: our schoolwork, our job, our parenting, etc. People are always evaluating us; do we measure up? Justification by faith reminds us that we need the Lord, that we can't make it on our own, that we are "poor in spirit" (Matt 5:3). There is something so beautiful about free grace that we seek it out when we are tired, exhausted, and spiritually empty. Thus, we need to return to this truth repeatedly so that we are full of praise and thanksgiving.

---

5   Luther, *Selected Psalms*, 37.

Justification Brings Assurance

A genuine understanding of justification brings assurance and comfort. If salvation is of the Lord, and we put our trust in Him, then God's grace comforts and consoles us in our doubts because we know that our salvation does not rest on us and what we do. We see in Galatians 3:1 that the devil can cast a spell over us, that the Galatians were beginning to listen to the wrong message, to the wrong gospel. Satan may wave a wand over us so that we forget about what it means to be right with God. We can forget that our righteousness isn't in ourselves but in Jesus Christ. We can forget about imputed righteousness.

Imputed righteousness might seem like a sterile academic doctrine, a doctrine that is restricted to seminary classrooms and academic discussions. Such academic discussions are vital, but we also need to understand that imputed righteousness provides soul comfort in the hardest times. One of the key texts for imputation is 2 Corinthians 5:21, "He [God] made the one who did not know sin [Christ] to be sin for us, so that in him we might become the righteousness of God." Here we see the great exchange where Christ took our sin, and we received his righteousness as we are united with Christ by faith.

Once we truly grasp biblical teaching on imputed righteousness, we don't have to wonder if we have done enough to be saved, for our job isn't to work *for* God but to *believe* in God. God does not ask us to *achieve* but to *believe*. He doesn't ask us to *work* for Him but to *rest* in Him (Rom 4:2–5). Unbelievers find such teaching difficult to believe since they are wired to do something to merit God's favor. Justification teaches us to cease striving and to give ourselves entirely to God. If we belong to Jesus, we know that Christ is our righteousness. Our righteousness doesn't reside in ourselves but in Christ crucified and risen.

Luther captures this truth well in his classic *Bondage of the Will*, expressing,

> Even if I lived and worked to eternity, my conscience would never be assured and certain how much it ought to do to satisfy God. For whatever work might be accomplished, there would always remain an anxious doubt whether it pleased God or whether he required something more, as the experience of all self-justifiers proves, and as I learned to my bitter cost through so many years. But now, since God has taken salvation out of my hands into his, making it depend on his choice and not mine, and has promised to save me, not by my own work or exertion but by his grace and mercy, I am assured and certain both that he is faithful and will not lie to me.[6]

In Roman Catholic theology, according to the Council of Trent, assurance is anathema (6.9 and Canon 9, 11, 16). However, 1 John 5:13 gives us the purpose of John's letter: "I have written these things to you who believe in the name of the Son of God so that you may know that you have eternal life." It could scarcely be clearer. The Lord desires believers to have confidence and assurance of their salvation.

The assurance imputed righteousness brings is illustrated in the life and especially the death of J. Gresham Machen. As Machen lay dying in the 1930s. he received comfort from the great truth of the imputation of Christ's righteousness. Machen, of course, was one of the luminaries among evangelicals in the first part of the 20th century. He founded both the Orthodox Presbyterian Church and Westminster Theological Seminary in Philadelphia. He was a godly

---

6   Martin Luther, *De Servo Arbitrio*, in *Luther and Erasmus: Free Will and Salvation* (trans. and ed. Philip S. Watson in collaboration with B. Drewery; LCC; Philadelphia: Westminster, 1969), 329.

man and wrote many books defending and explaining the faith, including *The Origin of Paul's Religion, The Virgin Birth of Christ*, and *Christianity and Liberalism*.

Machen was in his fifties and ministering in the Dakotas when he became mortally ill while traveling. What would you imagine Machen was thinking about as he was dying? Did he think about all that he had done for the kingdom, his tireless labors for the gospel, his devotion to the truth? On the contrary he almost certainly reflected on his sins! His many failings! The devil loves to bring our sins to mind in our last days and hours. But Machen knew the gospel. He knew the truth that our righteousness isn't in ourselves but in Jesus Christ, and thus he wrote to John Murray as he lay dying: "I'm so thankful for the active obedience of Christ; no hope without it."[7] The phrase "the active obedience of Christ" is technical, but it means that as Machen died he rested not in his own goodness but in the righteousness of God given to him in Jesus Christ, the imputed righteousness of Christ. As a result of this he died with assurance and comfort.

Justification Frees from Guilt

One of the most disabling experiences in life is guilt. Guilt and shame can paralyze us. In our hours alone instead of being at peace, we may think of our sin, our shame, and our weaknesses. Perhaps at certain times when we are isolated the guilt of our sins seems overwhelming. Such reflections may bring despair and even deep depression. Justification by faith alone reminds us that our sins are truly forgiven, that we are clean before God. As Romans 8:1 says "Therefore, there is now no condemnation for those in Christ Jesus." Paul goes on to say

---

7   Ned Stonehouse, *J. Gresham Machen: A Biographical Memoir* (1954; reprint, Grand Rapids: Eerdmans, 1978), 508.

in Romans 8:3, "For what the law could not do since it was weakened by the flesh, God did. He condemned sin in the flesh by sending his own Son in the likeness of sinful flesh as a sin offering." In Luther's day he was good friends with a man named Dr. Krause.[8] Tragically, Dr. Krause ended up committing suicide because he thought he denied Christ and became convinced that Christ was accusing him at the Father's right hand because of his defection. Clearly, Dr. Krause's suicide came from overwhelming feelings of guilt.

The flaw of such thinking was rightly refuted by Luther when he asserted that such despair was a lie of the devil. Christ is "not … a judge or tempter or an accuser but … the Reconciler, the Mediator, the Comforter, the Savior, and the Throne of grace."[9] If we think Christ accuses us before the Father, we are not hearing the gospel. For the gospel teaches that believers are God's beloved sons and beloved daughters. Satan whispers a false gospel to believers, insinuating that we are no good, that we are failures, that we are condemned before God. As believers we are prone to listen to the wrong message, forgetting that the good news is that we are saved by hearing the gospel with faith and not by the works of the law.

Paul declares in Galatians 3:13 that "Christ redeemed us from the curse of the law by becoming a curse for us." Guilt no longer defiles and stains us. Isaiah 1:18 prophesied, "Though your sins are scarlet, they will be as white as snow; though they are crimson red, they will be like wool." Furthermore, Micah 7:19 reveals God has thrown our sins into the deepest sea. Believers have assurance because we belong to the crucified and risen Christ.

---

8 See Martin Luther, *Lectures on Galatians, 1535: Chapters 1–4* (vol. 26 of *Luther's Works*, ed. Jaroslav Pelikan; St. Louis: Concordia, 1964), 195.

9 Luther, *Lectures on Galatians*, 195.

Justification Makes Us Realistic

Justification by faith fits with the "already" and "not yet" nature of our salvation. While we are new in Christ and indwelt with the Holy Spirit (Rom 8:1–17), we are not all that we should be, and we are certainly not all that we will be. We are like people who have come out of the freezing cold (the world) to what is warm (the love of God and righteousness). But we still feel the cold (our sin) as our hands are warming (we are becoming more like Christ). Faith does not transport us to paradise immediately because we still struggle with sin as Paul explains in Galatians 5:16–18 and in Romans 7:14–25. Luther famously recognized that we are righteous and sinners at the same time.

The paradoxical reality of Christian existence keeps us humble, reminding us that we still need the righteousness of Christ to stand before God. Luther remarks that the Christian "really and truly feels that there is sin in him and that on this account he is worthy of wrath, the judgment of God, and eternal death. Thus, he is humbled in this life."[10] Luther captures, better than any theologian, the weakness that still bedevils our lives. He catches and paints the tension so well because he experienced it himself. He says,

> "The words 'freedom from the wrath of God, from the Law, sin, death, etc.,' are easy to say, but to feel the greatness of the freedom and to apply its results to oneself in a struggle, in the agony of conscience, and in practice—this is more difficult than anyone can say."[11]

Living by faith is not easy in this fallen world since we are in battle between the flesh and the Spirit. We sigh and groan and

---

10   Luther, *Lectures on Galatians*, 235.

11   Martin Luther, *Lectures on Galatians, 1535: Chapters 5–6* (vol. 27 of *Luther's Works*, ed. Jaroslav Pelikan; St. Louis: Concordia, 1964), 5.

struggle against continuing sin, but we are also encouraged; we realize that our righteousness isn't in ourselves but in Jesus Christ crucified and risen.

Justification Unleashes Love

I have raised a practical question in this essay. Does justification by faith change the way we live? Does it make any difference in our everyday lives? I have been making the case that we live differently when we think and feel about ourselves differently. When we live with joy, assurance, and guiltlessness, then our lives will take on a radiant quality. We remain radiant even during suffering.

Still, justification by faith alone is not restricted to feelings; it also manifests itself in the way we live in the world. In Galatians 5:6 Paul speaks of "faith expressing itself in love" (NLT). In other words, faith unleashes love in our lives. When we truly trust God, when we depend upon Him for everything, then our lives are marked by love as the fruit of faith. Faith alone is not an abstraction but, so to speak, a productive machine. And if faith expresses itself in love, it shows up in a variety of ways. In Romans 13:8–10 we are told that all the law's commands, such as do not commit adultery or do not murder or do not steal, are summed up in the command to love. But if love is the fruit of faith, then keeping these commands is also the result and consequence of faith. Colossians 3:14 says that all the virtues of a godly life are captured in love that is shown to others. The virtues that capture the life of love are beautifully expressed in 1 Corinthians 13:4–7, and Paul encapsulates the Christian life with the words "walk in love" (Eph 5:2).

The faith that justifies is not idle but active and full of good fruit. Since we are already accepted and loved by God, we do not show love to others so that God will love us. We don't live a godly life with the motivation that God will then love us and accept us as his children. Our love is the overflow of God's grace. Since God has accepted us in Christ, we are freed up to love others. Since the God of the universe knows everything about us, all our faults and our sins, and the darkness of our hearts, and still loves us, our love is not an attempt to prove anything about ourselves to God or anyone else. God's grace in Christ forgives us, accepts us and loves us as we are, which leads us to respond in love. Our lives are changed. "We love," as 1 John 4:19 assures, "because he first loved us."

Epilogue

Justification by faith reminds us that we are loved by God, that we do not stand condemned before Him, and that we are free from guilt. When we recognize these truths, we are filled with praise, with joy, with radiance. The love and freedom that comes from justification touches every part of our lives, and in turn it affects the way we treat others. We live in a new way: with humility, grace, mercy, and joy because of what God has done for us in Jesus Christ, declaring that we stand in the right before Him based on Christ's saving work in his cross and resurrection.

Chapter two

Pray with Humility and Hope: Lessons from Hezekiah's Prayer in Isaiah 37:16–20

Mark Catlin

In the fall of 2019, my family and I moved to Memphis so that I could teach for Union University. As we were planning to move, one of the most important factors was where we would go to church. As we asked around about good churches in the Memphis area, one name kept popping up—South Woods Baptist pastored by Phil Newton. Friends we knew in Memphis *and all over the country* recommended we visit. Since we were looking for a church in a different area of Memphis, we did not visit there. Sometimes we lack wisdom. In the five years since we moved to Memphis, the Lord has been kind enough to let me get to know Phil. I have had a front row seat to Phil's life in "retirement." I now know why so many recommended that we entrust ourselves to Phil as our shepherd. He preaches the word faithfully with conviction and compassion; loves and leads his wife with gentleness and understanding; and cares for his elderly mother with joyful patience. Furthermore, in this so-called retirement, he continues to serve local churches in Memphis and around the world by raising up and training pastors to lead healthy churches. In short, Phil is a man who is worthy to imitate as he imitates Christ. So, I am thrilled to write an essay for this volume. My main area of study is the Book of Isaiah, and prayer is essential to the life of any faithful pastor. I trust this short offering on praying with humility and hope honors Phil, encourages and strengthens pastors, and most of all glorifies Christ.

The Book of Isaiah revolves around Sennacherib's invasion of Judah in Isaiah 36–37. Throughout Isaiah, God's people are beset by enemies from within and without. Their own idolatry and injustice have turned the faithful city into an adulteress. As a result, the Assyrians have become an instrument of judgment in the hand of Yahweh. Over the course of his ministry, Isaiah would witness the capture of all of Israel at the hands of Assyrian kings. Tiglath-Pileser III, Shalmeneser V, and Sargon II all contributed to taking the northern tribes of Israel by 722 BC. Then, in the fourteenth year of King Hezekiah (701 BC), Sennacherib took all the fortified cities of Judah (Isa 36:1). At this point, only Jerusalem remained out from under the boot of the Assyrian army. They would also set their sights on her, but the Assyrian army would be turned back, and Jerusalem rescued.

Sennacherib's invasion in 701 BC is the culminating historical reality behind the prophetic imagery of Isaiah 8:7–8,

> "The LORD will certainly bring against them the mighty rushing water of the Euphrates River—the king of Assyria and all his glory. It will overflow its channels and spill over all its banks. It will pour into Judah, flood over it, and sweep through reaching up to the neck."[1]

Or, as Sennacherib put it, he had Jerusalem surrounded and Hezekiah trapped "like a bird in a cage."[2] Yet, just as the waters rise

---

1   All biblical citations use the *Christian Standard Bible* version.
2   "Sennacherib's Siege of Jerusalem," trans. Mordechai Cogan (*Context of Scripture* 2.119B:303).

to the neck, they recede, and Hezekiah is freed from his proverbial cage. After decades of Assyrian dominance, the yoke of Assyrian oppression is broken by a single prayer. If the Book of Isaiah turns on the rescue of Jerusalem from Sennacherib's hand in Isaiah 36–37, then it also hinges around King Hezekiah's prayer in Isaiah 37:16–20. Hezekiah's prayer was God's orchestrated means to work his sovereign purposes for the good of his people and the glory of his name. God still empowers and uses prayer in similar ways and should shape how pastors pray today. The prayer of Isaiah 37:16–20 calls pastors to pray with humility and hope because our sovereign God sees, hears, and saves.

Hezekiah's Prayer

The immediate context of Hezekiah's prayer is a letter from Sennacherib to Hezekiah (Isa 37:10–15). In this letter, Sennacherib echoes the central thrust of his earlier propaganda. Sennacherib challenged the power of Yahweh to deliver Jerusalem from his hand, compared Yahweh to the other gods, and called the people of Jerusalem to place their trust in Sennacherib rather than in Yahweh or Hezekiah (Isa 36:4–10, 12–20). In response to these messages, Hezekiah tears his garment, goes to the temple, and sends this message to Isaiah, "Today is a day of distress, rebuke, and disgrace. It is as if children have come to the point of birth, and there is no strength to deliver them" (Isa 37:3).[3] Hezekiah then asks Isaiah to pray considering the situation.[4]

---

3   On the significance of these acts, see Gregory Goswell, "Royal Reactions: The Behavior of Hezekiah in Isaiah 36–37," in *Trinity Journal* (2021) 139–145.

4   Although asking for others to pray can certainly be a sign of faith, Brevard Childs is likely correct that in this context, Hezekiah's "request for the prophet to intercede in prayer is hesitant, uncertain, and tentative," idem, *Isaiah*, Old Testament Library series (London: Westminster John Knox, 2001), 274.

In his letter to Hezekiah, Sennacherib recalls that other kings trusted their gods to save them from Sennacherib. But they fell by the Assyrian sword. Sennacherib warns that the same fate awaits Hezekiah if he were to trust in Yahweh. In so doing, Sennacherib implies that Yahweh is no different from the gods of other nations, and therefore does not have the power to save. In direct opposition to Sennacherib's warning, Hezekiah now goes to the temple himself and prays to Yahweh. He places Sennacherib's words before Yahweh and prays:

> LORD of Armies, God of Israel, enthroned between the cherubim, you are God—you alone—of all the kingdoms of the earth. Listen closely, LORD, and see. Hear all the worst that Sennacherib has sent to mock the living God. LORD, it is true that the kings of Assyria have devastated all these countries and their lands. They have thrown their gods into the fire, for they were not gods but made from wood and stone by human hands. So they have destroyed them. Now, LORD our God, save us from his power so that all the kingdoms of the earth may know that you, LORD, are God—you alone (Isa 37:16–20).

In response to this prayer, Yahweh defeats Sennacherib and rescues Jerusalem (Isa 37:21–38). Hezekiah rightfully prays to Yahweh in faith because he believes that, despite Sennacherib's claims, his God is the sovereign one who sees, hears, and saves his people.

God is Sovereign

The beginning of Hezekiah's prayer stands in stark contrast to the claims of Sennacherib. Hezekiah's description of Yahweh in Isaiah 37:16 is a faith-filled confession that counters Sennacherib's challenge and expresses the universal kingship of Yahweh,[5] which is the central theological point of the whole narrative.[6] Hezekiah begins his prayer by calling upon the "LORD of Armies." The CSB translation highlights the military imagery of the phrase. Concerning this military connotation, John Oswalt notes, "All the hosts of heaven are at his beck and call; he can do whatever he wishes."[7] In the Book of Isaiah, this title most often occurs in the "context of Yahweh's covenant with Israel and His right and ability to judge persons and nations."[8] In other words, this phrase highlights the sovereignty of Israel's God over the powers of heaven and earth, including his power to defeat the strongest of military foes to save his people.

"Enthroned between the cherubim" recalls the Ark of the Covenant. When Yahweh instructs Moses on the design of the Ark of the Covenant, he says:

> Make two cherubim of gold … . Make one cherub at one end and one cherub at the other end. The cherubim are to have wings spread out above, covering the mercy seat … . Set the mercy seat on top of the ark. I will meet with you there above the mercy seat, between the two cherubim that are over the ark of the testimony (Ex 25:18–22).

Thus, "enthroned between the cherubim" recalls Yahweh's presence in the temple ("I will meet you there"), the precise location

---

5   For more on the kingship of Yahweh expressed in Isaiah 36–37, see Andrew Abernethy, *The Book of Isaiah and God's Kingdom: A Thematic-Theological Approach*, NSBT 40 (Downers Grove: IVP, 2016), 46–51.

6   Goswell, "Royal Reactions," 150.

7   John Oswalt, *Isaiah*, NIVAC (Grand Rapids: Zondervan, 2003), 413.

8   Paul House, *Isaiah: Chapters 28–66*, Mentor (Geanies House: Christian Focus, 2019), 2:213.

where Hezekiah prays this prayer.[9] Hezekiah's association of "enthroned between the cherubim" and "LORD of Armies" recalls the combination of these phrases in 1–2 Samuel, where this title seems particularly associated with the Ark of the Covenant (2 Sam 6:2); God's covenant with King David (2 Sam 7:27); and military victory (1 Sam 17:45). Isaiah shares similar concerns for God's covenant with David (e.g. Isa 9:1–7; 11:1–16; 37:35; 55:4), military victory (e.g. Isa 36–37), and God's presence with his people (e.g. Isa 7:14).

Hezekiah's invocation also explicitly articulates the incomparability of Yahweh among other so-called gods ("You are God alone"), especially since Yahweh is the creator of all things ("You have made the heavens and the earth").[10] Yahweh as creator stands above and over his creation. Yahweh, therefore, is not merely the God of Israel, but also the ruler of the kingdoms of the earth. He is God alone. Surely, then, this God is greater than the gods formed by *human* hands. This monotheistic confession anticipates the soaring theology of the following chapters of Isaiah. In Isaiah 40–55, Yahweh is the one who created the ends of the earth (Isa 40:28), founded the earth with his hand (Isa 42:5; 44:23; 48:13; 51:13, 16), created mankind upon it, and is able to gather those who have been scattered to the ends of the earth (Isa 41:5, 9; 42:10; 43:6; 45:22; 48:20; 49:6; 52:10). Therefore, Yahweh holds sway over creation and its rulers (Isa 40:12; 40:22, 23, 24; 46:11; 49:23), including Yahweh's servant who will bring justice to the earth (Isa 42:4). Because Yahweh is sovereign over all the earth and its inhabitants, he alone can bring salvation in which the earth both

---

9   On the significance of Hezekiah in the temple, especially in contrast to Sennacherib, see Gregory Goswell "Isaiah 36–39: Life and Death in the House of God" in *The Journal of Theological Studies* (April 2023), 1–19.

10   For the classic treatment of incomparability in the Old Testament, see C. J. Labuschagne, *The Incomparability of Yahweh in the Old Testament*, Pretoria Oriental Series 5 (Leiden: Brill, 1966).

participates (Isa 45:8; 49:8, 19; 53:2) and rejoices (Isa 41:18; 44:24; 49:13). Yahweh truly is God over all the earth (Isa 54:5).[11]

This God is the "God of Israel," whom Sennacherib has mocked. The God of Israel is the creator of the universe, the one who commands heaven's armies on behalf of his people. He is the King of kings, the sovereign one. Sennacherib has supposed that he will defeat and dispose of the God of Israel, as he has the gods of the nations. In so doing, Sennacherib has struck fear in the heart of Jerusalem and her King Hezekiah. Hezekiah's prayer settles his own troubled soul. Sennacherib has no authority, except that which has been given to him so that God might accomplish His purposes. Ultimately this is all for God's glory and the good of His people. Hezekiah, Jerusalem, and its inhabitants will be delivered by the hand of Yahweh (Isa 37:33–35). Gary Smith sums up well the point of Hezekiah's invocation:

> Hezekiah is not justifying his beliefs to others, developing an abstract doctrine of theology, or informing God at this point; he is primarily calling out to the only divine king who controls the world because Hezekiah needs Almighty God to use his power … . to rectify what Sennacherib has falsely claimed.[12]

Hezekiah prays to this Almighty God because he hears, sees, and saves.

God Sees and Hears

A prophet can rightly be understood, perhaps most fundamentally, as God's mouthpiece (see Ex 4:14–16; 7:1–2). Yet,

---

11 Matthew Seufert, "Reading Isaiah 40:1–11 in Light of Isaiah 36–37" in *JETS* 58 (2015), 266–67.

12 Gary V. Smith, *Isaiah 1–39*, New American Commentary 15A (Nashville: B&H, 2007), 618–19.

God does not simply speak into a vacuum, devoid of context. He speaks to his people in a particular time, place, and circumstance. When God speaks, he speaks to people he sees, whose voices he hears. God demonstrates that he hears Hezekiah's prayer as he responds through the prophet Isaiah, "Because you prayed to me about King Sennacherib of Assyria, this is the word the LORD has spoken against him" (Isa 37:21). Hezekiah's prayer, however, does not focus on his ability for God to hear the prayers of *his people*. Rather, Hezekiah petitions God to hear the words of *his enemy*.

The servants who meet with Sennacherib's messenger (Isa 36:3), the people in the city of Jerusalem (Isa 36:11–12), and Hezekiah, have all heard the mocking words of Sennacherib. Their knowledge of his mockery and intent to destroy the people of God matters not since they are powerless to stop the Assyrian king and his army. Hezekiah has admitted as much, as his initial response to Sennacherib demonstrates (Isa 37:3). He seems to admit his weakness in this prayer as well, as he recounts the Assyrian kings' track record of success and shows no confidence in his own ability to save Jerusalem from Sennacherib (Isa 37:18–20). If left to his own strength, Hezekiah would face the same end as the kings of other nations. So, he calls upon Yahweh because he knows that if Yahweh sees his people's situation and hears the mocking voice of his enemy, Zion will have a chance to be rescued (Isa 37:20). Then he cries out for the living God to see and hear—and God does.

Immediately following Hezekiah's prayer, Yahweh reveals that He has heard Sennacherib's blaspheming (Isa 37:23–24, 29) and knows Sennacherib's movements (Isa 37:28). Yahweh further reveals that He is no mere observer of Sennacherib's actions, nor is He forced into action unwillingly by Hezekiah's pesky prayer. Yahweh has been in control the whole time. He says, "Have you not heard? I [Yahweh] designed it long ago; I planned it in days gone by. I have now brough it to pass, and you [Sennacherib] have crushed fortified cities in to piles of rubble" (Isa 37:26). Yahweh, therefore, knows every detail of Sennacherib's actions, even before they come to pass, including Sennacherib's defeat and return to his own land. Yahweh continues, "I know your sitting down, your going out and your coming in, and your raging against me. Because your raging against me and your arrogance have reached my ears, I will put my hook in your nose and my bit in your mouth; I will make you go back the way you came" (Isa 37:28–29). Apparently, Yahweh not only sees and hears, but He also speaks and acts on behalf of his people.

On a pastoral note, one of the most comforting truths for the people of God is that He sees and hears both us and our enemies. Our God is keenly aware that we need to be confident of these truths, so He speaks to us. By the end of the episode with Sennacherib, only Isaiah, Hezekiah, and a few messengers are aware of Yahweh's response to Sennacherib. Others still have concerns about God's care for them. The God of Israel quotes the complaint of his people, "Jacob, why do you say, and, Israel, why do you assert: 'My way is hidden from the LORD, and my claim is ignored by my God'" (Isa 40:27)? Yahweh has heard their cry and will provide an answer. Isaiah 40–55, in large part, should be read as God's response to let *all* of those who have experienced the terror of Sennacherib, including the inhabitants of Jerusalem (Isa 40:1–2) and the cities of Judah (Isa 40:9–11), know that the living God sees and hears them. Yahweh does this to comfort his people by showing his incomparability among the gods and his divine rule over the kings of the earth.

Yahweh quotes Sennacherib, saying, "You have said, 'With my many chariots I have gone up to the heights of the mountains, to the far recesses of Lebanon. I cut down its tallest cedars, its choice cypress trees. I came to its distant heights, its densest forest. I dug wells and drank water in foreign lands.[13] I dried up all the streams of Egypt with the soles of my feet'" (Isa 37:24–25). Isaiah 40–55 takes up the language that describes Sennacherib and ascribes it to Yahweh in greater measure to show that Yahweh is superior to Sennacherib. Therefore, Yahweh has the power to save Jerusalem from Sennacherib's hand. Although Sennacherib has gone to the heights of the mountains, Yahweh holds the mountains in a scale (Isa 40:12) and can lay them waste (Isa 40:4; 41:15; 42:15; 49:11; 54:10).

Furthermore, the mountain top will be the place from which God's redeemed people will proclaim the good news that Yahweh is king (Isa 40:9; 42:11; 52:7), even as the mountains themselves give praise to Yahweh (Isa 44:23; 49:13; 55:12). Although Sennacherib cut down Lebanon's cedars and cypress trees, Yahweh is the one who can cause cedars to grow in the wilderness and cypresses in the desert (Isa 41:19; 55:13), and for whom "Lebanon would not suffice for fuel, nor are its beasts enough or a burnt offering" (Isa 40:16). Whereas Sennacherib provides water from wells and dries up the streams of Egypt, Yahweh is the one who dries up the deepest waters (Isa 44:27) and the sea in the exodus out of Egypt (Isa 50:2; 51:10). Indeed, He holds all the waters of the earth in his hands (Isa 40:12).

Yahweh further echoes his response to Sennacherib by the way He asks questions in Isaiah 40–55. Yahweh responds to Sennacherib by posing the question: "Whom have you mocked and blasphemed"

---

13   Stéphanie Anthonioz, "Water(s) of Abundance in the Ancient Near East and in Hebrew Bible Texts: A Sign of Kingship," in *Thinking of Water in the Early Second Temple Period,* eds. Ehud Ben Zvi and Christoph Levvin, BZAW461 (Berlin: De Gruyter, 2014), 60–62, argues that the ability to enable waters to gush forth is a unique attribute of the king in Mesopotamia.

(Isa 37:23)? Yahweh also asks Sennacherib if he understands that Yahweh handed the fortified cities of Judah over to him, introducing the question, "Have you not heard" (Isa 37:26)? In Isaiah 40–55, Yahweh uses "Have you not heard?" to introduce Yahweh's absolute superiority (Isa 40:21, 28). Isaiah 40–55 also uses very similar phrasing to speak of things that Yahweh planned long ago and has now accomplished (Isa 45:21; 46:10; 51:9).

The central texts that form Isaiah's polemics against idolatry all begin with "Who?" questions (Isa 40:18–20; 41:2, 4, 6–7; 44:7–20; 46:5–7) in which Isaiah and Yahweh invite an explicit comparison between Yahweh and the idols.[14] Furthermore, "Who?" questions occur frequently throughout Isaiah 40–55, almost always inviting a direct comparison with Yahweh, in which Yahweh is clearly vindicated either over other gods or unbelieving Israel (Isa 40:12, 13, 14, 25; 41:26; 42:19, 23, 24; 43:9; 44:10; 45:21; 48:14; 49:21; 50:8, 9; 51:19). As He expands his response to Sennacherib to speak to his people, Yahweh uses these questions to argue that He is the one true God worthy of trust.

These concerns are not merely academic. They rest at the heart of our hope in God. The sovereign one who sees and hears our specific situations also speaks specific words of comfort and acts for our salvation. Yahweh is nothing like the idols that the Assyrian kings have destroyed on their way to Jerusalem. The God of Israel is the Unmade Maker, the one true and living God. These truths are not for the few, but for the many, as Hezekiah makes clear at the end of his prayer.

---

14   Knut Holter, *Second Isaiah's Idol-fabrication Passages*, BBET 28 (Frankfurt am Main Peter Lang, 1995), 29.

God Saves (Isa 37:20)

Hezekiah ends his prayer much like he began. He recognizes Yahweh as the only true God and king over all the earth. Considering who God is, Hezekiah makes known his final petition and his purpose—the salvation of Jerusalem for the glory of God: "Now, Lord our God, save us from his power so that all the kingdoms of the earth may know that you, LORD, are God—you alone" (Isa 37:20). Yahweh answers immediately, "Because you prayed to me about King Sennacherib of Assyria, this is the word the LORD has spoken against him" (Isa 37:21–22). Yahweh goes on to speak a word of salvation for Jerusalem and defeat for Sennacherib. Sennacherib, however, will not lose *in battle*. His army will be defeated *before* any fighting takes place in Jerusalem. Yahweh says, "He [Sennacherib] will not enter this city, shoot an arrow here, come before it with a shield, or build up a siege ramp again sit. He will go back the way he came, and he will not enter this city" (Isa 37:33–34). Yahweh then defeats the Assyrian army in a way that demonstrates his superiority to the Assyrian king: "Then the angel of the LORD went out and struck down one hundred eighty-five thousand in the camp of the Assyrians. When the people got up the next morning—there were dead bodies! So, King Sennacherib of Assyria broke camp and left" (Isa 37:36–37). Yahweh has fulfilled his word to his people and demonstrated that He alone is God. He has accomplished this for the purpose stated in Hezekiah's prayer, "I [Yahweh] will defend this city and rescue it for my sake and for the sake of my servant David" (Isa 37:35). Isaiah, however, is not content to leave his readers with the deliverance of Jerusalem.

Isaiah lets his readers in on an event that will take place twenty years from the time of rescuing Jerusalem from Sennacherib's hand. The account of Sennacherib's invasion of Judah ends with

Sennacherib's death at the hand of his own sons (Isa 37:38). Ironically, Sennacherib himself dies by the Assyrian sword, and another king takes his place on the Assyrian throne (Isa 37:38). Sennacherib is dethroned, while Yahweh still rules over all the kingdoms of the earth. Sennacherib is dead, Yahweh lives. The true king and God of all the earth offers salvation from Jerusalem to the ends of the earth (e.g. Isa 49:6). His offer of salvation still stands today.

Pray with Humility and Hope

Given the richness of Hezekiah's prayer and the surrounding context in Isaiah, one could draw innumerable applications from the text. Here, I will offer two main applications for today's pastor that I hope can shape his life and ministry in multiple ways. Pastors should pray with humility because our God is sovereign. We pray with humility by recognizing our king, understanding our own weaknesses, and committing everything to prayer. Pastors should pray with hope because our sovereign God still sees, hears, and saves. We pray with hope by entrusting ourselves, our people, and unbelievers to the God who has promised to save.

Pray with Humility

Pastors should pray with humility by recognizing our sovereign king. Like Hezekiah, we should go to God in prayer with the posture that He is the king overall and that we are not. This posture relieves us of the burden that building the kingdom on earth as it is in heaven rests upon our shoulders. While we can sow and water, only God brings the increase. We should also recognize a difference between us and Hezekiah. We are not kings over the people we shepherd. The promised son of David and Abraham who will rule faithfully forever over all of creation to bless all nations is Jesus of Nazareth, our Messiah (Matt 1:1; 28:16–20). He is our Chief Shepherd.

The author of Hebrews tells us that our king is also our high priest. As high priest, Jesus ever lives to intercede for us (Heb 7:25). Since He is our perfect high priest, we should be comforted by Him and go to His throne of grace with boldness, knowing that He will sympathize with us in our weaknesses, and He will supply mercy and grace to help us in our time of need (Heb 4:14–16). This approach to the throne of grace may especially include confession of our own sin, as the author of Hebrews focuses on the high priest as the one who has atoned for our sins once and for all. This sentiment coheres with the idea of Jesus as our advocate in 1 John. There John writes that He does not want us to sin, but if we do, "we have an advocate with the Father—Jesus Christ the righteous one. He Himself is the atoning sacrifice for our sins, and not only for ours, but also for the those of the whole world" (1 John 2:1–2). When we recognize Jesus as our king and high priest, we are free to acknowledge or weaknesses and confess our sin. In so doing, the redeeming work of Jesus for His churches begins with our humble submission to our king. When we struggle to come to God in prayer to submit to our king, acknowledge our weaknesses, and confess our sin, we may have lost sight of who our enemy is.

We might be tempted to believe that the Assyrian army that Hezekiah faced is a bigger threat than anything we might face in our ministry. But just because we cannot see our enemy standing outside the window of the church surrounding the people of God with swords drawn while we worship, does not make him any less real. The Scriptures are clear that we face an enemy far more powerful than Sennacherib. Peter writes, "Your adversary the devil is prowling around like a roaring lion looking for anyone he can devour"

(1 Pet 5:8). It is no mistake that Peter speaks of our adversary after speaking about elders shepherding the flock and calling the flock to submit to their elders (1 Pet 5:1–5). Peter then tells the elders and flock alike to *clothe themselves with humility* because God resists the proud but *gives grace to the humble* (1 Pet 5:5).

Peter then writes, "Humble yourselves, therefore, under the mighty hand of God, so that he may exalt you at the proper time, casting all your cares on him, because he cares about you" (1 Pet 5:6–7). Peter goes on to say that we should "be sober-minded," "be alert," "resist," and "be firm in the faith" (1 Pet 5:8–9). One main way that we can do all these things is casting our cares on Him through prayer. As we go to Him, we should expect the God of all grace to "restore, establish, strengthen, and support" us (1 Pet 5:10). Given the power of prayer against our enemy, we can show humility by beginning everything we do with prayer.

The Book of Isaiah is riddled with ostentatious displays of arrogance. Ahaz, Assyria, Babylon, and, of course, Sennacherib. The nearly complete absence of prayer is striking. God is continually speaking to his people, but they, especially their leaders, do not seek communion with their God. While Hezekiah sets himself apart by humbling himself in prayer, he does not *begin* with prayer. Before Hezekiah prayed, he relied on other strategies for war. He relies on Egypt for an unholy alliance (Isa 36:6), and he tries to pay off Assyria with silver and gold (2 Kgs 18:13–16). When the Assyrian King kept marching toward Jerusalem, Hezekiah was left with no army, no money, no more bargaining chips. What could Hezekiah possibly do? Pray. He only turns to prayer when he has no other option. We would do well to learn from his mistake and begin everything we do with prayer.

Marketing strategies, carefully planned Sunday services, youth ministries, building campaigns, and well-run committees can be useful for the work of the local church. Apart from prayer, however, these can be expressions of arrogance and pride, believing that we can build God's kingdom apart from humbling ourselves under the mighty hand of God. By beginning with prayer, we remind ourselves that we are not the ones in control, and we entrust ourselves, our ministries, and our people to the one who is. Perhaps this is why Paul, after he commands the Ephesians to put on the full armor of God to stand against the schemes of the devil (Eph 6:10–17), also reminds them of the power of prayer during wartime. Once the people have clothed themselves with the full armor of God, Paul commands them to pray three times in the next three verses. Paul commands them to "pray at all times" (Eph 6:18) and twice he commands them to pray for him that he might preach the gospel with boldness (Eph 6:19). Paul acknowledged his own weaknesses, understood his enemy, and submitted himself in humility before his king in prayer. We should do the same, as we also pray in hope.

Pray with Hope

Praying with hope is difficult because, by definition, praying with hope means praying for what we do not see. The good news is that we can pray with confidence for what we do not see because we serve a faithful God. He will bring all his promises to fulfillment in Christ, including our salvation. Because our faithful God sees, hears, and saves, we should pray with hope for salvation.

We often discuss and speak of salvation in the past tense, as in "God saved me." And, of course, this is true. Praise be to God that we *have been* saved from our sins and raised to walk in newness of life! Therefore, we should pray that this initial act of salvation, whereby God regenerates and justifies someone by faith through the preaching of the gospel, continues to take place for those who have not yet come to a saving knowledge of Christ. In other words, we should pray similarly to Hezekiah, who prayed that what God has done for his people would be made known to all nations, including those who do not yet know Him, and that they would trust in Christ alone for salvation. We pray in hope that the salvation we do not currently see in the world around us will spring forth because the God who created all things by his Word still saves through the proclamation of his Word. While this is a wonderful and necessary aspect of God's salvation, God has promised us more than a one-time decision to follow Him in the past. He continues to work out his salvation in us and will bring it to completion with the new heavens and the new earth. So, there is more to pray for in salvation than unbelievers putting their faith in God for the first time.

Paul writes to the Philippian church, "I [Paul] am sure of this, that he who started a good work in you will carry it on to completion until the day of Christ Jesus" (Phil 1:6). We can see past (he who started a good work) present (will carry it on to completion) and future (until the day of Christ Jesus) in this one verse. Paul later describes this work in terms of salvation. After he describes the Incarnation and saving work of Christ in his life, death, resurrection, and ascension, he writes, "Therefore, my dear friends, just as you have always obeyed, so now, not only in my presence but even more in my absence, work out your own salvation with fear and trembling. For it is God who is work in you both to will and to work according to his good purpose" (Phil 2:12–13). Our Sovereign God calls us to work out our salvation because God is at work in us. Pray with hope that God's people can work for his good purpose. According to the natural eye and worldly way of thinking, Hezekiah should have had no confidence for victory over Sennacherib. The strength of those who oppose God's work, the weakness of your flesh, difficulty of your location, the pastoral issues you face in your church, persecution from the world, and even your own shortcomings in ministry cannot keep God from working out his salvation in his people. So, pray with confidence. Pray boldly. Pray with the hope that God is at work to put to death the deeds of the body, conform you and your people the image of Christ, and sanctify you by the Holy Spirit. God has promised these things, so pray in the hope that He will bring them to pass, and do not lose sight of the glory of the consummated new creation.

Revelation 21–22:5 is a breathtaking vision of the new creation to which we are headed. Although we do not see it yet, God is making a world in which "death will be no more; grief, crying, and pain will be no more, because the previous things have passed away" (Rev 21:4). These things will take place because God will make his dwelling with humanity and "He will wipe every tear from their eyes" (Rev 21:4). In this vision of the new creation, all our enemies have been defeated, including Satan, death, and our own sin, never to ruin the goodness of God's world again. When we look up from the page, of course, we see that we are surrounded by death, grief, crying and pain. The "previous things" remain. So, what should we do? Persevere by praying with hope in God's promise of a new creation. Pray with joy during your suffering, knowing that suffering in the name of Jesus leads to resurrection. Cry out to God in a prayer of lament, weeping and calling God to action against injustice, sickness, sin, and death, while trusting his infinite wisdom and timing. To pray with hope means to pray with confidence in what we do not yet see because we trust that the God who sees our current situation and hears our prayers, is also faithful to save his people. In this way, Hezekiah's prayer is exemplary.

Conclusion

In the Lord's kindness, He moved Isaiah to record Hezekiah's prayer in Isaiah 37:16–20. During a seemingly hopeless situation in which the promise of God's land, presence, and people seemed nearly null and void, Hezekiah cried out to God in faith. He cried out to Him in humility, submitting to God as the one true God and divine king. He cried out to Him in honesty, acknowledging the power of the enemy over him if left to his own strength. And he cried out to Him in hope, believing that the sovereign God of the universe would save his people from the enemy that mocked and reviled the living God. Hezekiah's prayer in 701 BC calls pastors to pray in similar ways for the people of God today. We should pray with humility by recognizing that Jesus as our king, understanding our weaknesses, and committing everything to prayer. We should pray with hope in the work that God is doing to save his people, even when we cannot see it.

Chapter three

Pastors, Love Your Wives: An Exposition of Ephesians 5:25–33

Todd Wilson

Husbands, love your wives …
Ephesians 5:25a[1]

Introduction: The Higher Call of Husband/Pastor

1 Timothy 3:2—Therefore an overseer must be above reproach, *the husband of one wife*

Titus 1:6— If any be blameless, *the husband of one wife*

In the verses above, the Apostle Paul began his list of qualifications for overseers (or *elders* or *pastors*[2]) in both pastoral letters. While "the husband of one wife" has been interpreted in various ways[3], the explanation that seems to best fit Paul's meaning of "husband of one wife" is that a man cannot be guilty of unfaithfulness in

---

1   All citations of Scripture are from the English Standard Version (ESV).
2   The title "overseer," "elder," and "pastor" are used interchangeably and describe the same office in the church. See Phil A. Newton, *40 Questions About Pastoral Ministry* (Grand Rapids: Kregel, 2021), 20.
3   See Newton, *40 Questions*, 38.

marriage. Fidelity, a singular devotion for and toward his spouse, is not an option for a husband to consider among other options, but a command to be obeyed, both joyfully and humbly. Captivating the mind (Song 7:5), keeping the heart (Prov 4:23), and a covenant with the eyes (Job 31:1) ought to be the spiritual routine of the husband. Of course, for the Christian husband, this routine flows from his ultimate and primary relationship with his Lord and Savior, Jesus Christ. And for the husband who is also called to pastor, the command has both a deeper meaning and a higher standard.

By this, Paul did not mean that a pastor must be married. However, if married, a pastor must be faithfully devoted to one woman, that one woman being his one wife. Note that this serves as the first of the things necessary for a pastor to be considered "above reproach" or "blameless." A pastor must have an unblemished reputation concerning his marriage and sexuality. There can be no question that his wife is the only woman he desires. In the home and in the church, his wife is his primary ministry!

The church should understand that their pastor has this biblical responsibility to his wife (and children as well if so blessed). Of course, this does not mean that a pastor can use his family as an excuse to neglect the flock. This has caused great turmoil in the life of a church. The opposite extreme is also dangerous. A pastor can be more "married to ministry" than "married to wife." And this has brought destruction to many a household. For the pastor, it takes the wisdom of the Holy Spirit to know how to live both of his callings as husband and as pastor. This is done in a way that honors and glorifies the Lord and is good for his church and his family. It takes a deep, devoted love to Christ as all in all (Eph 1:23). In Christ, in His bride, in the Church, a pastor finds the supreme example or model for a marriage that honors and glorifies God. If a pastor loves his wife "as Christ loved the church" (Eph 5:25), then he will not fail to be "above reproach" or "blameless" in his calling as husband *and* pastor. So, what does the phrase "as Christ loved the church" look like in Ephesians 5:25–27?

Christ's Love Is a Sacrificial Love

> *Eph 5:25*—Husbands, love your wives, as Christ loved the church and *gave himself up* for her.

The greatest expression of love is not that it gives things or even that it gives up things, but that it gives itself. I trust you recognize how counterintuitive this idea is in a culture that bombards us with selfishness everywhere we turn. In fact, such a statement would be considered absurd to say, even more to practice. We are inundated with images that promote the self, often at the expense of others. We are told to live for self because it is our right; to love ourselves and only be lovers of ourselves. This is what is known as *narcissism*. A narcissist might give the appearance of love, "giving of things" or even "giving up things," but these are only masked attempts to cover their selfishness.

This is not the love that the believer is to emulate, or the love that a husband, especially a pastor, is to have for his wife. [Note: For the rest I will use "pastor" in place of "husband" to emphasize the high calling described earlier] Christ's love was, and is, and forever will be, a sacrificial love, a selfless love. He "gave himself up" in sacrifice to the Father (Eph 5:2) for the church (Eph 5:25). The pastor is to have a similar sacrificial, selfless love, not a selfish love that abuses his headship at every turn.

Of course, Christ's sacrificial love accomplished what the pastor's love for his wife cannot. Christ's sacrifice for His bride was *penal*, satisfying the penalty required for sin, which being death (Rom 3:23; 6:23). Christ's sacrifice for His bride was *propitiatory*, satisfying God's righteous wrath and holy justice for sin (Rom 5:8–9; 1 John 2:2). Christ's love for His bride was *substitutionary*, satisfying the curse associated with sin as He Himself became a curse for her (Gal 3:13). Christ's love for His bride was *redemptive*, satisfying the price required for sin as her ransom (Mark 10:45; 1 Tim 2:6). His calling was to provide salvation as reconciler of those at enmity because of sin.

But while a pastor's love for his wife cannot accomplish what Christ accomplished for His bride; that is, her salvation. He is, nevertheless, to "love his wife" even "as Christ loved the church and gave himself up for her." How is a pastor to love his wife like that? If not for salvation, in what way is his call to sacrifice like that of Christ's sacrifice? J. Ligon Duncan gives the answer:

> It means loving our wives in light of the sacrifice of Christ. It means loving our wives in light of the self-giving sacrifice of Christ in the cross. It means loving our wives in light of the atonement.
>
> The cross is first and foremost about what God has done on our behalf, something that we could never do for ourselves. The cross is first and foremost about God's glory. It's a matchless action that cannot be repeated. But having seen that great work of God's love and that great work of God's redemption, the Apostle Paul himself is telling Christian husbands here to look at the cross and learn how to love your wife. The Apostle Paul is saying Christ lived and suffered and died for His bride; so, Christian husband, *you live, and if necessary, suffer and die* for your wife's good.[4]

---

4   J. Ligon Duncan, https://fpcjackson.org/resource-library/sermons/god-s-new-family-an-exposition-of ephesians-li-god-s-household-rules-marriage-and-family-6-love-your-wife-3/, accessed May 28, 2024 (emphasis mine).

There it is … living, and if necessary, suffering and dying for your wife's good. That is what is needed from you, pastor; for you to love your bride as Christ loved His … sacrifice! Your wife should know that you love her, first and foremost, in Christ. You are one flesh in marriage and part of the one body of Christ. So, you love her as you love Christ. As He is your Head, you are to be her loving and lovely head (Gen 3:16; 1 Cor 11:3; Eph 1:22–23; 4:15–16).

Pastor, your wife must know that you *cherish* her in Christ, not just in word, but in deed as well. She must see that you love her more than your ministry and the church to which you have been called. As mentioned above, you can quickly fall into the snare of the evil one and be married to ministry. Might I offer a simple reminder here of what Paul said: Christ is married to the church! She is His bride. In your glorious calling, you are a part of that. His church, His bride, will grow in Him and be glorified in Him. You rightly fulfill your ministry in the church and in your marriage. The church should grow and mature as they see your devotion to your wife *as part of* your ministry, as should you. Your marriage to your bride is to reflect Christ's marriage to His church. And your church, and your wife, should experience that reflection of sacrificial love.

Your wife must also know that you look to *protect* her in the church. As a pastor you know that the saints often have unrealistic expectations of you in the church and how burdensome this can be. The same can be true concerning your wife. She might be expected to teach the Ladies Sunday School class *and* head the childcare *and* sing in the choir *and* lead Vacation Bible School. Because she is the pastor's wife. I think you will agree that this is both unfair and unrealistic. The Holy Spirit has gifted your wife to serve the church according to those gifts. And expecting her to serve in ways contrary to her calling and giftedness is detrimental to her personally, to your marriage and home, and to the church. You must remember this yourself and remind others, that *you* are the pastor, not your wife. And she must know that you are protecting her from unrealistic expectations. These can come from saints who mean well and/or misunderstand your wife's role in the church and in the home.

Christ's Love Is a Sanctifying Love

Eph 5:26—that he might *sanctify her, having cleansed her* by the washing of water with the word

Of course, all of this comes in the context of a sinful world, which includes the church and the home. You, pastor, are a sinner in need of sanctification and so is your wife. In pre-marital and marital counseling, I often remind a couple that they are merely two sinners coming together as one. This is where it is critical to understand that just as Christ loved you when you appeared unlovely (not unlovable!) and continues to love you when you are unlovely, so too are you to love your wife. Not only are you to love your bride when she is unlovely, but you are called by God, as her bridegroom, as a means of God's grace, to *make* her lovely. That is how Christ, who is our example in this matter, loved and continues to love His bride! Pastor, note Spurgeon's wise words:

He (Christ) did not admire her because there was no spot in her. He did not choose her because she had no wrinkles. He fixed His affections where there were multitudinous spots and wrinkles—where everything was deformity. He still set His heart and would not withdraw till He had loved the spots away and loved every wrinkle out of her who was the object of His choice.

And now He seems to say to every Christian man, however unhappily he may have fared: "If perhaps, in the lot of Providence, you have been yoked to one who deserves but little of your affection, yet if you cannot love because of esteem, love because of pity. If you cannot love because of present merit, then love because of future hope, for possibly, even there, in that bad soil, some sweet flower may grow. Be not weary of holy tillage and of heavenly plowing and sowing, because at the last there may spring up some fair harvest that shall make your soul glad." He loved His Church and gave Himself for her that He might present her to Himself a glorious Church.[5]

That is what *sanctification* entails. In justifying us, God *declares* us holy and righteous in Christ and the *penalty* for sin is settled, the debt is paid in full: "There is therefore no condemnation for those who are in Christ Jesus" (Rom 8:1). In sanctifying us, God is *making* us holy and righteous, and the *power* of sin, though it stays, is broken and being weakened. That is what Christ at present is conducting for His bride. We were and are, unlovely – *but we were not, and are not, unlovable.* He justifies us (Eph 5:25) so that He might sanctify and glorify us (Eph 5:26), where Christ will finally *make* us holy and righteous with no taint or spot or blemish or wrinkle of sin. There will be no *presence* of sin, nor will there be any effects of sin, in eternity. We will forever be *lovely!*

But that is not yet the case. So, the Apostle Paul's point in all of this is that you, pastor, who are held to a higher standard, are called to love your wife—as Christ loves His bride. You are called to a selfless, sacrificial love that looks not simply to make your life more comfortable and pleasurable (or your wife's). But to make your wife more spiritually lovely, to make her more holy and righteous. With Christ as his example, a pastor is to always love his wife, even

---

5   C. H. Spurgeon, Metropolitan Tabernacle Pulpit, vol. 11. Sermon #628, "A Glorious Church" (spurgeongems.org), accessed May 29, 2024.

when she is unlovely. And Paul gives how this sanctification is done: a pastor sanctifies his wife as he *sets her apart* and as he *purifies her*.

First, he *sets her apart*. This aspect of holiness is found in the language concerning the temple in the Old Testament. These inanimate objects were said to be holy or sanctified unto the Lord. As such, a table that might have once served as a setting for a feast no longer served that function. What was commonly used to eat upon was set apart for now uncommon purposes and devoted entirely to the Lord. A tent that might have provided shelter in common use was set apart to belong completely to the Lord. It had the uncommon purpose of sheltering those objects that had been set apart. And along with and before the tabernacle and its objects had been set apart for devotion to Him, the Lord set apart as holy unto Him the people of Israel. They belonged to Him; they were to live in a relationship with Him. In covenant, steadfast love, He was their God, and they were His people (consider His covenant name). As such, they were to reflect His holy character in the home, in their worship, and in the world.

In like manner, a pastor is to set his wife apart for devotion to the Lord. You do this as you see her as the apple of your eye, as you cherish her, lead her, guard her, and provide for her. If this sounds familiar to you as a pastor, it should. This describes your calling as a pastor/shepherd of the church—to lead, feed, and protect. The same is true in your role as husband. You are, as Sam Waldron rightly suggests, a "priest in your own home."[6] As said earlier, your wife is your primary ministry, your greatest sheep!

This is done as you fulfill the second idea associated with sanctification—*purifying*. You *purify* her as you lead her in the

---

6   Samuel E. Waldron, *A Man as Priest in His Home*, (Greenbrier, AR: Free Grace Press, 2023).

spiritual disciplines of Christ and his Word, "by the washing of water with the word." Spurgeon again captures the meaning:

> The water which washes away sin, which cleanses and purifies the soul is the Word. The Word of God has a cleansing influence. It comes and convinces the man of sin. It makes him see his impurity so as to hate it. When applied with power by the Holy Spirit, it works repentance. It leads the man to weep and bewail himself before God. That same Word leads to faith in Christ Jesus, and faith works by love and purifies the soul. The Word is preached, the Word is believed. And as soon as ever that Word is believed, it begins to act like water in the heart of man. You cannot receive the Gospel and yet be as filthy as you were before. My brother, if you really welcome the truth, those grosser sins will be washed away at once. Next, as you discover them, your besetting sins will be cleansed away and constantly, as you understand the Word better, believe it more firmly and feel its effect more powerfully, you will by it, as by water, be washed and cleansed from all indwelling sin till you are sanctified and cleansed and made fit to enter into heaven![7]

Pastor, in the home, it is your responsibility to sanctify your wife. The husband is not to wait for the wife to start sanctifying love in the home. This is especially true of the pastor. It is his responsibility, commanded by God, to lead his wife in spiritual things, to protect her from the ways of the world, to direct her in the way of godliness. You do this as you intentionally and persistently pour the Word into her. Of course, that can only happen as *you* grow in grace and are shaped and molded into the image of Christ by His Word.

Unfortunately, this is often either overlooked or taken for granted in the pastor's home. He assumes that this leading/feeding/protecting takes place at church, in the preaching and teaching of

---

7   C. H. Spurgeon, Metropolitan Tabernacle Pulpit, vol. 11. Sermon #628, "A Glorious Church" (spurgeongems.org), accessed May 29, 2024.

the Word. And while that is certainly a part, and an important part, it is not the whole. Pastor, *at church* you plead with your men to lead *in the home* as husbands and fathers, and rightly so. And you do so to prepare them to lead their families the other six days of the week. Pastor, you are not excluded here, and you (we) might need to listen to your own preaching! You must bathe your wife in Word and prayer at home, daily, to sanctify her as commended. Do not take your spiritual leadership in the home for granted!

Christ's Love Is a Perfecting Love

> *Eph 5:27*—so that he might present the church to himself in *splendor, without spot or wrinkle or any such thing, that she might be holy and without blemish*

"So that" is a purpose clause, completing the thought that Paul had as the master logician. The purpose that Christ gave up Himself for His bride, the reason that presently He is sanctifying her, is so that He might present her *to Himself*. He gave Himself to get her, a much better her! He left her on this earth for a time and He will come again and receive her unto Himself and present her to the Father (1 Cor 15:24). Here and now, His bride is being prepared for that great day! Picture a wedding, your wedding, or a wedding you have officiated as a pastor. See the woman as she comes down the aisle in her magnificent wedding gown of pure white. She is dressed for the occasion, and she is meant to be the center of attention!

That describes Christ's devotion to His bride. He has already dressed her in His righteousness. That could only be true if He Himself is without spot or blemish (1 Pet 1:19). He is righteous, and His bride wears His righteousness like that bright white wedding gown (Rev 7:9). But there are still some spots and wrinkles! They might not be seen by the natural eye, but they are there in the eye of the Bridegroom. So, Christ is preparing His bride for a perfect presentation that will occur on the last day: "And I saw the holy city, new Jerusalem, coming down out of heaven from God, prepared as a bride adorned for her husband" (Rev 21:2). The church at present is being "adorned." While it is difficult to capture what this looks like, D. Martyn Lloyd-Jones was certainly on the right track:

> "Dare I put it like this? The Beauty-Specialist will have put his final touch to the church, the massaging will have been so perfect that there will not be a single wrinkle left. She will look young, and in the bloom of youth, with colour in her cheeks, with her skin perfect, without any spots or wrinkles. And she will remain like that for ever and ever."[8]

That is what Christ has done, and is doing, in giving Himself up for her. The goal (which will be done!) is "splendor"—a glorious church full of honor and beauty, worthy of the love of the bridegroom. She is "without spot"—not a stain, a defect, or impurity. She still retains the allusion of a bride and to the care taken to remove every blemish. There is no "wrinkle"—the vigor and beauty of youth like a bride in whom there is no wrinkle of age—"or any such thing." There is nothing to deform, disfigure, or offend.[9] All of this is to make her like Him, "holy and without blemish," made worthy of Him!

That is what the husband and you, pastor, are to be involved in as a means of grace that God has provided for the woman, the one woman, who is your wife. The purpose of *sanctifying* love is *perfecting* love, a love that prepares for glory. You are to be actively and joyfully

---

8   D. Martyn Lloyd-Jones, *Life in the Spirit in Marriage, Home, & Work: An Exposition of Ephesians 5:18–6:9*, repr. (Grand Rapids: Baker, 2000), 175–76.

9   Definitions from Albert Barnes, *Commentary on Ephesians*, https://www.studylight.org/commentaries/ eng/bnb/ephesians-5.html, accessed May 30, 2024.

engaged, intentionally involved, in preparing her, in dressing her up, of adorning her, of perfecting her. You do this as you wash her with the Word and as you pray for her and with her. You should wish your wife's purity and holiness—as much as your own. While perfect holiness cannot be gained this side of eternity, it ought to be the goal of all individuals (1 Pet 1:16) and the desire of all Christians for the church ... especially a pastor for his wife.

Conclusion

So, pastor, love your wife! Pastors ought to love their wives in the same way that Christ loves the church (Eph 5:25). The day you said, "I do," you agreed before God and the church of Christ that you would love your wife, not only in an earthly way, but in the way that God and Christ love you and her. Your promise was to "die for her" if necessary. Your promise was to shepherd her, to lead her and to feed her and protect her. Your promise was to grow her into the greatest holiness possible. This satisfies Paul's command—both as husband as pastor. May God give us strength! *Soli deo gloria!*

THE PASTOR

Chapter four

Layering in Pastoral Ministry: The Need for Repeating and Reminding

Drew Harris

Introduction: Can You Say That Again?

I had considered the words carefully in my mind, but it was the first time I said them out loud. "I think I am a Calvinist," I told my friend as he listened quietly. "What changed?" he asked. I had been following Christ for about a year and studying the doctrines of grace for several months. There had been hours of reading Scripture and theology books, as well as talking with my friend who was already convinced of God's sovereignty in salvation.

I recently had listened to a sermon series that left me convinced that Reformed soteriology expressed biblical doctrine. I explained to my friend what the pastor had said, the arguments he made, and the Scripture supporting his views. After I articulated my newfound understanding, my friend said with a lighthearted chuckle, "That is what I have been telling you for three months." He was right. There was nothing in the sermon series that I had not previously heard or read. But it was only after hearing the same truths, repeatedly over time, that I came to embrace them in my mind and my heart. As Thomas Wolfe wrote, "I have to see a thing a thousand times before

I see it once."[1] That's often our unfortunate condition, but the Lord works in mysterious and gracious ways.

Fast-forward about a year: I had joined South Woods Baptist in Memphis, Tennessee, where Phil Newton was the senior pastor. I participated in the church's pastoral mentorship program, where Phil discipled and trained men with an interest in pastoral ministry. We read books, prepared and preached sermons, and met regularly to discuss topics related to church leadership. But what impacted me most was the wealth of real-life ministry experience Phil shared. During those years, I remember Phil saying over and over again, as if practicing what he preached: "Always layer biblical truth and the gospel. Pastoral ministry is layering. Look for opportunities to layer the truth."

Layering is Reminding

In pastoral ministry, layering is reminding the church of biblical truth using various modes of communication over an extended period of time. Layering uses preaching, teaching, counseling, informal conversations, emails, and much more. Layering is repetition, but it is not mere repetition. It employs appropriate illustrations and applications to share truth from different perspectives, aimed at changing hearts and minds. Layering is an essential pastoral tool that God uses in His sovereignty to bring people to embrace—and persevere in—truth.

The Bible is replete with examples of God teaching His people through layering. In Deuteronomy 6:4–9, God tells His people to continually remind one another of His law throughout their daily lives. The prophets layer God's truth using preaching and teaching,

---

1   Thomas Wolfe, *You Can't Go Home Again* (Harper & Row, Publishers: New York, 1940), 355–356.

frequently repeating themes of judgment, repentance, and salvation. Wisdom literature reminds us over and over of certain themes, and historical books recount narratives of God's gracious deliverance. In the New Testament, layering is first evident in the presence of four Gospels in the canon of Scripture—repeated accounts of Jesus' life from different perspectives. Examples of layering continue all the way through Revelation, which reminds us of a central biblical theme: God's purposes will stand, and Jesus will reign forever. The Bible is God's masterwork of layering from beginning to end.

My aim in this chapter is to show that layering is integral to pastoral ministry and to help pastors begin to think about how they can employ it with their churches. First, I will show that the apostle Paul practiced layering in his ministry and instructed pastors under his care to do the same. Second, I will show how Jesus used layering in His earthly ministry, especially to help His disciples understand difficult truths. Third, I will consider a few ways pastors can layer God's Word in their ministries.

Peeling Back Paul's Layers:
Preaching, Writing and Sending

The apostle Paul's ministry was defined by layering gospel truths. His message focused on Jesus, the cross, and its application to the church. His mission was to take that message to unbelieving Jews and Gentiles. His method was to bring people to saving faith through the proclamation of the gospel and then regularly remind them of that truth through preaching, teaching, writing and sending emissaries.

Paul characterizes his preaching ministry in Corinth as a glorious broken record, stuck on the greatest lyrics known to humankind. He writes, "For I decided to know nothing among you except Jesus Christ and him crucified" (1 Cor 2:2).[2] Apparently Paul struck this note over and over again while in Corinth. Did Paul mean that he never spoke on any other topics? Of course not. Paul's point is that he focused on the message of Jesus—restating it often—illustrating and applying it according to the audience and situation. He preached the gospel and then reminded them of it again and again. In other words, he layered the gospel message in his preaching. Commenting on this passage, Jim Shaddix said Paul and other New Testament writers "saw themselves as responsible for reminding God's people about things they had previously been told. They knew it was necessary if the human mind was ever going to embrace the truth and enable it to sink into the heart."[3]

Paul's layering of the gospel message to the Corinthians was not limited to his preaching and teaching. He ensured the church continued in truth by writing letters and sending emissaries. After preaching the gospel in Corinth, Paul emphasizes the importance of repeating it in his first letter to the church: "Now I would remind you, brothers, of the gospel I preached to you, which you received, in which you stand, and by which you are being saved, if you hold fast to the word I preached to you—unless you believed in vain" (1 Cor 15:1–2).

In the verses that follow, Paul rehearses the facts around the death and resurrection of Christ as prophesied in the Old Testament. Without doubt, the Corinthian church knew these truths about Christ. Paul had preached to them in person, and many had believed. That is why he addresses the letter to "the church of God that is in Corinth, to those sanctified in Christ Jesus, called to be

---

2   All Scripture are references from the English Standard Version.

3   Jim Shaddix, "The Preacher as Reminder," accessed June 8, 2024, https://www.preaching.com/articles/the-preacher-as-reminder/.

saints" (1 Cor 1:2). Paul writes to people who already believe in the death, burial and resurrection of Christ. Why, then, does he take the time to remind them of these things? Paul must believe the gospel is applicable to the issues at hand, namely divisions in the church, pride, sexual sin, love toward one another, and proper worship. Paul reminds them of gospel truths as a means of application to their current situation.

In addition to preaching and letter writing, Paul layers the gospel message by sending Timothy to reiterate and apply the truth he previously delivered. What was Paul's purpose in sending his trusted companion? Paul tells the Corinthians plainly, "That is why I sent you, Timothy, my beloved and faithful child in the Lord, to remind you of my ways in Christ, as I teach them everywhere in every church" (1 Cor 4:17). In contrast to the belief that the gospel is primarily for unbelievers as the way to become a Christian, Paul shows the gospel is the way to continue as a follower of Christ. He emphasizes this point to the young church by sending letters and Timothy.

Paul uses this same strategy with other New Testament churches. Writing to the church in Rome, Paul tells them, "On some points I have written to you very boldly by way of reminder, because of the grace given me by God" (Rom 15:15). While Paul had not yet visited this church personally, he apparently knew many believers there (see Rom 16:1–16) and refers to the church as those "loved by God and called to be saints" (Rom 1:7). These believers needed reminders regarding justification by faith and sanctification. Likewise, Paul does not have any qualms about repeating truth to the church at Philippi. He presses, "Finally, my brothers, rejoice in the Lord. To write the same things to you is no trouble to me and is safe for you" (Phil 3:1). Peter O'Brien explains that "the same things" refers to "those things the apostle had already spoken about previously in his ministry among the Philippians."[4] As Paul ministered to young churches, his standard procedure included frequently layering truth to shepherd God's people.

Commending and Commanding: Layering with Timothy

Paul employed the same techniques as he discipled other leaders in the early church. In 1 and 2 Timothy, Paul presses upon Timothy the importance of faithfulness to the gospel, and he commends Timothy to do the same with the Ephesians. In the first epistle, Paul explains his reason for Timothy staying in Ephesus: "As I urged you when I was going to Macedonia, remain at Ephesus so that you may charge certain persons not to teach any different doctrine ..." (1 Tim 1:3). In this example, Paul reminds Timothy of his mission as an encouragement to him. Undoubtedly, Timothy knew why he was to stay in Ephesus, but Paul brings it back to memory to buoy his confidence in the face of opposition. Paul also implies that Timothy should use layering in his ministry. How would Timothy go about charging people "not to teach any different doctrine"? He must remind them of central truths, calling them from erroneous doctrine back to the truths of the gospel.

Furthermore, Paul models layering for Timothy by quoting concise statements of truth that were circulating around the early church. Four times Paul introduces these statements with the phrase "the saying is trustworthy" [e.g. "The saying is trustworthy and deserving of full acceptance, that Christ Jesus came into the world to save sinners, of whom I am the foremost" (1 Tim 1:15; see also

---

4   Peter T. O'Brien, *The Epistle to the Philippians*, New International Greek New Testament Commentary (Grand Rapids: Eerdmans, 1991), 352.

1 Tim 3:1, 4:9; 2 Tim 2:11–13)]. George Knight points out that "in each occurrence the statement to which the formula refers has a 'saying' quality," and the formula thus serves as a commendation of the quotation.[5] In other words, certain truths had been repeated frequently over a period of time so that they had become familiar sayings within the early church.

Even though these truths were well known, Paul is not shy to repeat them to Timothy to strengthen his pastoral resolve. Paul intends for Timothy to emphasize these truths to the Ephesians, and the apostle makes that explicit in 2 Timothy 2:14. After repeating the faithful saying about resurrection and endurance in 2 Timothy 2:11–13, Paul tells Timothy: "Remind them of these things" (2 Tim 2:14). In other words, Paul commands Timothy to repeat the faithful sayings the Ephesians already knew. Thus, we see a biblical command to layer truth within the church. The apostle Paul reminds Timothy who in turn reminds "faithful men who will be able to teach others also" (2 Tim 2:2). Knight sums up verse 14, explaining: "Timothy is commanded to bring to the minds of these men the very things that Paul has just brought to his mind."[6] Layering is not suggested—it is a commanded method for passing truth down to God's people.

Layering by the Master

In the Gospels, Jesus employs layering throughout his earthly ministry, reminding his disciples—especially the Twelve—of difficult truths. Jesus repeatedly addresses certain themes in his preaching, teaching, and conversations to press important points

---

5   George W. Knight III, *The Pastoral Epistles, New International Greek New Testament Commentary* (Grand Rapids: Eerdmans, 1992), 99.

6   Knight III, *The Pastoral Epistles*, 410.

93

into the hearts and minds of his followers. One example is Jesus' focus on the high cost of discipleship. Sometimes He explains this truth clearly and without equivocation to the twelve disciples: "Beware of men, for they will deliver you over to courts and flog you in their synagogues … and you will be hated by all for my name's sake" (Matt 10:17, 22). Later in the chapter, Jesus puts it in different terms: "I have not come to bring peace, but a sword" (Matt 10:34). He goes on to explain that even the closest familial relationships will be divided because of allegiance to Him.

Another time Jesus gathers the Twelve and tells them that to be his disciple meant the person must "deny himself and take up his cross and follow me" (Matt 16:24). Persecution will certainly follow, but only those who see Jesus as more valuable than their own lives find eternal life. Jesus layers this truth again in the parables of the hidden treasure and the pearl of great value. Preaching to large crowds, Jesus emphasizes that His disciples must be willing to forsake everything to follow Him—and receive much more in return (Matt 13:44–46).

Jesus uses layering consistently throughout the gospel accounts, but another is worth pointing out because it illustrates the importance of restating difficult truths. Matthew records three accounts of Jesus telling the disciples that He must go to Jerusalem, be killed and be raised on the third day (Matt 16:21–23; 17:22–23; 20:17–19). In the first instance, Matthew emphasizes that this is the beginning of something new in Jesus' ministry, an essential and soon-to-be repeated message: "From that time Jesus began to show his disciples that he must go to Jerusalem and suffer many things from the elders and chief priests and scribes, and be killed, and on the third day be raised" (Matt 16:21). As Leon Morris points out, "this was a lesson the disciples found very hard indeed. This may be the point of Matthew's *began*; it would be a long, slow process."[7]

Again and again, Jesus teaches about the importance of his death and resurrection to help the disciples grasp what He had come to do. The disciples are slow to grasp Jesus' point, as evidenced by their response. Jesus' first declaration comes with pushback—rejection and rebuke from Peter (Matt 16:22). After the second declaration, the disciples are "greatly distressed" (Matt 17:23). When Jesus tells the disciples a third time, Matthew immediately records a scene where the mother of James and John requests that her sons be honored in Jesus' kingdom (Matt 20:20–21). Clearly the disciples were slow to understand Jesus' mission and its implications, but the Lord patiently layered the message to press the truth upon them.

In the Gospel of John, Jesus tells the disciples that the Holy Spirit would "bring to your remembrance all that I have said to you"—another example of layering (John 14:26). They finally grasp the fullness of Jesus' death and resurrection after the Holy Spirit comes at Pentecost, as evidenced by the evangelistic preaching of Acts. The resurrection is now the central focus of their preaching, the gospel message first proclaimed in Jerusalem and then to the Samaritans and Gentiles (Acts 2:1–36, 8:4–13, 10:34–48). Without a doubt, encounters with Jesus after his resurrection, combined with the witness of the Holy Spirit, were essential to the disciples' understanding of Jesus' words. God's supernatural work in the hearts and minds of sinners is always necessary for people to believe biblical truth. But God uses the conjunction of the Spirit and the Word—often repeated and layered over time—to help his people fully understand truth.

---

7   Leon Morris, *The Gospel According to Matthew, The Pillar New Testament Commentary* (Grand Rapids: Eerdmans, 1992), 428. Italics in the original.

Putting It into Practice

Even from a cursory overview, it's clear that layering was important in the early church, employed and modeled by both Jesus and the apostles. As noted above, Paul taught Timothy to layer gospel truths as he ministered to young Christians, and Timothy was to teach other faithful men to do likewise. If layering was vital to pastoral ministry in the early church, how much more should pastors take this approach today? Our sinful hearts and minds are still quick to wander. Additionally, we have seen a massive increase in potential distractions made possible by technologies of the modern age. We can easily forget truths or, more specifically, forget to apply truths that we already know and believe.

In his book *Preaching as Reminding*, Jeffrey Arthurs says reminding is God's means to help us when we are prone to forget: "Remembering can be tough for a harried brain in the age of distraction with an idol-making heart tempted by the world, but God has provided help through the ministry of remembrances."[8] How can a pastor proceed?

Preaching and teaching should be the foundational ways a pastor uses layering with his congregation. As noted above, God has layered themes and doctrines throughout the Bible to remind his people of central truths. Therefore, expositional preaching and teaching will naturally offer opportunities to remind congregations of the person and work of Christ, justification by faith alone, God's grace and love, human sinfulness, and much more. Layering through preaching urges people to apply the truths they already believe. For example, people may believe in God's sovereignty over all things but struggle to see how their current trial or difficulty fits into God's

---

8   Jeffrey D. Arthurs, *Preaching As Reminding: Stirring Memory in an Age of Forgetfulness* (Downers Grove, IL: InterVarsity Press, 2017), 46.

plan. Frequent reminders help people apply God's Word to their situation. Or God may use the repeated preaching and teaching of a hard-to-grasp doctrine to convince people of its biblical truth. This was my experience with the doctrines of grace. People often come to the Bible with preconceived ideas that need reshaping. Jensen and Grimmond remind us that "we cannot change people's lifelong presuppositions by merely mentioning them in passing."[9]

Pastors may question how to repeatedly layer truths without boring their hearers with the same message over and over again. In an age when novelty gets the most attention, will repetition cause people to lose interest? Pastors should first remember that their primary task is to proclaim, not entertain—to preach God's truth in God's way. The Holy Spirit can take well-worn truths and blaze them into the hearts and minds of congregation. Secondly, pastors should work hard to communicate truths creatively, finding new avenues to deliver truths in striking ways. Application is one of the best means of accomplishing this. For example, the doctrine of justification by faith can be emphasized in numerous ways: warning unbelievers of their sinful record and pointing to hope in Christ; comforting believers struggling to believe God's acceptance; or urging a congregation to look to Christ instead of leaning on their own good works. In each case, the pastor layers the doctrine of justification by faith alone by applying it from different perspectives.[10]

Counseling is another way pastors can layer God's truth to the people under their care. If preaching and teaching give opportunities for general applications, counseling gives the pastor a chance to

---

9   Phillip D. Jensen and Paul Grimmond, *The Archer and the Arrow: Preaching the Very Words of God* (Matthias Media: Kingsford, Australia, 2010), 113.

10   Timothy Keller, *Preaching: Communicating Faith in an Age of Skepticism* (Viking/Penguin Random House: New York, 2015), 186.

layer in very specific ways. One-on-one discussions help people understand how they can apply biblical truths to their current situation. Regarding counseling, Paul Tripp explains that "Scripture must become the basis for interpreting life ... you want to bring that biblical perspective to your counselee, because when God's truth becomes the lens through which everything is examined, life changes."[11] Counseling provides the opportunity to remind someone of biblical truth and apply it in very tailored ways.

Baptism and the Lord's supper are additional opportunities for layering, using the symbols of water, bread, and wine as tangible reminders of Christ's work on the cross and our union with Him. The ordinances provide pastors with ample opportunities to emphasize the gospel and connect the symbols in fresh ways to biblical doctrines. When commanding "Do this in remembrance of me," Jesus teaches his disciples to see the Lord's Supper as a means of continually reminding the church of his work on the cross (Luke 22:19).

Finally, pastors can layer biblical truth through informal conversations and by modeling faithful obedience. In the thirteen years that Phil was my pastor, I remember countless conversations with him in the church foyer or over lunch. "That reminds me of something I read in my quiet time this morning," he might say. Then he would proceed to share something applicable by way of reminder from God's Word. Had I heard that truth before? Yes, it was almost always something I had heard previously from his preaching and teaching. But Phil used the opportunity to remind me of truth in a casual way that pressed the point home. Although the formal preaching of God's Word takes priority in pastoral ministry, God

---

11   Paul David Tripp, *Instruments in the Redeemer's Hands: People in Need of Change Helping People in Need of Change* (P&R Publishing, Phillipsburg, NJ, 2002), 290.

uses the continual layering of those truths—in counseling, hallway conversations, even e-mail updates—to grow and sanctify the church.

Conclusion: Remind So They Will Recall

We crave novelty. The desire for something new, combined with pride, led to the Fall. But chasing novelty in pastoral ministry is not the way of Christ. The old way, the worn-out path, the trusted trail of gospel truths and biblical doctrine is the only road for a pastor to travel. That means pastors must have a ministry marked by layering truth—repeating and reminding their congregations of "the faith that was once for all delivered to the saints" (Jude 3). This is the pastoral calling, and it is how sinful people will repent and believe— and keep on repenting and believing until we see Jesus. Pastors should aim for a ministry marked by the heart of the apostle Peter, who made no qualms about layering the truth time and time again:

Therefore I intend always to remind you of these qualities, though you know them and are established in the truth that you have. I think it right, as long as I am in this body, to stir you up by way of reminder, since I know that the putting off of my body will be soon, as our Lord Jesus Christ made clear to me. And I will make every effort so that after my departure you may be able at any time to recall these things (2 Pet 1:12–15).

Chapter five

The Essential Role of Pastoral Leadership in Biblical Church Discipline

David Lawrence

Introduction

"Jesus is worthy of a pure bride." For years I had quoted that phrase and believed it was true. Yet, I knew that there was something missing from the churches of my youth. And especially those where I had served as pastor for many years. The missing biblical practice in these and most churches familiar to me was Biblical Church Discipline. I do not remember hearing a sermon on this subject. I never learned about church discipline in Baptist college classes or from my seminary alma mater. Occasionally, I would hear about incidents of moral failure or financial misconduct involving church leaders. But these cases were often managed quietly by other leaders and then announced afterward to the church. I once sought counsel from a retired Baptist pastor who was a member of our church concerning an issue in which I felt church discipline was warranted. He counseled me against acting. He stated, "You cannot lead an older, established church to practice church discipline." He offered this counsel out of concern for potential church division.

Reading the business meeting minutes from many years ago in the church I now serve, the reading revealed some form of church discipline had been exercised in the past. It appeared that some of the procedures of church discipline may have been harsh and legalistic. It is for this reason that the practice of church discipline gradually became neglected. Instead of reforming the procedures to align with Scripture, our church and others completely abandoned the Biblical doctrine of church discipline. While this practice was almost non-existent in familiar churches; I knew Jesus had established this discipline and that his instruction was being neglected. As I preached through New Testament books and came to texts dealing with church discipline, I endeavored faithfully to teach and acknowledged that we were neglecting this practice. But to no avail—little changed.

Over ten years ago, I had the opportunity to attend a training conference for church leaders in North Mississippi. One of the breakout sessions was led by a Memphis pastor named Phil Newton. In this forum, Phil taught the biblical principles of church discipline. He shared practical steps for implementing this practice in the local church. His training led me to think and pray about how to begin church discipline in our context. At this time, our church was c. 140 years old. Sometime later, other leaders from our church with me met with Phil and his church's pastors for lunch. We asked numerous questions about how to begin the process of church discipline. I will always be grateful to Phil Newton for his faithful example and encouragement in this essential biblical doctrine and practice. I have sought his counsel on numerous other church ministry issues. In every instance he remains biblical, helpful, and encouraging.

It is understood that church discipline is conducted in two forms: formative and corrective. This essay will focus on the dynamic of corrective church discipline. Our church leaders have gleaned from other pastors, churches, and resources to implement faithfully what we have learned. We have made mistakes along the way and still have a lot of room for growth in our application of the doctrine. However, churches which have abandoned or neglected church discipline must be led by their pastors to establish and maintain this important practice. That is, if they desire to be biblically healthy churches. Consider with me the pastor's essential leadership role in establishing and maintaining church discipline.

Accept Responsibility for Each Member

One of the metaphors chosen by the Holy Spirit to identify Christ's church is that of a flock. The members are sheep, and the pastors are their shepherds. Paul charged the Ephesian elders, "Pay careful attention to yourselves and to all the flock, in which the Holy Spirit has made you overseers, to care for the church of God, which he obtained with his own blood" (Acts 20:28).[1] This verse contains several directives for pastors. They must "pay careful attention." This is one word in the Greek text and is translated "Be on guard" (NASB95) and "Keep watch over" (NIV). Pastors are to pay careful attention first to themselves and then "to all the flock." Paul declared that "the Holy Spirit has made you overseers, to care for the church of God, which he obtained with his own blood." Polhill says that the term overseer in this text is not a reference to the office but to a function. He explains that "the Ephesian leaders were not designated as bishops but rather as elders who functioned to 'watch over the flock of God.'"[2] Pastors are not responsible for all of God's sheep,

---

1   Unless otherwise noted, all citations of Scripture are from the English Standard Version (ESV).

2   John B. Polhill, *Acts, Vol. 26. The New American Commentary* (Nashville: Broadman & Holman Publishers, 1992), 427.

only the flock under their care. This does include, however, *every* member of their local church. The magnitude of this task should lead every local church to follow the biblical pattern of a plurality of pastors.

Hebrews 13:17 corroborates pastoral responsibility and accountability for the care of each member. The Scripture instructs us, "Obey your leaders and submit to them, for they are keeping watch over your souls, as those who will have to give an account. Let them do this with joy and not with groaning, for that would be of no advantage to you." While the writer directs these words to the church members, he assumes that pastors know that their responsibility is "keeping watch over" the soul of each of their members. Each pastor should know they will have to give an account to Christ for each sheep. Church members should aim for pastoral accounting to be given with joy and not with groaning.

Teach the Biblical Basis and Necessity of Church Membership

The practice of church membership is closely tied to church discipline. Pastors must know for whom they are responsible. Pastors and churches cannot discipline those who are not members of their local churches; any more than parents can discipline other peoples' children. I preached a sermon series on "the church" as our leadership began to nudge the church body toward biblical church membership and discipline. These messages included the basic biblical idea(s) of what it meant to be a member of a local assembly. Preaching and teaching these biblical texts enabled our members to understand and accept their own personal responsibility. They began to understand their accountability to the church of which they were members. It helped them to see membership in a local church is not a human invention but is a biblical necessity. And that for every genuine disciple of Christ. While the terms church membership or membership roll are not specifically used in the New Testament, they are certainly implied. The metaphor of "flock" employed in Acts 20:28 and 1 Peter 5:2 implies an extremely specific group of people for whom the under-shepherd was responsible. In *40 Questions About Pastoral Ministry*, Phil Newton writes,

> One does not find "membership" in the New Testament. Yet when we consider the word expressing *belonging or being a part of a group or people or a commitment to others centered in common cause*, then we see "membership" throughout the NT. The church emerging at Pentecost reinforces the idea of belonging … . Belonging may not have included a membership roll, but it displayed a clear sense of membership with one another.[3]

Pastors should also teach their churches about their responsibilities as members of the local church. Among those responsibilities as members is faithfulness to its gatherings. This is clearly taught in Hebrews 10:24–25, which says, "And let us consider how to stir up one another to love and good works, not neglecting to meet together, as is the habit of some, but encouraging one another, and all the more as you see the Day drawing near." The *New Bible Commentary* comments on the seriousness of neglecting the church's gatherings:

> The writer uses a term for their meeting (Gk. *episynagōgē*, 'assembly') that is parallel in sense to 'church' and suggests a formal gathering of some kind. A few of their number are *in the habit* of neglecting this responsibility. The warning about apostasy that follows (26–39) implies that people who deliberately and

---

3   Phil A. Newton, *40 Questions About Pastoral Ministry*, (Kregel Academic, 2021), 284.

persistently abandon the fellowship of Christian believers are in danger of abandoning the Lord himself![4]

As members grow older, some will become physically unable to assemble due to their health. These homebound members provide an opportunity for ministry by the pastors, deacons, and other church members. Those who can meet must do so to be under the ministry of the word; to utilize their spiritual gifts in serving, to fulfill all the "one another" commands in Scripture, and to be accountable to the church.

Teach Biblical Truth
Concerning Church Discipline

Pastors who seek to lead their churches to establish and maintain biblical church discipline must preach and teach texts in Scripture which give instructions on this doctrine. This is especially vital for churches which have a long history of neglecting this biblical practice. As pastors patiently preach and teach these texts, they are helping the church to understand that church discipline is just as important for the church in our day as when the church was first established. Faithful pastors will lovingly declare to their congregations that neglecting church membership and discipline is disobedient to the Scripture and to the Lord of His Church.

One of the clearest texts on church discipline is Matthew 18:15–20. Here, Jesus gave a step-by-step process for confronting another believer who sins against you personally. This passage teaches the accountability members of a local church have to one

---

4   D. G. Peterson, "Hebrews," in *New Bible Commentary: 21st Century Edition*, 4th ed., eds. D. A. Carson, R. T. France, J. A. Motyer, & G. J. Wenham (Inter-Varsity Press, 1994), 1345.

another. It also instructs concerning their personal responsibility to lovingly confront sin in each other's lives. It affirms that the goal of church discipline is repentance, reconciliation, and restoration to fellowship. It also demonstrates the church's corporate responsibility to discipline the unrepentant members.

The process begins with a personal confrontation by the offended member to lead the brother or sister to repent. If he or she repents, then restoration has occurred, and the offense is resolved. If the person is unwilling to repent, then the offended member is to take one or two others from the church in another effort to confront and restore the member. If the brother or sister repents, reconciliation occurs. However, if the member continues in an unrepentant sin, then the church is to be informed of the member's sinful state. At that time, the person is to be brought to the church. If the church congregation is unable to lead the member to repentance; Jesus says, "let him be to you as a Gentile and a tax collector" (v. 17). This means that the unrepentant member is to be treated as an unbeliever and to be removed from church membership. This is commonly known as excommunication. While the sin described here is personal, this process can also be applied to sin(s) of a public nature. Jonathan Leeman applies this passage concerning the church to other types of sin where discipline might be necessary. He writes:

> The larger point in these verses is that the local churches have the authority to assess professions of faith and to act accordingly: "if two of you agree on earth about anything they ask" (Matt18:19). In other words, churches can employ the process of discipline described in verses 15 to 17 to sins more broadly.[5]

---

5   Jonathan Leeman, *Church Discipline: How the Church Protects the Name of Jesus* (Wheaton, IL; Crossway, 2012), 29.

Other biblical texts concerning the practice of church discipline include 1 Corinthians 5:1–13, Galatians 6:1–2, 2 Thessalonians 3:14–15, and Titus 3:10. Pastors must carefully address these in the preaching. It should be noted that Paul directed the church to take immediate action to remove the immoral member in the 1 Corinthians 5 passage. Thomas Schreiner explains the swift response which differs from Jesus' slower process in Matthew 18:15–17: "The public and gross character of the sin demanded a public and immediate response by the church."[6] Newton points out that what these two texts have in common is that "the final authority for removing from membership is not with the elders but the assembled church taking action."[7] As pastors consider the swiftness of exercising church discipline upon a member; the level of seriousness of the sin, the potential harm to the church, must be welded to the community testimony of the church before a member is removed.

Seek God in Prayer
While Establishing Church Discipline

One of Jesus' most often quoted promises on prayer is found in Matthew 18:19–20 where Jesus instructs, "Again I say to you, if two of you agree on earth about anything they ask, it will be done for them by my Father in heaven. For where two or three are gathered in my name, there am I among them." Jesus' promise is given in the context of his teaching on the process of church discipline and restoration. Pastors and other church leaders must plead with God in prayer as they lead the church to establish church discipline and

---

6   Thomas Schreiner, "The Biblical Basis for Church Discipline" in *Those Who Must Give an Account: A Study of Church Membership and Church Discipline,* eds. John S. Hammett & Benjamin L Merkle, (Nashville, TN: B&H Academic, 2012), 114.

7   Newton, *40 Questions About Pastoral Ministry,* 271.

to practice it faithfully. Andrew Davis emphasizes the vital necessity of prayer in church discipline:

> Prayer is a clear declaration of dependence on the part of a pastor, saying, "Apart from you, I can do nothing!" Prayer appeals to the sovereign power of God to change hearts and minds, to direct them to love and obey God's Word. Without this change in the majority of the hearts of the local church, that church will never do church discipline. Furthermore, as various difficult cases of church discipline come up in the life of the church, prayer will be vital as church leaders (elders) appeal to God for supernatural wisdom (Jas 1:5) to navigate often complex discipline cases.[8]

Demonstrate Patience
when Establishing Church Discipline

Pastors must be especially patient with the church when seeking to establish church discipline as new congregational polity. Mark Dever gives wise counsel to pastors concerning the patience they need to make these necessary changes. He states: "Once you've discovered that corrective church discipline is biblical, hold off on practicing it for a while." He goes on to explain his counsel and reasoning:

> I'm trying to help you do what Jesus instructed his disciples to do (see Luke 14:25–33): count the cost before you begin. Make sure your congregation sufficiently understands and accepts this biblical teaching. Your goal is not immediate compliance followed by an explosion, but rather a congregation being reformed by the Word of God. You want them going in the right direction. And that requires patient shepherding.[9]

---

8   Andrew M. Davis, "The Practical Issues of Church Discipline," in *Those Who Must Give an Account: A Study of Church Membership and Church Discipline*, eds. John S. Hammett & Benjamin L Merkle, (Nashville, TN: B&H Academic, 2012), 163–164.

9   Mark Dever, "'Don't do it!!' Why You Shouldn't Practice Church Discipline," 9Marks Journal, Volume 6, Issue 6 (2009): 6–7.

Exercising patience may delay progress with church discipline temporarily. But it will provide growing believers with time to understand how critical it is as a key role to a biblically healthy church.

Lead the Church to
Adopt Necessary Policies and Procedures

To implement biblical church discipline and to continue this process in a clear, consistent, and orderly manner; pastors will need to examine their church's written policies. Necessary changes will need to be recommended. Leeman makes the following statement about the need for written church documents. He argues:

> It's an act of kindness to let people know what standards they are going to be held accountable to before you discipline them. A statement of faith lets them know what they are expected to believe. A covenant lets them know how they are expected to live. A constitution lets them know how membership and discipline work. Such documents also provide unity. Agreed-upon documents spare the church from controversies over the methods or rules every time a disagreement arises.[10]

As our pastors began preparing our church to establish these new policy changes, we realized that our church's written policies did not support this practice. Many members were no longer attending, as many no longer lived in our area. We established a team consisting of pastors and members to review our constitution and bylaws. They were to bring recommended revisions that included a more biblical church membership and church discipline policies to the congregation. We obtained copies of bylaws from

10   Leeman, *Church Discipline: How the Church Protects the Name of Jesus,* 133–134.

like-minded churches that contained robust policies concerning church membership and church discipline. After months of working through this process, a revised constitution, bylaws, and church covenant were recommended in a church business meeting and were approved. These new policies were essential. They became the basis of what was done when the church began seeking to contact and restore absentee members. Then and only then could we remove those who were unrepentant, absent, dead, or moved away.

Lead the Church to Implement
Biblical Church Discipline

When a church has a membership roll which includes members who no longer attend or who no longer live in the area, this can become the springboard for implementing church discipline. When we began this process, we had over 750 members. Almost four hundred of these were resident members and over 350 were nonresident. One of our nonresident members, who is now a famous entertainer, joined the church with his family as a child. But he had long since left our church and community.

To accomplish all this, it was necessary to enlist the participation of our staff, deacons, and faithful members. We attempted to visit the non-attending members within a reasonable distance of our campus. As we visited, we asked absentee members if they had joined or were attending another church. We presented them with a letter from the pastors. It briefly explained what the Scripture taught about church attendance. Along with it, we presented them with our newly adopted membership polices and revised church covenant. We asked them to complete and return a card indicating their intention to return to active church participation. When possible, we shared the gospel and encouraged them to return. In this process, we discovered a member who had begun attending a Buddhist temple and no longer claimed faith in Christ. He was polite but quite ready to be removed from our church's membership.

This process of visiting and contacting the absentee members took several months. We sent letters to those whom we were unable to contact personally that included this same information and requested a personal response. Many never responded. Those who did not return and demonstrate repentance were removed from the membership by a vote in congregational business meetings. In the process of visiting these members, other public sins were exposed. Those exposed led to church discipline and eventually to excommunication for the unrepentant. We also sent letters to nonresident members explaining our membership policy. We included our church covenant and asked them to inform us if they had united with another church. If not, we lovingly urged them to search for a biblically healthy church and offered to assist them in locating one. We eventually removed these nonresident members. We were most careful not to remove a few homebound members who were physically unable to attend a local church in their area.

After nine years of ongoing church discipline, our church membership and attendance are much more closely aligned. A small number of previously non-attending members have returned to active participation and have given evidence of repentance and spiritual health.

Execute a Plan for Faithful Member Care

It is when shepherds are not guarding their sheep that they are most vulnerable to attack. Shepherds of God's church must remain vigilant in their care of the flock so that they are not neglected or lured into sin. This is why faithful member care is essential. When church membership rolls are managed well and we know the members of our church and their spiritual condition, we are much more able to care for their souls. The church is also more able to minister to any practical needs they may encounter. The writer of the epistle of Hebrews instructs us how desperately the members need to care for one another. "Take care, brothers, lest there be in any of you an evil, unbelieving heart, leading you to fall away from the living God. But exhort one another every day, as long as it is called 'today,' that none of you may be hardened by the deceitfulness of sin" (Heb 3:12–13). Andrew Davis offers an application of this passage to pastors and church members' care for one another:

> The pastor/elder must "watch" over the whole flock to be sure that none of their hearts is hardening and turning from Christ. This ministry is so vital and so difficult that it will involve the full effort of all elders, especially in motivating all church members to care for one another spiritually. The only way to tell that someone is, under the influence of sin's deceitfulness, developing a hardened heart is by knowing that person well.[11]

As we care for the soul of each member, we have implemented a plan for our pastors to visit each member's household on a rotating basis. The purpose of this visit is to strengthen our relationships with our members, to learn the state of their relationship with Christ, and in the case of married couples, observe the state of their marriage and family. We give them an opportunity to ask questions related to Scripture, concerning our church, or our ministry as their pastors. During this visit we also pray for any spiritual or physical needs the members have. Our pastors get to know their members

---

11 Andrew M. Davis, "Those Who Must Give an Account: A Pastoral Reflection," in *Those Who Must Give an Account: A Study of Church Membership and Church Discipline*, eds. John S. Hammett & Benjamin L Merkle, (Nashville, TN: B&H Academic, 2012), 212.

better through member care; they can more faithfully disciple, serve and pray for them. It leads to greater accountability and enhances spiritual health which may minimize the need for corrective church discipline in the lives of members.

Conclusion

Every pastor who desires to obey the whole counsel of God will seek to lead his church to practice church discipline. Pastors may be leading churches which have neglected this practice for so long that they do not know where or how to start. Undoubtedly, pastors who neglect church discipline do so because they are concerned about division if implemented. They are rightly concerned that the practice of church discipline could lead to such. Some may even be tempted to think that the church has gotten along okay without church discipline all these years and ask, "Why start now?" They may observe other churches which are growing without practicing church discipline. While many excuses may be offered for the neglect of church discipline, the truth is, it is clearly taught in Scripture. What God has instructed us to do, He will enable us to do. "Jesus is worthy of a pure Bride."

Chapter six

Worship that Leads to Missions

Jim Carnes

What a joy and privilege to author this chapter in honor of Phil Newton, my long-time friend and brother in Christ. We met for the first time in the spring of 1987 and then again in early 1995. We served together from 1995 until 2023 at South Woods Baptist Church, where he became like a brother to me—certainly, a friend and mentor. He was my pastor, and a fellow elder. We thought each other's thoughts and finished each other's sentences; we shared a common theological foundation: We belonged to the same Christian era (the Jesus Movement of the 1970s). We enjoyed church history; we were moved deeply by the study of God's Word; we loved worshiping the triune God; we appreciated the rich tradition of hymns and enjoyed writing. and composing new ones; we longed for the victorious return of Christ. His friendship was and has continued to be a deep encouragement to me.

I have benefited from his preaching and teaching and pastoral ministry, especially in the areas of missions. When I began attending the church I noticed the emphasis on short term mission trips. Certainly, I had seen this in other churches, but never to the degree as in South Woods. Those early years witnessed an extremely high percentage of church members serving on trips to South America, Romania, Kiev, southern France, etc. And it was not long before

Central Asia became a major focus. I mention this because this was always part of Phil's heartbeat. It was the beginning of my personal rethinking of missions. Those trips—coupled with some amazing meetings with servants from the mission field, Phil's solid exposition of biblical texts, and a shared love for Christian history and biography—began to change my missiological vision. I am thankful for the opportunity to minister to God's people with someone who loved (and loves) all these things.

Like many other pastors, Phil led the church to think biblically about evangelism and missions as an outworking of worshiping the Triune God. I hope to demonstrate early influences on Phil's ministry from people like John Piper et al. But also, to show that his thinking continued to develop as he focused on Word-centered texts.

Even though I will reference several texts, I will spend most of the time with one of Phil's most loved (and preached) texts: Revelation 5:1–14. I do not know how many times he preached from this passage—five or six times. But he always emphasized the connection between the great redemptive purpose of God and the worship of the Lamb by those from every tongue, tribe, and people group. This is the great gospel emphasis. I have been blessed over the years to hear this refrain and have my heart stirred for the continuing gospel commission. May we all be so encouraged.

Prelude

As we begin to consider this foundational text, I will list some of the thematic motifs and show how Phil's understanding and concerns of the application of Scripture for all the church began to develop.

Even though Phil had been leading the church in missions from the formation of South Woods, it was not until 2004 that some of his thoughts were codified in a book entitled. *Dear Timothy. Letters on Pastoral Ministry*.[1] The essay written by Phil is called "Care for the Nations." As is the other chapters in the book, this one is written as pastoral advice for younger ministers, although old and new pastors alike can treasure these truths. The third paragraph lays out his concern:

> ... But as your pastor and friend, I want to remind you of an area that can easily be left out of the hectic pace of pastoral life—namely, *missions*. I know that you will diligently observe the emphases of our denomination on missions but that can almost be done unconsciously. Pastors tend to relegate missions to the denomination's mission agency or to parachurch organizations, but you must see this as *your* work, leading your flock to have a passion for the world. The local church must be the launching pad for global missions. As pastor of a local church, you are the key to launching missions from your congregation.[2]

As a seasoned pastor, Phil works through the temptations of a minister and the opposition from others to neglect this emphasis. He reminds "Timothy" to find his confidence to continue, even during persecution, by "standing upon God's Word."

> The term that Luke uses for "preaching the word," comes from the same root word as "gospel." I like to think of it as "they were *gospelizing*" (Acts 8:4). Persecution brought about the spontaneous proclamation of the gospel outside the familiar trappings of Jerusalem.[3]

At this early point in the account Phil mentions a key influence on his thinking: John Piper, *Let the Nations Be Glad! The Supremacy*

---

1   Phil Newton, "Care for the Nations," in *Dear Timothy: Letters on Pastoral Ministry*, ed. Tom Ascol, (Cape Coral, FL, Founders Press, 2004), 331.

2   Newton, "Care for the Nations," 331.

3   Newton, "Care for the Nations," 331.

of God in Missions.[4] Piper's persuasive book impacted many people to rethink missions. God only knows the number of pastors and churches were helped to develop a heart for the world. Even though Phil was certainly moved by the book he also influenced others to get a passion for the advancement of the kingdom.

> This fire must be communicated to your congregation. They must see in you a man with the world on his heart. Like John Wesley who said, "The world is my parish," you must feel the burden of the nations on your shoulders. While building your own congregation up in a most holy faith, you must likewise see the broader work of God's kingdom to the ends of the earth.[5]

Phil explained that Timothy could increase his congregation's heart for the nations through his faithful exposition of God's Word.

> As you work your way through one passage after another, you will squarely face the missionary mandate for the people of God. Expound it and apply it with passion. Work your way through Genesis 12, 17 and 22. Preach through the Psalms, especially the Messianic Psalms 2 and 110, as well as the kingly Psalms 93–99. Exegete Isaiah's multiplied missionary texts in chapters 40–66. Study through the little missionary Book of Jonah and then Habakkuk's promise of the earth being filled with the knowledge of God (2:14). The Gospels demonstrate Christ's passion for all people. Luke gives numerous examples of Jesus dealing with the Gentiles (or peoples). The prologues to John and Romans provide missionary motivation. Expound the Book of Acts, and in doing so teach your congregation to think missiologically. The Epistles

---

4   Newton, "Care for the Nations," 331; John Piper, *Let the Nations Be Glad! The Supremacy of God in Missions,* (Grand Rapids: Baker Books, 1993), 96.

5   Newton, "Care for the Nations," 333.

> give clear examples of the gospel message being applied in missionary settings. Revelation is an extraordinary missionary book, especially chapters 4–5.[6]

And there it is. Phil's last sentence. "Revelation is an extraordinary missionary book, especially chapters 4–5." I want to pivot here to discuss one of Phil's favorite chapters for teaching about missions: Revelation 5. But before doing so, I want to mention that Phil would continue to advise young Timothy with various ideas that have helped him in addressing the Bible's missionary message. These three points are extremely helpful precepts for ministers. "First, as you expound a text you will be showing the missionary mandate within a biblical context … . Second, prove from the Scriptures that missions are central to a true, New Testament church … . Third, exhort the congregation to total involvement in missions."[7]

Under the first precept Phil once again references the help of John Piper and this is central to my emphasis.

> As you expound a text you will be showing the missionary mandate within a biblical context. That way you are never reduced to manipulation or gimmicks to motivate God's people for missions. In this manner, you are setting forth the eternal Word that becomes our highest motivation. Show the church that the ministry of missions is to call the nations to the worship of God so that His glory might be displayed throughout the earth. John Piper explains that worship "is the fuel and goal in missions. It's the goal of missions because in missions we simply aim to bring the nations into the white-hot enjoyment

---

6   Newton, "Care for the Nations," 333–334. As a side note, this essay could be built around several other biblical expositions, certainly the Book of Acts where much of Phil's mature missiological thinking can be seen.

7   Newton, "Care for the Nations," 334–335.

of God's glory. The goal of missions is the gladness of the peoples in the greatness of God."[8]

Notice Piper's emphasis that worship "is the fuel and goal in missions." That resonated with Phil personally and impacted his ministry. The church would often hear this emphasis. And that is why, as his minister of music, I would be so excited to work on the orders of worship for upcoming Sundays. I knew that if we were focused in worship that glorified God there would be ancillary effects in every area of the church, including evangelism and missions. What a joy to work with a pastor who is motivated by that goal. And what a joyful experience to read Scripture and pray and sing the songs of the Lamb our Redeemer! What a blessing to see the church passionately worshiping Christ and desiring to see the kingdom advanced!

So, what were some of the principles that Phil drew from Revelation 5 that so influenced and encouraged South Woods? For the sake of brevity, I will divide the chapter into three sections: 5:1–7; 5:8–10; and 5:11–14.

Fugue
Theme and Exposition: Revelation 5:1–7

During 2006 Phil preached through the Book of Revelation, and by November 19 he arrived at 5:1–14. The sermon title was "The Lion & the Lamb."[9] Once again he leaned heavily upon Piper's *Let the Nations Be Glad!*

---

8   Newton, "Care for the Nations," 334.

9   Phil Newton, "The Lion & the Lamb. Revelation 5:1–14. Part 2." November 19, 2005. https://south woodsbc.org/media/fzqs9vz/revelation-5-1-14a.

> Missions is not the ultimate goal of the church. Worship is. Missions exist because worship doesn't. Worship is ultimate, not missions, because God is ultimate, not man. When this age is over, and the countless millions of the redeemed fall on their faces before the throne of God, missions will be no more. It is a temporary necessity. But worship abides forever [John Piper, *Let the Nations Be Glad!*].[10]

In the first section of the sermon (A call to worship) Phil helps us to understand the opening theme concerning *a book written inside and on the back, sealed up with seven seals* (v. 1). And this book is in the right hand of Him who sat on the throne (v. 1). What is so important about the book? What is in this book? "All of human destiny is found in the book. All of God's purposes and plans for His creation—including redemption and judgment—are contained in this book."[11] The apostle John longs to investigate this book, but there is a problem. There is no one able or worthy to open the book (vv. 2–4).

> "No one … was able to open the book or to look into it" because no one was worthy. For one to mediate both redemption and judgment found in the book, He must be worthy to exercise both. He must be of such righteousness that He can judge humanity; He must also be of such righteousness that He can redeem sinners through propitiating God's eternal justice and wrath.[12]

Is there not anyone worthy enough to open the book? The angels want to know. John wants to know. He begins to weep that no one can be found to open the book. And this points us to the primary focus for the book:

---

10   Newton, "The Lion and the Lamb," 1.

11   Newton, "The Lion and the Lamb," 1.

12   Newton, "The Lion and the Lamb," 2.

One of the elders, upon hearing John's profuse weeping over no one being found in all the universe worthy to open the book, said, "Stop weeping; behold, the Lion that is from the tribe of Judah, the Root of David, has overcome so as to open the book and its seven seals." We understand as the text progresses that "overcome" has to do with the atoning and substitutionary death of Christ on the cross. He overcame sin, Satan, and death at the cross. He satisfied God's Law by His obedience and God's justice by His death. He purchased God's elect by the price of His bloody death.

From that vision of a Lion in John's mind, he turned to see "a Lamb standing, as if slain." John uses that title of Christ over two dozen times in this book, showing that the focus of his instruction aims at the redemptive death of Jesus Christ by which He overcame the enemies of our souls. Understanding this leads to worship.[13]

This is the heartbeat of worship. "Look at the crucified and risen Lamb of God, and hear the call to worship!"[14] "The Lamb is all the glory of Immanuel's land."[15] This is the great refrain of the Scriptures: *the Son of God, who loved me and gave Himself up for me (Gal 2:20); just as Christ also loved you and gave Himself up for us (Eph 5:2); To Him who loves us and released us from our sins by His blood (Rev 1:5).* This is the prelude to our worship but like a magnificent orchestral arrangement what comes next develops and expands the theme.

Development: Revelation 5:8–10

Let us worship the King! And we can only do that if we get a good glimpse of the Lord whom we worship ... let the Word serve to fuel

13   Newton, "The Lion and the Lamb," 2.
14   Newton, "The Lion and the Lamb," 2.
15   Hymn: "The Sands of Time Are Sinking." Last verse. Words by Anne Ross-Cousin, based on the letters of Samuel Rutherford.

our worship.[16] Phil continues his exposition of the second section of Revelation 5:8–10.

> [I]n the previous chapter, two songs of worship declaring the holiness and worthiness of "Him who sat on the throne" are led by the four living creatures and echoed by the twenty-four elders. Chapter 5 adds three more songs of worship with the first led again by the four living creatures who represent the created order in heaven and the twenty-four elders who represent the redeemed in heaven. Creation untainted by sin, conscious of the holiness of God, rapt with devotion to God and the Lamb, and awed by the worthiness of the Lamb by reason of His redemptive death, initiates worship in heaven. The church's representatives, the twenty-four elders, "fell down before the Lamb, each one holding a harp and golden bowls full of incense, which are the prayers of the saints," join in this litany of praise to the Lamb of God.[17]

The subject is the same: The Lamb is worthy of taking the book and He did take it. So, what is the right response to this revelation? It is a development of the theme. Let us join in worship of his slain Lamb. First the four living creatures lead out; then the twenty-four elders fall prostrate before the throne of God and join the chorus, *and they sang a new song, saying, Worthy art Thou to take the book, and to break its seals* (v. 9). And why is Christ so worthy? *For Thou wast slain* (v. 9). Just like the angels in Revelation 4, now the creatures and elders join in singing the mighty redemptive refrain.

And what other reason is given for such worship? *and didst purchase for God with Thy blood, men from every tribe and tongue, and people and nation* (v. 9). There it is. Christ is worthy because He opened the book, because He came and fulfilled the redemptive

---

16   Phil Newton, "The Lamb Rules, Let's Worship. Revelation 5:1–10." July 8, 2018.

17   Newton, "The Lion and the Lamb," 2.

purpose of God, because He purchased for God His blood bought people from every tribe and tongue. Why is He worthy? Because Christ *hast made them to be a kingdom and priests to our God, And they will reign upon the earth.* (v. 10).

And thus, we see the great missiological theme which leads to further worship.

Recapitulation and Finale: Revelation 5:11–14

And now comes the last section of Revelation 5:11–14 which recapitulates the theme and leads us to the great choral finale:

> The circles of praise and worship widen. It begins with the four living creatures and twenty-four elders in vv. 8–10; then it moves to the innumerable host of angels in vv. 11–12; and finally, "And every created thing which is in heaven and on the earth and under the earth and on the sea, and all things in them, I heard saying, "To Him who sits on the throne and to the Lamb, be blessing and honor and glory and dominion forever and ever." In chapter 4, the four living creatures, representing the created order, lead the way in worshiping God as the sovereign Creator. Now, John shows us that ultimately, when final redemption takes place all of the universal created order will be given expression to worship God as Creator and the Lamb as Redeemer. Paul only hints at what John pictures in Revelation 5, that "the whole creation groans and suffers the pains of childbirth together until now," awaiting the day of final redemption (Rom. 8:22–23). The Psalmist declared, "The heavens are telling of the glory of God; and their expanse is declaring the work of His hands" (Ps. 19:1). That's happening at present but John tells us that more is to come. Universal worship of our Sovereign Creator and Redeemer will echo throughout eternity![18]

---

18   Newton, "The Lion and the Lamb," 3–4.

Did you notice who was worshiping? *Angels, and creatures, and elders, and myriads of myriads, and thousands of thousands.* There they are, all around the throne and what were they saying? Here is the refrain once again: Worthy is the Lamb that was slain. But notice the amplification of His worth. He is so worthy. He deserves to receive power and riches and wisdom and might and honor, glory, and blessing.

And that is not the final list of worshipers. Notice who else was worshiping? *And every created thing which is in heaven and on the earth and under the earth and on the sea, and all things in them* (v. 13). And what were these saying? *I heard them saying, To Him who sits on the throne, and to the Lamb, be blessing and honor and glory and dominion forever and ever.*

The grand old hymn captures the worship as well as can be here before the consummation of all things:

> Let every kindred, every tribe On this terrestrial ball,
> To Him all majesty ascribe, and crown Him Lord of all.
> O that with yonder sacred throng We at His feet may fall,
> We'll join the everlasting song, and crown Him Lord of all.[19]

What could be added to such worship? What else were the four living creatures saying? *And the four living creatures kept saying,* amen (v. 14). What else were the elders doing? *And the elders fell down and worshiped* (v. 14).

---

19   Hymn: "All Hail the Power of Jesus' Name." These stanzas written by John Rippon.

Postlude

What are the redeemed from every tribe and tongue, people, and nation supposed to be doing? What are all of God's created beings supposed to be doing?

Therefore, worship is the goal and the fuel of missions: Missions exist because worship doesn't. Missions is our way of saying: the joy of knowing Christ is not a private, or tribal, or national or ethnic privilege. It is for all. And that's why we go. Because we have tasted the joy of worshiping Jesus, and we want all the families of the earth included.

All the ends of the earth shall remember and turn to the Lord, and all the families of the nations shall worship before you (Ps 22:27). Seeking the worship of the nations is fueled by the joy of our own worship. You can't commend what you don't cherish. You can't proclaim what you don't prize. Worship is the fuel and the goal of missions.[20]

Conclusion

What have I learned from my brother in Christ, my friend, and my mentor? That God's mercy and grace and love lead a believer to a deep-rooted appreciation for the preaching and teaching of God's Word. Which leads to gratitude for God's faith, love, and hope. And that leads to love, not only for God's people, but for the world. Worship is indeed the fuel and the goal of missions. For me, until I met Phil, worship was the most important thing in the church. It was what I was trained for and what I enjoyed. But I had never made the connection between worship and everything else, especially

---

20   John Piper, Missions Exists Because Worship Doesn't. https://www.desiringgod.org/messages/missions-exists-because-worship-doesnt-a-bethlehem-legacy-inherited-and-bequeathed.

missions. Those connections developed during my time with Phil and continue to grow. I am richer indeed to think more deeply about the Singer, His Song, and the upcoming Finale. *Soli Deo Gloria*!

The closing words of Phil's sermon, "The Lamb Rules, Let's Worship," sum it all up for me:

So, keep writing new songs because the realities of Christ's mercies and grace and power and love are inexhaustible. Our worship must never, never be dull or thoughtless or perfunctory when we have such a King that reigns over us with wisdom and power, and who is worthy to be praised for all eternity.[21]

---

21   Newton, "The Lamb Rules, Let's Worship," 7.

Chapter seven

Pastoral Ministry in Dying Churches

Brian Croft

Introduction

I had just arrived at an invite only pastor's retreat in 2012. There were about twenty-five pastors privileged with this invite. Some pastors I knew. Others I did not know. But I was filled with gladness when I looked up and saw my friend, Phil Newton, walking towards me. He had that warm look and smile as he approached, a demeaner so many of us have come to love. He greeted me with a hug and some kind words. Then, I was surprised by what came out of his mouth next.

> Hey Brian! Would you want to write a book on funerals together? I grew up in a funeral home and I have done hundreds of funerals in my ministry. But I have also attended many poorly done funerals throughout the years, and still have not found a good little book to address this issue. We need an accessible book that makes the gospel clear, and yet explains how to also care for the grieving families well. I thought you would be the perfect person to work together on this book.

I was intrigued for two reasons. First, I had just published my second practical ministry book but was not at all a credible and widely known author. And I was a young pastor in my late thirties with a fraction of the three decades of pastoral ministry experience of my friend. So, his eagerness to write with me was a bit of a shock. Second, the next practical ministry book I had already planned to write was a book on funerals—but had told no one. So, I began to wonder if the providence of God was at work in this divine moment, both to affirm my right choice of what was to be my next book project, as well as provide an older, wiser friend as a co-author.

It proved to be a most providential appointment. By the end of the retreat, Phil and I had a title, subtitle, working outline, and the assigned sections for each of us to write. Hence, *Conduct Gospel-Centered Funerals: Applying the Gospel at the Unique Challenges of Death* was born. It was my first book with a co-author, and because of my wonderful experience with Phil in writing this book together, over half of my 25+ books published are with a variety of co-authors.

Writing this book with Phil was a wonderful experience for many reasons. First, writing with a friend is a unique joy. The "give and take" of the writing process with each other was an encouraging and sharping experience. Second, the fruit was undeniable. We have seen God use this book all over the world over the last ten years. This little book remains one of the only short, accessible books to help pastors think through how to conduct funerals in a balanced manner where the gospel is clear, and yet grieving people are cared for well. This funeral book has sold over 20,000 copies around the world and has been translated into multiple languages.

Finally, this was such an encouraging experience because of the chance to learn from a wise, seasoned pastor. I was a pastor approaching a decade in my church and still had much to learn. Phil Newton was the pastor of one local church for thirty-five years and by the time he transitioned from there, he had established a faithful pastoral ministry that should and does act as a model and example for any pastor.

This chapter seeks to honor the long, faithful pastoral ministry of my friend, Phil Newton, by demonstrating how his entire pastoral ministry modeled the biblical paradigm from the New Testament. It will additionally show how that example of faithful ministry can be a blueprint to help struggling and dying churches. We will first consider what that New Testament paradigm for pastoral ministry is, then apply how that understanding can help dying churches.

The Biblical Paradigm for Pastoral Ministry

Busyness marks the lives of all of us in our culture, especially those in ministry. Some wear it like a badge of honor while others try to avoid it like the plague, but no one escapes it. The work to be done, people to contact, possessions to maintain, activities to schedule and attend, friendships to cultivate, guests to host, and appointments to keep are endless. Regardless of age and interests, most people have more to do than can reasonably be done. When Christians add meaningful participation—including regular worship attendance, volunteer service, and special events—to the list of normal busyness, their calendars fill to the point of bursting. Life in twenty-first century Western culture feels like an unending rat race that only slows down when crisis or sickness force it to a screeching halt.

Pastors not only observe the pressures, demands, and responsibilities that push and pull-on church members, but experience them firsthand. Because the pastor's call to shepherd God's people requires involvement in their lives, he must juggle his own schedule with the added pressure of working around the hectic schedules of God's flock. The convergence of all this busyness creates expectations that bring tremendous tension for those in pastoral ministry, which sets them up for failure from the start.

This pressure yields two traps that sabotage the faithful work of a proper pastoral ministry. In some cases, a pastor quickly realizes that he cannot provide adequate care for his congregation, so he fails to attempt it. Even with a smaller congregation, it's impossible to attend *every* surgery, ball game, funeral, doctor's visit, home invitation, ministry activity, church workday, and counseling request. Discouraged, they stop trying altogether. While some languish in laziness, most redirect their attention to focus more broadly on administrating large activities, managing busy programs, and overseeing the practical functioning of the local church, leaving the work of "relational ministry" to others—or neglecting it altogether.

On the other hand, some determined pastors recognize that they cannot do it all, but they commit to pushing through the pain to do as much as is humanly possible. They set an ambitious hand to the plow, hoping that with enough effort they can please at least *some* people. This approach is fraught with dangers, too. Now enslaved to the demands and needs of his church, the pastor allows the congregation to dominate his life. Whether directly or indirectly, other people's desires largely determine the investment of his time and energy. The measure of his ministry's faithfulness and fruitfulness becomes intertwined with the congregation's expectations and his ability to meet them. While some are pleased some of the time, none are ever fully satisfied, and most find a reason to criticize him regardless. Pursuing human approval will inevitably lead to exhaustion and emptiness.

A Call to Faithful Ministry

While called to fulfill a robust ministry, the pastor is tasked by God neither to run programs for the masses nor to satisfy every expectation. God, who alone can set men aside for this ministry, has the authority to establish the terms and responsibilities of their calling. Thankfully, he outlines the pastor's marching orders in his word. The pastor's path to steadfast faithfulness, which avoids the pitfalls of distraction and misdirection, is to know and do *what* God has truly called him to do. Peter exhorts elders/pastors to shepherd—care for—God's people when he writes:

> So I exhort the elders among you, as a fellow elder and a witness of the sufferings of Christ, as well as a partaker in the glory that is going to be revealed: shepherd the flock of God that is among you, exercising oversight, not under compulsion, but willingly, as God would have you; not for shameful gain, but eagerly; not domineering over those in your charge, but being examples to the flock. And when the chief Shepherd appears, you will receive the unfading crown of glory. (1 Pet 5:1–4)[1]

To summarize the pastor's calling in a single sentence, "Shepherd the souls of God's people under your care until the Chief Shepherd appears." Note the what, who, how, and when of this important work.

What: Shepherd the flock of God.

Who: The flock of God that is among you.

How: Not because you must, but because you are willing, as God would have you; not pursuing dishonest gain, but

---

1 All citations of Scripture are from the English Standard Version (ESV).

eager to serve; not domineering over those entrusted to you but being examples to the flock.

When: Until the Chief Shepherd, Jesus Christ, returns for his flock placed in your care.

A pastor's true calling, then, is to shepherd the souls of God's people humbly, willingly, and eagerly, and on behalf of the Chief Shepherd, Jesus Christ. Despite sweeping cultural changes that make life today quite different than in the first century, this task has not changed since the time Peter wrote these words. The basic responsibilities of pastoral ministry remain.

God's word is sufficient to equip a man for every good work (2 Tim 3:17), including the work of pastoral ministry. The Scripture outlines the responsibilities of this divine calling and instructions for the man's daily priorities. Drawing on shepherd imagery, the Bible consistently highlights the central concerns for faithful pastors as leading, feeding, protecting, and caring for the souls of God's people entrusted to your care. In the face of the unbiblical demands, pressures, and expectations foisted upon a pastor that often crush his spirit, we hope studying and meditating on the biblical directives will solidify a conviction to the what, who, how, and when of pastoral ministry.

Phil Newton felt those unbiblical demands and pressures for four decades and yet was faithful to embody this biblical calling throughout his entire ministry. This is evidenced in a healthy local church that remains in Memphis, TN. It is also evidenced by a massive number of grateful souls who heard the word, were prayed for, were visited when they were sick, cared for when widowed, comforted while dying, encouraged when weak, guided when lost, protected when in danger, and confronted when careless.

Additionally, Phil took this paradigm and taught other pastors and continues to raise up another generation of pastors to shepherd the souls of God people until the Chief Shepherd appears. This is the biblical call of every pastor for every generation regardless the country, context, or culture.

The Epidemic of Dying Churches

We have reached an unprecedented crisis in North America. Four thousand churches close every year in North America, while close to 1,000 of those churches are Southern Baptist churches as reported by the North American Mission Board. The problem of declining and dying churches has created unique challenges for all mainline denominations scrambling to search for answers on how to address this growing crisis.

I am convinced the biblical call to shepherd the souls of God's people modeled by Phil Newton's own pastoral ministry is the blueprint to bring dying churches back to life.

My Experience with a Dying Church

Many readers have likely heard the story of my seventeen-year pastorate. The first five years were brutal. When I arrived, this Southern Baptist Church consisted of thirty elderly people on the southside of Louisville, Kentucky. The virtually non-existent ministry was matched only by the church's finances. Although I did not know it when I was hired, they could only afford to pay my salary for about six months, and even without the commitment to my compensation, they were headed toward closure in two to three years. The situation actually deteriorated after my arrival. I faced three different efforts from within to fire me in those first five years.

The first of these attempts happened only three months into my ministry, and it was initiated by a staff member I had inherited. He boasted of getting my predecessor fired, and he tried to do the same with me. The second firing attempt came at the two-and-a-half-year mark when I led them to find the 580 people on the membership roll who had not been to church in over ten years. I will never forget receiving the phone call warning me about these maneuvers while I was on a family vacation. The third, and thankfully final, firing attempt arose at the five-year mark and ultimately led to an exodus of 25 percent of the congregation. Some of the folks who left had come under my ministry during the previous five years and had become dear friends. When the smoke cleared, I was beat up, discouraged, and ready to leave.

As I look back, I persevered in that field for two reasons. First, I sensed God, in faithfulness to his church, would not abandon us after bringing us so far. We could identify evidence of his grace and work, even amid the hostility. Second, I was haunted by the realization that I would "have to give an account" for every soul under my care, even those who did not like me very much (Heb 13:17). So, I stayed, along with some of the hostile members. In that sixth year God displayed his power and grace in turning the ship. This change of course led the church to flourish over the next decade.

The church grew numerically and, more importantly, spiritually. We adopted a church leadership structure that included the two biblical offices of pastors/elders and deacons, and we affirmed men to serve in these roles who grasped their scriptural responsibilities and excelled in them. We celebrated conversions from the people in our neighborhood. We experienced ethnic diversity that mirrored our community, having previously been a multi-generational but all-white congregation. This diversity even included refugees. The change was not only inwardly focused but outwardly as we raised up pastors and missionaries and sent them out. Most significantly, the spiritual temperature of our gatherings shifted as the angry, scowling faces I had grown accustomed to seeing as I preached now softened. People who had been hostile to me began to trust me, and even grew to love me. They accepted my preaching in ways they had resisted and developed love for biblical exposition. They received my efforts to shepherd their souls in some of the most significant events of their lives. I am so thankful I stayed, and even more, I'm grateful for the previously hostile members who stayed with me. Our perseverance together laid the groundwork for God's sovereign, stunning work of redemption in the lives of a young, broken pastor and a discouraged, hurting people. Through it all, God revealed his desire to revive dying churches.

The Blueprint to Revive Dying Churches

God brought spiritual life back to a dying church. This story is particularly significant for this occasion because of Phil Newton; he was one of my trusted counselors, prayerful supporters, and pastoral encouragers all throughout my ministry at this church. He did not just model this biblical paradigm in his own life. He had confidence that this same model of pastoral ministry to shepherd the flock through the word of God, by the Spirit of God, would be what God would use to help us revitalize our dying church.

This biblical paradigm fully trusts that the word of God is powerful enough to build a church and breathe life into cold hearts and dying churches as we shepherd the flock. Despite the power and sufficiency of God's word to create life by reviving the dead, he rarely hurries to complete his work based on our measure of time. He always acts, but rarely as quickly as we would want.

In fact, according to Jesus' parables in the gospel accounts, God's design for building his kingdom is intentionally slow, subtle, often hidden, and generally unimpressive. Herein lies the profound paradox related to God building his kingdom through the preaching of his word: while pastors should sense an urgency for his work, God contentedly plays the long game. Understanding this idea helps the pastor balance his urgency to preach with the necessary patience to wait for God to work on his timescale. Jesus captures this concept so well in the parable of the sower:

> Again he began to teach beside the sea. And a very large crowd gathered about him, so that he got into a boat and sat in it on the sea, and the whole crowd was beside the sea on the land. And he was teaching them many things in parables, and in his teaching he said to them: "Listen! Behold, a sower went out to sow. And as he sowed, some seed fell along the path, and the birds came and devoured it. Other seed fell on rocky ground, where it did not have much soil, and immediately it sprang up, since it had no depth of soil. And when the sun rose, it was scorched, and since it had no root, it withered away. Other seed fell among thorns, and the thorns grew up and choked it, and it yielded no grain. And other seeds fell into good soil and produced grain, growing up and increasing and yielding thirtyfold and sixtyfold and a hundredfold." And he said, "He who has ears to hear, let him hear."
>
> And when he was alone, those around him with the twelve asked him about the parables. And he said to them, "To you has been given the secret of the kingdom of God, but for those outside everything is in parables, so that they may indeed see but not perceive, and may indeed hear but not understand, lest they should turn and be forgiven.
>
> And he said to them, "Do you not understand this parable? How then will you understand all the parables? The sower sows the word. And these

are the ones along the path, where the word is sown: when they hear, Satan immediately comes and takes away the word that is sown in them. And these are the ones sown on rocky ground: the ones who, when they hear the word, immediately receive it with joy. And they have no root in themselves, but endure for a while; then, when tribulation or persecution arises on account of the word, immediately they fall away. And others are the ones sown among thorns. They are those who hear the word, but the cares of the world and the deceitfulness of riches and the desires for other things enter in and choke the word, and it proves unfruitful. But those that were sown on the good soil are the ones who hear the word and accept it and bear fruit, thirtyfold and sixtyfold and a hundredfold." (Mark 4:1–20)

Because Jesus interprets this parable, we have no doubt about its meaning and significance. The sower's seed is God's word (v. 14). Like natural seed, it falls on different kinds of soil that receive it with greater and lesser success. When it finds the good soil of a receptive heart (v. 20), it takes root, germinates, and grows, even yielding a massive harvest. God's word is powerful, and He uses the spreading of it to build his kingdom.

The metaphor unmistakably conveys deliberateness that can feel like downright slowness. Farming does not deliver a quick return. Everything about this example reinforces patience and dependence on God. After the seed is scattered, the sower is helpless in speeding up the rooting and growth process. He must wait to see if the seeds produce sprouts, let alone a fruitful harvest. The incredible sight of produce comes only after the long and grueling process of growth.

Jesus teaches several valuable lessons in this simple parable. It reinforces both that the word of God builds the kingdom of God and that we can trust that God's timing always perfectly accords with his purposes. Sowers of the word must be faithful to play their part and then wait for God to do his work by his Spirit. Jesus exhorts pastors to patience.

This balance of urgency and patience is a difficult and critical aspect of persevering in a faithful pastoral ministry. While most pastors begin with a tremendously eager resolve, the most common reason they fail to persevere stems from a lack of patient endurance in the absence of visible results. In the parable of the sower, Jesus clarifies that urgency without patience is not his design, and often leads to discouragement and despair. The power of God's word does not guarantee it will act quickly. This period of waiting leads many pastors to frustration, questions of personal effectiveness, doubt in God, and a wavering commitment to his word. All this can culminate in the pursuit of another foundation for ministry or another field of ministry. In contrast, pastors who persevere in a difficult ministry post embrace both urgency and patience.

This blueprint to a long, faithful pastoral ministry and the solution to revive dying churches was captured beautifully in the thirty-five-year pastoral ministry of Phil Newton and the way he continues to support pastors all over the world seeking to remain faithful in their call. This blueprint of shepherding souls through the centrality of the word of God pictured by Jesus in the parable of the sower, can be summarized and applied best with these "Five P's": preaching, prayer, patience, presence, and picking.

Preaching

Under the umbrella: "Shepherd the flock that is among you" is this most important task if we believe the Word of God builds any church—that is, the weekly public preaching of God's Word. This is the most important way the "seed is sown" among those we are entrusted to shepherd. The sower sows the word. That's the role of the pastor. There are few men you will find who so diligently sowed the seeds of the word week in and week out, for decades in the same place through faithful expository sermons like Phil Newton.

Prayer

Prayer reminds us of our deep dependance upon God. Jesus brilliantly uses this parable to demonstrate the clear role of the sower, and yet the sower's complete inability to make it grow. Only God makes it grow. Only God can make the seed find good soil and eventually bear fruit. The pastor sows but then is completely reliant upon God to do with his word whatever God chooses. So then, the pastor sows, prays, and waits—captured well in the consistent and persevering prayer life and ministry of Phil Newton.

Patience

Patience is arguably one of the most important traits of any pastor. Pastors love to preach. Many embrace the need to pray and declare their reliance upon God in their labors. But no pastor likes to wait. This is why this parable is such an important blueprint for dying churches. The work of church revitalization is never quick. It is a slow work, and the impatience of a pastor can sabotage the very impact he is seeking to have from his ministry. But patience appears to be a key aspect to the way God builds his kingdom in this world.

Just because God's word is powerful does not mean it works quickly. This captures the interesting paradox of this paradigm of pastoral ministry. We preach the word with urgency but wait on it to work patiently. Phil Newtown labored for thirty-five years in the same church. No pastor makes it that long in any church without a clear conviction and resolve to be patient and pray for God to build his church in his time.

Presence

Never underestimate the power of presence. Pastors mistakenly spend too much time running and talking instead of sitting and listening. This too is implied in the parable of the sower. What are pastors to do as they preach, pray, and wait? They engage in the private daily grind of caring for the souls of their people. One of the most essential ways to care for souls is to be with your people, one at a time. Shepherds who effectively shepherd, smell like sheep. Undoubtably, Phil Newton was with his people and present in some of the most important moments, tragedies, and events in their lives. Everyone knew he smelled like his sheep. And they loved him for it.

Picking

This last aspect to this blueprint points to the need for pastors serving dying churches to pick their battles wisely. Pastors in dying churches will find all kinds of problems and issues they will want to change or fix immediately. Some will even be convinced God demands they change these things ASAP. But an important principle in church revitalization is the need to earn the trust of the people before you can fight a bunch of the needed battles for change. Dying churches are full of sacred cows that cannot be slaughtered simply by a new, charismatic pastor quoting passages from the Bible. But they can be addressed once an ordinary, faithful, pastor loves and shepherds those people for several years, who through that faithful shepherding then earns their trust and has demonstrated his is worthy to follow. No one survives thirty-five years in the same church and still leaves a beloved pastor, without knowing how and when to pick the right battles to fight at the right time. Phil Newton exuded that wisdom and patience and in doing so prove this biblical paradigm that planted and established a healthy thriving church, and likewise, could also revive the most lifeless church.

A Final Tribute

This project has brought a unique joy for me as one of so many helped and impacted by knowing Phil Newton. It has caused me to reflect on God's kind providence in my life to bring a co-author, co-laborer, and wise counselor for my benefit and the benefit of others. I thank God for a man who became the embodiment to so many of us of what a biblical pastoral ministry looks like. It has aided me in my own ministry, as well as the hundreds of dying churches I have advised, counseled, and served.

But to be honest, I am most thankful to God to have a friend who points me to Jesus, still greets me with a warm smile and hug, and takes a true genuine interest in me and how God is at work in me and my ministry. Phil Newton has been that counselor, example, and friend for me and countless others and for that—is worthy of the unique honor of this book.

Chapter eight

The Spiritual Formation of Ministerial Trainees

Matthew W. Moore

Introduction

As Phil Newton moved into the most recent phase of his ministry after stepping out of the pulpit at South Woods Baptist Church, several conversations generated about what a blessing he has been to other, generally younger, pastors. One recurring sentiment within those conversations is that Phil Newton was church planting before church planting was "cool." I believe it is safe to say that throughout his pastoral ministry Phil was a pioneer. Not only as a church planter in the 1980s but also as a trainer of pastors and church leaders. Phil led the church he planted to prioritize training leaders before it was in vogue.

I will argue that Phil was ahead of the curve, even when compared to seminaries. His experience, later research, application throughout, and argumentation in both a dissertation and a book,[1] led him to a decisive conclusion that the best context for training is the local church. In recent years, seminaries began to adopt the same

---

1 Phillip A. Newton, "Local Church Leadership Development: Its Effects and Importance on Church Planting and Revitalization" (Ph.D. diss., Southeastern Baptist Theological Seminary, 2013); Phil A. Newton, *The Mentoring Church: How Pastors and Congregations Cultivate Leaders* (Kregel: Grand Rapids, 2017).

conclusion. It is now commonplace to find graduate degree program formats that place the student within the context of the local church for the duration of the degree.

The push—or return, rather—to local church-based training naturally results from a recovery or strengthening of ecclesiology. In what might be described as a resurgence, many evangelicals are rediscovering the critical role the church plays in the formation of Christ's followers. To say it another way, the local church is an essential, formative factor in training Christians for ministry.

Through the following explanation of church-based training, it will become apparent how the church is uniquely equipped to train church leaders. Jesus established a training foundation for the church to adopt. The apostle Paul then connected training to local church settings. Then the churches of the NT began to execute their training responsibilities. Through God-appointed interaction with Scripture and in divine construction as the body of Christ, local churches function as the best training ground and steward of ministerial trainee formation.

Foundation: The Lord Jesus

Jesus created a pattern in calling the first generation of disciples that stands in contrast to rabbinic teachers of his day. Certain features remain intact, but many new features appear. Jesus' selection of disciples, the multiplication of disciples, the prominence of women, the prophetic layer to His ministry, the communal aspect of following Him, and His self-awareness as the God-man all corroborate the uniqueness of His training method.[2] Cues from Jesus' pattern may

---

2   Matthew W. Moore, "New Testament Norms for the Great Commission: A Framework for Disciple-Making as a Communal Function of the Local Church," (Ph.D. diss., Southeastern Baptist Theological Seminary, 2022), 46–56.

have benefits when adapted to various methods and models of training. However, the best application of Jesus' model may be found in the local church's responsibility to train leaders.

The apostles were the leaders of the first local church expression. In their obedience to Christ's commands, these men pioneered the movement and multiplication of the church. The church's self-propagating nature implies—even demands—the reproduction of qualified leaders. The apostles represent the prototypical disciples, but they also "were examples of how Jesus trained the leadership of the church."[3] Phil points to Jesus' method as essential for training. He agrees that the development and apostleship of the original twelve disciples and other Christian disciples in the New Testament, serve as "an appropriate template ... for training church planters and revitalizers."[4] Just as Jesus was training the apostles for a specific role in unfolding the plan for the church, so churches must be intent on reproducing qualified leaders to lead healthy local churches.

While the focus of this essay is the spiritual formation of trainees, we must acknowledge its integration with discipleship in general. In fact, the natural overlap of Jesus' discipleship model and leadership training finds its way into many "modernist" approaches to discipleship. Modernist approaches, which try to directly replicate Jesus' model, often end up being rigidly "mechanistic" and "managerial" as well as individualistically program-oriented rather than community-oriented and animated by the Holy Spirit.[5] Phil likewise identifies flaws in "*content*-driven training, such as is found

---

3   Wilkins, *Following the Master*, 134.

4   Newton, "Local Church Leadership Development," 25.

5   Don Little, *Effective Discipling in Muslim Communities: Scripture, History and Seasoned Practice* (Downers Grove: IVP Academic, 2015), 76–84, critiques the comparable approaches of Leroy Eims, Allen Hadidian, Robert Coleman, and Kenneth Boa, categorically identifying them all as "modernist."

in seminary classrooms, lectures, or conferences."[6] These practices attempt to directly apply Jesus' model, but they neglect the essential ecclesial application of leader training evident in the remainder of the NT. Phil's labors, which are meticulously applied ecclesiology, lead us to recover the local church's role as the essential context for ministerial training.

Connection: The Apostle Paul

The best training practices pick up where the apostle Paul left off, as he aimed to strengthen local churches for the training task. Paul refers to himself as an apostle "untimely born" (1 Cor 15:8), but in God's providence he functioned as a critical transition from the original twelve to the multiplicity of local churches in the NT and those throughout church history. In that sense, we must admit the timeliness of Paul's ministry. Practically, he connects Jesus's training pattern to the training responsibilities of pastors and local churches. The clearest evidence lies in Paul's relationship and exhortation to Timothy.

Timothy spent much time with Paul traveling, preaching, and church planting. Timothy's experiences, even before leading the church at Ephesus, were intended by Paul to be reproduced in others based on Paul's own words. In his last letter to Timothy, written with his imminent death looming, Paul instructed, "What you have learned from me in the presence of many witnesses entrust to faithful men, who will be able to teach others also" (2 Tim 2:2). This text is repeatedly used to champion disciple-making and certainly has implications touching personal discipleship. But the context of

---

6   Newton, *40 Questions about Pastoral Ministry*, 162. See also D. Michael Crow, "Multiplying Jesus Mentors: Designing a Reproducible Mentoring System—A Case Study," Missiology: An International Review, 36, no. 1 (January 2008): 93.

these pastoral epistles indicates the priority need for leaders in local churches. Timothy was instructed to do that work within the local church.

Upon Paul's instruction in 2 Timothy 2:2, Bill Hull argues leadership development ranks among the most important tasks of church leaders. In contrast to frequently used earthly measurements of identifying leaders, Hull exalts proven gospel propagation as a requirement of worthy leaders, who will receive greater responsibility once shown faithful.[7] Several other passages of Scripture reveal that Paul prepared numerous people to serve as leaders in local churches (see Acts 15:22–33; 18:18–19, 24–28; 19:22, 29; 20:1–5; Gal 2:1–10; Rom 16:3; 2 Cor 8:23). Eckhard Schnabel comments, "Of the approximately one hundred names that are connected with Paul in the Book of Acts and in the Pauline letters, thirty-eight are coworkers of the apostle."[8] Schnabel further identifies many of those coworkers who became leaders in the church and disciplers in their own right, which supports Paul's focus on leadership.[9] Even when traveling with a deep entourage, Paul's focused investment and instruction to Timothy highlight the importance of leadership training.

Execution: The Local Church

Consider 2 Timothy 2:2 once more to gain a bit of context and borrow one of Paul's metaphors. His exhortation to Timothy is

---

7   Bill Hull, *The Disciple Making Church: Leading a Body of Believers on the Journey of Faith*, Kindle ed. (Grand Rapids: Baker, 2010), ch. 11, "The Pastoral Priorities." See Luke 16:10.

8   Schnabel, *Paul the Missionary*, 248–9. See also Robert Banks, *Paul's Idea of Community: The Early House Churches in Their Historical Setting* (Grand Rapids: Eerdmans, 1980), 153–4.

9   Schnabel, *Paul the Missionary*, 250–5, names Barnabas, Timothy, Luke, Aquila, Silas/Silvanus, Titus, Tychicus, Apollos, Phoebe, Priscilla, Mary, Junia, Tryphaena and Tryphosa, Persis Apphia, Euodia and Syntyche, all of whom were coworkers with Paul, and he identifies how and where they went on to lead and participate in local churches.

paralleled to the athlete who "competes according to the rules" (v. 5). Along with a soldier and a farmer, the athlete requires the suffering part and parcel to a disciplined life if he wishes to succeed at his chosen athletic competition. If I may extrapolate from this athletic metaphor, two fields for discipline come to the forefront of trainees' formation: diet and exercise. At this point, I might lose the readers who have recently heard these words from their doctors, but hear me out! Indeed, these two analogous foci describe how the church is best equipped for training leaders.

Diet: The Scriptures Properly Interpreted[10]

Diet describes the spiritual nourishment that comes from rightly understanding and applying the Word of God. Jesus solidified a lasting relationship between food and the Bible when He quoted to the Devil from Deuteronomy, "Man shall not live by bread alone, but by every word that comes from the mouth of God" (Matt 4:4). The enemy is happy to use Bible verses, if they are stripped of their intended meaning, thus, wrongly interpreted. Jesus would not fall for that trick; nor should we. Scripture must be properly interpreted if it will bring the spiritual nourishment and sustenance God intends. By God's design, it is the local church that stewards interpretation to its best, transformative conclusions.

Christian Scripture is the preserved revelation of the triune God to mankind. Yet, God's self-revelation is not simply a record of information to be transferred to its readers or hearers, as if Christianity's goal summarily amounts to data transmission or increased knowledge. Scripture interactively moves its believing subjects in ways consistent with God's ongoing work in the world,

---

10 This section has been adapted from Moore, "New Testament Norms for the Great Commission," 129–64.

not the least of which is the complete salvation of His people. As such, the Bible holds the place of the most basic earthly content available to the local church.

The apostolic testimony, according to Acts 2:42, holds an authoritative position from the start of the church and continues in that authoritative role with the completion of the New Testament. The result was, local churches assumed responsibility for "the faith that was once for all delivered to the saints" (Jude 1:3). And they maintained this commonly held faith by upholding Scripture as the "authority in the common life of the Christian community."[11] God's Word communicated through the apostles organized and equipped a lasting community with the content essential to making disciples and training leaders.

Not only does the Word of God "[create] for itself a church which remains steadfast in it," but the resulting church depends on Scripture for continual confirmation in its faith and theological development.[12] In doing so, the church utilizes biblical content for the preservation of its identity, making and maturing disciples and training leaders. The church—created, sustained, and grown by the Word of God—fundamentally labors in faithful interpretation in order to accomplish its mission.

Christian Scripture holds a place that is finally authoritative for faith and practice but is not the object of faith. It testifies to the Word incarnate, Jesus Christ, who is the object of faith and in whom resides the transformative power. Through the revelation of God's written Word, one comes to know the person of Christ. The apostle Paul describes what begins in conjunction with saving faith

---

11   David H. Kelsey, *Proving Doctrine: The Uses of Scripture in Modern Theology* (Harrisburg, PA: Trinity Press International, 1999), 164.

12   Dietrich Bonhoeffer, *The Cost of Discipleship*, trans. R. H. Fuller, 2nd ed. (London: SCM Press, 1959), 225; Kelsey, Proving Doctrine, 99–100.

in 2 Corinthians 3:18, declaring, "And we all, with unveiled face, beholding the glory of the Lord, are being transformed into the same image from one degree of glory to another." Such a faith-filled sight comes through an encounter with the truth of God's Word. Donald Bloesch rightly concludes that the most appropriate symbol of God's Word is "the cross of Christ shining through the pages of the open Bible."[13] Christ and His work must be the aim of trainees.

New Testament Scripture received by the church as God's self-communication interacts with the believing community. This is done by way of interpretation to ensure the end to which it labors, namely, transformation into the likeness of Jesus Christ. "This comes from the Lord who is the Spirit" (2 Cor 3:18).[14] Accordingly to the revelatory Word of the triune God who "has shone in our hearts to give the light of the knowledge of the glory of God in the face of Jesus Christ" (2 Cor 4:6).

The long-term goal of apprehending truth and transforming believers into the likeness of Christ can only be carried out by the "community of inquiry," which is the local church. Robert Corrington explains, "The community now stands at the place where knowledge is won or lost, and the community can work across large stretches of time to ensure that knowledge will indeed be won."[15] The local church possesses every resource necessary to engage the content of Scripture faithfully. Only the nourishing content of God's Word

13   Donald G. Bloesch, "The Primacy of Scripture," in *The Authoritative Word: Essays on the Nature of Scripture*, ed. Donald K. McKim (Grand Rapids: Eerdmans, 1983), 120.

14   Murray J. Harris, *The Second Epistle to the Corinthians: A Commentary on the Greek Text*, NIGTC (Grand Rapids: Eerdmans, 2005), 318, credits Christlike transformation to the person of the Holy Spirit.

15   Robert S. Corrington, *The Community of Interpreters: On the Hermeneutics of Nature and the Bible in American Philosophical Tradition* (Macon, GA: Mercer University Press, 1995), 13.

ecclesially received[16] provides the balanced diet necessary to ministerial training.

Through the local church, ministerial trainees learn to view Christ through the Scriptures and lead others to do the same. This is where training intensifies in the preparation to lead and care for others. One appointed for the task of church leadership is required to handle the word in a trustworthy way (2 Tim 2:15). Those who teach will be "judged with greater strictness" (Jas 3:1). They will "give an account" for those souls of whom they have been entrusted by God (Heb 13:17). Phil has argued this kind of preparation "goes beyond homiletical structure." For example, it reaches full and true formation in the Christian-walk, discerning application, and passionate teaching.[17] The life-on-life nature of church-based training reveals the presence or absence of faithful interpretation; that is, if the trainee truly excels in understanding *and* application.

Exercise: The Body Properly Functioning[18]

Each local church, as an outpost of Christ's kingdom, has the honor and responsibility of seeing the Spirit's work bear kingdom fruit in its midst. The new humanity made visible in the local church stewards trainee formation, in part, as its primary context. J. Gary Millar accurately claims, "The church is the context in which (and a means by which) God transforms us."[19] By examining images used for the church in the NT, the ecclesial context for training becomes clear.

---

16 Craig Bartholomew, *Introducing Biblical Hermeneutics: A Comprehensive Framework for Hearing God in Scripture* (Grand Rapids: Baker Academic, 2015), 9, uses the phrase "ecclesial reception."

17 Newton, *40 Questions*, 161.

18 This section has been adapted from Moore, "New Testament Norms for the Great Commission," 80–128.

19 J. Gary Millar, *Changed into His Likeness: A Biblical Theology of Personal Transformation*, NSBT, ed. D. A. Carson (Downers Grove: IVP Academic, 2021), 240.

Of particular importance, images serve a crucial role in the church's self-understanding. John Hammett suggests the "primary way" the NT communicates ecclesiological truth is through images and metaphors.[20] Similarly, Jonathan Leeman credits the images with "reflecting the church's manifold splendor" as they "work together" to describe the people chosen, purchased, and empowered by the persons of the triune God, respectively.[21] A well-informed understanding of church images esteems the ecclesial centrality of NT norms for training. Here I will focus on the most recognizable image of the church in the NT, the functioning body of Christ.[22]

Body imagery extraordinarily communicates the church's diverse interdependent life together and Christ's intentions for discipleship and leader training. According to Rudolf Schnackenburg, the image "forcefully suggests itself as the most mature result of New Testament thinking about the church."[23] In the body, "[Jesus] is now alive to give [the Church] his very life by his Spirit so that they might continue the mission of Jesus in the midst of the world."[24] Jesus' training method, once again, finds its continuation in the context of a healthy, functioning local church.

---

20 John Hammett, *Biblical Foundations for Baptist Churches* (Grand Rapids: Kregel, 2009), 31.

21 Jonathan Leeman, *The Church and the Surprising Offense of God's Love: Reintroducing the Doctrines of Church Membership and Discipline* (Wheaton: Crossway, 2010), Kindle edition, ch. 5, "The Covenant of Love."

22 Claude Welch, *The Reality of the Church* (New York: Charles Scribner's Sons, 1958), 183; Craig Van Gelder, *The Essence of the Church: A Community Created by the Spirit* (Grand Rapids: Baker Books, 2000), 110–11; Kevin Giles, *What on Earth Is the Church? An Exploration in New Testament Theology* (Eugene, OR: Wipf & Stock, 1995), 11, 103; Alfred Kuen, *I Will Build My Church*, trans. Ruby Lindblad (Chicago: Moody Press, 1971), 93; Lee C. Camp, *Mere Discipleship: Radical Christianity in a Rebellious World* (Grand Rapids: Brazos Press, 2008), 114.

23 Rudolf Schnackenburg, *The Church in the New Testament* (London: Burns and Oats, 1974), 165.

24 Michael Goheen, *A Light to the Nations: The Missional Church and the Biblical Story* (Grand Rapids: Baker, 2011), 173.

In light of Paul's usage, the image's metaphoric nature prominently speaks to the functional ideal of local churches. Romans 12:4–5 offers a single functioning human body to speak metaphorically to the variety of functions within the local church. Paul writes, "The members do not all have the same function," then expounds on the diversity of functions (vv. 6–21). Two practical keys stand out. *First, church members differ from one another on purpose.* God graciously gifts differences in the church like the parts of a body. The church is designed this way. *Second, church members are connected to one another, making them interdependent.* Robert Yarbrough observes, "They form a coherent social organism" in a way that "optimizes body flourishing."[25] Although Paul does not explicitly mention growth, no member is superfluous but "contribute[s] to the growth of all."[26] This way, designed interdependence advances discipleship and training.

Paul's letter to the Colossians contains four uses of body-church imagery (1:18, 24; 2:19; 3:15). To say Christ is "the head of the body, the church" (1:18) is to uniquely connect Him to the church in a way that He is not connected to "all things" (1:16). In 1:24 Paul explains his own motivation for "filling up what is lacking" as being "for the sake of his [Christ's] body, that is, the church." The genitive of the Greek "his" points to a straightforward statement of Christ's possession of the church; it belongs to Him.[27]

The physiological detail of Colossians 2:19 develops the imagery further, in relation to "the head," who nourishes and knits the body together. In Christ, different members unite around this

---

25 Robert W. Yarbrough, "Romans," in *Expository Commentary, Vol. X Romans–Galatians*, eds. Iain M. Duguid, James M. Hamilton, Jr., and Jay Skylar (Wheaton: Crossway, 2020), 177.

26 Anders Nygren, *Commentary on Romans*, trans. Carl C. Rasmussen, 2nd printing (Philadelphia: Muhlenberg Press, 1949), 423.

27 Gosnell L. O. R. Yorke, *The Church as the Body of Christ in the Pauline Corpus: A Re-examination* (Lanham, MD: University Press of America, 1991), 88.

nourishment, maintaining structural connection through "joints" and "ligaments" for its own functional benefit.[28] In 3:15, the head is not mentioned, but only the peace He provides, which ought to "rule" in hearts corporately, because the church was "called in one body." The need for peaceful harmony assumes the presence of different and complementary members within an integrated whole.[29] Colossians adds two additional practical keys. *Third, the church body is clearly identified as the body of Christ*, a direct connection not present in Romans 12. *Fourth, the complexity of the metaphor advances with Christ designated as the head, who is the source of the body-church's growth.*[30]

Church members come together for the expressed purpose of growth, both numerically and characteristically. Their interconnectedness and interdependence are strategic when considered along with the "joints" and "ligaments" crucial to body function. Church relationships, both with Christ and with one another, cannot be construed as "mere nominal attachment" but meaningful for development.[31] The presentation of fully transformed members (Col 1:29) requires constant functional engagement in and through local churches.

Ephesians 2:14–16 is a good instance where the body imagery of metaphor is described in terms of the cross's effects. Paul declares the reconciliation of Jews and Gentiles to be "in one body." Frank

---

28 James D. G. Dunn, *The Epistles to the Colossians and to Philemon: A Commentary on the Greek Text*, NIGTC (Grand Rapids: Eerdmans, 1996), 186, explains these are "medical technical terms" describing the interconnectedness of the church.

29 Dunn, *The Epistles to the Colossians and to Philemon*, 235.

30 Richard R. Melick, *Philippians, Colossians, Philemon*, NAC 32 (Nashville: Broadman and Holman, 1991), 273; Frank Thielman, *Ephesians*, BECNT (Grand Rapids: Baker Academic, 2010), 113.

31 Mark G. Johnston, *Let's Study Colossians and Philemon* (East Peoria, IL: Versa Press, 2013), 73.

Thielman shows that "Paul refers not to the crucified body of Christ but … a body of people unified with each other across ethnic lines and at peace with God."[32] Subsequently, Ephesians 3:6 credits this mystery of unity in the same bodily terms. Ephesians 4 builds on the gifts given to the church for the members' growth (vv. 11–14) by aiming the growth at Christ, "who is the head" (v. 15). We must note from this that "all" individuals equipped for ministry then carry out that ministry in and through the church, and the "whole body" grows corporately when each part functions properly (v. 16). In the body, Christ's stature advances in each individual and the whole church.

Ephesians 5:22–33 pictures the gospel through the institution of marriage. The husband parallels Christ as the head with the wife and the church submitted to their authoritative positions, respectively. Here, too, the mutually maturing interactions of the body-church rely on Christ's provisions, which include "everything necessary for its nourishment and support."[33] Ephesians supplies one more interpretive key. *Fifth, members of the body bear the responsibility of ministering to one another, which results in individual and corporate growth.*

In summary, these passages offer five interpretive keys to body imagery, which are also all present in the body imagery of 1 Corinthians, which is the most explicit, functional explanation of the image (see 10:16–17; 11:17–34; 12:12–26): 1) The body-church is made up of different members on purpose; 2) The body-church's members depend on one another; 3) The body-church belongs to Christ; 4) The body-church grows through nourishment supplied by Christ; and 5) The body-church stewards its members on the way to maturity in Christ.

---

32   Thielman, *Ephesians*, 172.

33   Thielman, *Ephesians*, 388.

God provided what the body needed for the upbuilding of the church (1 Cor 14:5, 12, 26) in love (1 Cor 13:1–13). In fact, the test of loving, local church edification governed and authenticated all the "manifestations of the Spirit" (1 Cor 14:7, 12).[34] Paul's long explanation of body imagery, spanning three chapters and corroborating and expounding in practice his usage in Romans, Colossians, and Ephesians, heralds the controlling "intention of the Spirit" to build up the church.[35] This supreme goal upholds the growth and maturity of the whole body (1 Cor 12:7) as well as the individual members that make it up (1 Cor 12:25–27).

The body-church provides the regular, essential atmosphere wherein a trainee's preparation intensifies. Congruent with the image, I suggest a few body parts for trainee's focused preparation. Each applies to the individual and to the whole church body. First, the *heart* must develop after the likeness of Christ's shepherding heart. Pastorally, the heart that loves will be the heart that cares deeply and diligently for the sheep. Second, the *voice* needs training for leadership through the proclaimed Word of God. The habits of teaching and preaching "prep" paired with the benefit of kerygmatic "reps" allow the trainee room to hone the craft of biblical exposition. Third, the *knees* ought to be toughened by supporting the discipline of prayer.

Conclusion

Phil Newton is a pioneer. I have benefitted in various ways from his counsel, preaching, conversations, books, articles, and the example he set for younger pastors like me. Apart from his influence, I might have never come to love the local church and my calling to

---

34   Paul Minear, *Images of the Church in the New Testament* (Philadelphia: Westminster, 1960), 252.

35   Minear, *Images of the Church*, 252–53.

shepherd it as I do today. The training I received under his ministry and as a member of the church he pastored prepared me well. His taught me faithful interpretive practices and modeling before my eyes what the life of the body of Christ should be. It was in the local church that I saw my greatest advancements as a young man called to lead God's people. Though many entities and strategies complement training, they will never exceed the ability of a healthy local church to train leaders.

Chapter nine

Pastoring by the Book: The Centrality of Scripture in Gathered Worship

Chris Spano

Introduction: We Must Pastor by the Book

It was Christmas Eve. I had never been so eager to attend the evening's worship service at a local church because my grandparents had agreed to attend. For years I had shared the gospel with them and prayed for God to save them. To my knowledge, my grandparents had not attended a church worship service during my lifetime. So, I wondered what God might do when they heard the gospel message preached from God's Word by God's servant, the pastor. Instead, the pastor ascended to the pulpit and read a heart-tugging Christmas story from a magazine, which contained as much gospel as a figgy pudding. Both for good and for ill, I burned with anger. Then, when we got back to the house, my grandma smiled and said something like, "That was wonderful! If church was always like that, I would be happy to go!" My heart was broken.

Now that I serve as a pastor myself, I sometimes still think of that evening as I plan and lead gathered worship services. In such services, what is our primary duty as pastors? What is our primary duty as men of God called to shepherd the sheep of Jesus Christ, our Chief Shepherd (see 1 Pet 2:25; 5:4)? Are we to lead gathered worship and, if necessary, to use the Bible? Not at all. In gathered worship, we must pastor by the Book. From beginning to end, both in substance and in structure, Scripture must be central.

In this chapter, I will start by showing that we must pastor by the Book because Jesus Christ pastored by the Book. Then, I will apply the principles learned from Christ's ministry to local church ministry—specifically, to the ministry of God's Word in key aspects of gathered worship. Finally, I will conclude with a word of exhortation.

The Centrality of Scripture in the Pastoral Ministry of Jesus Christ

Jesus' public ministry began in some surprising ways. For example, right after Jesus gathered his first disciples, He entered the city of Capernaum and taught in the synagogue. Yet even before Jesus left the synagogue, desperately needy people began to interrupt his teaching. "All who were sick or oppressed by demons" came to Him (Mark 1:32).[1] Then into the night, Jesus cast out demons and healed sick people. When dawn arrived, more needy people came seeking help, but Jesus was nowhere to be found. While it was still dark, He had departed to a desolate place to pray. Eventually, Jesus' disciples found Him and said to Him, "Everyone is looking for you" (Mark 1:37). Having witnessed the previous night's signs and wonders, they assumed Jesus would want to continue his ministry by doing such mighty works. Surprisingly, they were wrong. "[Jesus] said to them, 'Let us go on to the next towns, that I may preach there also, for that is why I came out'" (Mark 1:37). By design, Jesus' ministry

---

1 All citations of Scripture are from the English Standard Version (ESV).

was primarily a ministry of the Word, not a ministry of doing mighty works.

This pattern continued. After Jesus crossed the Sea of Galilee and stepped out of the boat, "He saw a great crowd, and he had compassion on them, because they were like sheep without a shepherd" (Mark 6:34). So, Jesus became a shepherd to these sheep. He went on to perform the mighty work of feeding this crowd of five-thousand men with five loaves and two fish but only *after* "he began to teach them many things" (Mark 6:34–35).

Jesus' pattern raises the question: Why did the Chief Shepherd prioritize Word ministry over all other aspects of ministry? Jesus Himself answers this question in John 10. He prioritized Word ministry because Word ministry is how He gathers his sheep and grows his flock—numerically and spiritually. "The sheep hear his voice, and he calls his sheep by name and leads them out ... and the sheep follow him, for they know his voice" (John 10:3–4; see also vv. 14–16).

At the conclusion of his earthly ministry, Jesus clarifies that even though He is no longer physically present to lead his sheep, He still speaks to his people through his under shepherds. This is why Jesus thrice commanded the apostle Peter, "Feed my lambs ... tend my sheep ... feed my sheep" (John 21:15–17). And this is why ordinary, faithful pastors have inherited Christ's calling to go and do likewise (see 1 Pet 5:2). As we oversee the right ministry of God's Word in gathered worship, Christ speaks to his people "the things concerning himself" from the Old Testament (Luke 24:27). In the New Testament, Christ obviously speaks about Himself to his people in the Gospels, through the ministry of the Holy Spirit, and through the apostolic ministry to local churches (see John 16:13–15; 2 Pet 3:15–16).

What, then, is the problem with Word-*less*—or at least Word-*light*—worship services? Such services silence Jesus. They replace the milk and honey of the Word of Christ with the soda and pork rinds of merely human opinions. God's people are not rightly led in such services. At best, those who have already been called to Christ are left spiritually underfed. At worst, those who have not yet been called to Christ are left spiritually dead. That's why we must pastor by the Book—especially when the whole church gathers in the spiritual presence of Christ to hear from pastors the Word of Christ (see Matt 18:20; 28:20).

The Centrality of Scripture in Gathered Worship

What, exactly, does it mean to maintain the centrality of Scripture in gathered worship? Mark Ashton and C.J. Davis correctly note, "Being biblical [in gathered worship] is not just a matter of including Bible readings and extracts … but of faithfully reflecting the Bible's own teaching, which interprets and draws them together."[2] This means every part of the worship service should be considered an aspect of Word ministry. Furthermore, every aspect of Word ministry should promote God's glory in salvation through judgment, accomplished by Jesus Christ, then applied by the Holy Spirit.[3]

I. The Public Reading of Scripture

Last year, I attended a funeral led by a Roman Catholic priest. Although the liturgy was replete with false teaching, it was also full of Scripture readings. This is in sharp contrast to many protestant, evangelical churches I have visited over the years. Perhaps often, the

---

2   Mark Ashton and C. J. Davis, "Following in Cranmer's Footsteps," in *Worship by the Book*, ed. D. A. Carson (Grand Rapids: Zondervan, 2002), 70–71.

3   See James M. Hamilton Jr., *God's Glory in Salvation through Judgment: A Biblical Theology* (Wheaton: Crossway, 2010).

only Scripture read during the service was the sermon text. It should not be so, and it has not always been so.

According to Hughes Oliphant Old, "The [public] reading of the Law in Nehemiah 8 can safely be regarded as the oldest description we have of the liturgy of the word."[4] It was an historically crucial moment. Nearly one hundred years before, God's people began returning to the Promised Land from Exile. The Jerusalem temple had been rebuilt. The city wall had been rebuilt. Now, the time was ripe to reform the nation's worship. And this reform began with the public reading of Scripture to God's people.

> All the people gathered as one man into the square before the Water Gate. And they told Ezra the scribe to bring the Book of the Law of Moses that the LORD had commanded Israel. So Ezra the priest brought the Law before the assembly, both men and women and all who could understand what they heard, on the first day of the seventh month. And he read from it facing the square before the Water Gate from early morning until midday, in the presence of the men and the women and those who could understand. And the ears of all the people were attentive to the Book of the Law (Neh 8:1–4).

Most likely, this reform movement set the stage for centuries of liturgical practice in Jewish synagogues, and thus also, in early Christian churches.[5] By the time of Christ's first advent, most Jewish synagogues had developed the habit of publicly reading through the Torah in a regular cycle. Synagogues also added regular public readings from the Prophets (see Luke 4:16ff). Similar habits made their way into early churches. Presumably, this is why Paul commands Timothy, a younger pastor, "Devote yourself to the public

---

4   Hughes Oliphant Old, *The Reading and Preaching of the Scriptures in the Worship of the Christian Church, Volume 1* (Grand Rapids: Eerdmans, 1998), 96.

5   See Old, *The Reading and Preaching*, 99ff.

reading of Scripture" (1 Tim 4:13). According to Justin Martyr, the second-century church father,

> "on the day which is called Sun's Day [i.e., Sunday] there is an assembly of all
> who live in the towns or the country; and the memoirs of the Apostles [i.e.,
> the New Testament] or the writings of the prophets [i.e., the Old Testament]
> are read, as much as time permits."[6]

Many Reformation-era churches maintained these traditions by publicly reading from multiple parts of Scripture during gathered worship.[7]

Certainly, Scripture itself does not specify how much Scripture should be read and for how long it should be read in gathered worship. So, I do not intend to bind the conscience where the Bible does not. Yet, where is the wisdom in jettisoning the traditions of our forefathers in the faith by whittling away at the public reading of Scripture? To this end, I offer the following suggestions. First, if the Bible commands pastors to devote themselves to the public reading of Scripture, then seasoned pastors should train novice pastors how to do this well. When I served as an intern with Phil Newton, he led me one afternoon into the empty sanctuary. He put me behind the pulpit and told me to start reading the Bible aloud. Then, for the next hour or so, he offered criticism, correction, and encouragement. That afternoon has paid dividends for years to come. Second, consider simple ways in which to add Scripture readings to the service. As a suggestion, begin and end the service with a call to worship and a

---

6   Quoted in Henry Bettenson, ed., *The Early Christian Fathers: A Selection of Writings of the Fathers from St Clement of Rome to St Athanasius*, trans. H. Bettenson (Oxford: Oxford University Press, 1956), 62–63.

7   See Jonathan Gibson and Mark Earngey, eds. *Reformation Worship: Liturgies from the Past for the Present* (Greensboro: New Growth Press, 2018).

benediction that come from the Bible. Or, perhaps read a text from the opposite testament from the sermon text. Maybe even consider reading through books of the Bible on a consistent cycle. Third, I would encourage you to make sure the preacher is the person who reads the sermon text. After all, in addition to commanding Timothy, "Devote yourself to the public reading of Scripture," Paul immediately adds, "To exhortation, to teaching" (1 Tim 4:13). This is because, "In the end, the point of the sermon was to make clear the reading of the Scriptures."[8]

II. The Preaching of Scripture

I once watched the recording of a sermon delivered by one of the most popular preachers in America. While he spoke, he walked around the stage without a Bible. Well into the sermon, he introduced half a verse from Romans, which was projected on a screen. Yet, before doing so, he apologized to his hearers for complicating his message. How very different from the biblical precedent!

When Ezra and his fellow priests gathered the people of God, "They read from the book, from the Law of God" (Neh 8:8). Nehemiah then specifies that they read "clearly"—or, as the ESV footnote puts it, "with interpretation"—so that the people understood the reading.[9] Once again, this set the stage for centuries of liturgical practice in Jewish synagogues, and thus also, in early Christian churches. In synagogues, "The sermon was supposed to be a learned interpretation and application of the text. It was supposed to teach, admonish, inspire, and comfort the congregation."[10] Even a cursory reading of Acts confirms that Paul preached like this in Jewish

---

8   Old, *The Reading and Preaching*, 99.

9   J. Gordon McConville, "Nehemiah," in *ESV Study Bible* (Wheaton: Crossway, 2008), 837.

10   Old, *The Reading and Preaching*, 103.

synagogues. The same can be said for the Book of Hebrews, which is the closest thing to an early church sermon that is available to us (see Heb 13:22). And once again, the post-apostolic church maintained this tradition of preaching. According to Justin Martyr, "When the reader has finished the president gives a discourse, admonishing us and exhorting us to imitate these excellent examples."[11] During the patristic period, there was a strong tradition of preaching consecutively through books of the Bible. Consider for example, the sermons of John Chrysostom and Augustine of Hippo. Under the influence of Roman Catholicism, this tradition faded in medieval churches. But it did not disappear. It became the pattern for teaching in medieval universities. Another example is the commentaries of men like Thomas Aquinas and Martin Luther which are essentially their published lecture notes. During the Protestant Reformation, the consecutive exposition of biblical books was returned to the churches by men like Ulrich Zwingli and John Calvin. Famously, when Calvin resumed his ministry in Geneva after several years in exile, he resumed by preaching the very next text from where he had left off previously.

Numerous methods for preaching faithful sermons from the Bible, such as consecutive exposition, doctrinal exposition, topical exposition, can all be employed. Whichever method is chosen, we must strive to stay in line with the Scripture. Preachers must strive to say no more and no less than the Bible itself says: the truth, the whole truth, and nothing but the truth, so help us God.[12] If you persist in doing this, and if you persist in godliness, then "by so doing

---

11   Quoted in Bettenson, *The Early Christian Fathers*, 62–63.
12   I learned this idea of "staying on the line" from The Charles Simeon Trust, which runs Workshops on biblical exposition (see https://simeontrust.org/courses/first-principles/).

you will save both yourself and your hearers" (1 Tim 4:16). For this reason, Herman Melville was right to declare:

> The pulpit is ever the world's foremost part; all the rest comes in its rear; the pulpit leads the world. From [the pulpit] ... the storm of God's quick wrath is first [perceived] ... . From [the pulpit] ... the God of breezes fair or foul is first invoked for favorable winds. Yes, the world's a ship on its passage out, and not yet a voyage complete; and the pulpit is its prow.[13]

Even though the reading and preaching of God's Word is the foremost part of the ship, it's not the only part of the ship. The ministry of the Word also extends to other parts of the ship (as it were).

III. The Singing of Scripture

Before I became a pastor, I attended a conference at which a well-known Baptist pastor argued that singing during gathered worship is a ministry of the Word. Thus, pastors should oversee the selection of songs to be sung in gathered worship. During the subsequent time for questions, I asked, "What if I am not familiar with the tradition of Christian hymnody?" He responded, "You should find a new vocation." I countered, "What if I do not want to find a new vocation?" He said, "Buy a bunch of hymnals and start reading them." At the time, I did not buy it. Then, I became a pastor. By a series of unfortunate events, I not only became the person who selects music, but I also became the person who leads the congregational singing during gathered worship. Now, I agree with that man; singing is a ministry of the Word, which pastors should oversee in some way.

---

13   Herman Melville, *Moby Dick* (New York: Barnes and Noble, 1993), 33.

In the Old Testament, God's people gathered to sing new songs in response to each new act of salvation and judgment (see Ex 15:1–21; Judg 5:1–31). The Psalms, many of which were used for congregational singing, remembered God's past acts and looked forward to God's future acts. In the New Testament, examples of singing are sparser, but certainly not absent. The night before He died, Jesus and his disciples sang together—probably a traditional, biblical Psalm sung by Jews during Passover (see Matt 26:30). Paul and Silas sang hymns to God while in prison (see Acts 16:25). And the Corinthian Christians included singing of some kind in gathered worship (see 1 Cor 14:26). Furthermore, scholars reasonably speculate that the apostles allude in their letters to a number of new hymns, which remember the work Christ already accomplished during his first coming and look forward to the work Christ will accomplish at his second coming (see 1 Tim 3:16).[14] Indeed, Paul commands Christians, "Let the word of Christ dwell in you richly, teaching and admonishing one another in all wisdom, singing psalms and hymns and spiritual songs, with thankfulness in your hearts to God" (Col 3:16; cf. Eph 5:19–20).

Since Christians are supposed to minister the Word to one another through singing, it might seem obvious that this should happen when we gather to worship God. Surprisingly, congregational singing was not a common part of early, post-apostolic worship services. It only became common in the fourth century.[15] Most often, congregations sang biblical Psalms. Eventually, they also added in extra-biblical hymns. At the outset of the Protestant Reformation, Luther was especially enthusiastic about singing in church. To that

---

14 Peter T. O'Brien, *The Epistle to the Philippians,* NIGTC (Grand Rapids: Eerdmans, 1991), 188–193.

15 Nick Needham, *2000 Years of Christ's Power: Volume 1, The Age of the Early Church Fathers* (Geanies House: Christian Focus Publications, 2016), 73–74.

end he wrote many hymns, including "A Mighty Fortress." At first, the reformed tradition stuck to biblical Psalms. But eventually, most branches of Reformed Protestantism eventually included extra-biblical hymns as well. Thus, in our own day, it is hard to imagine a Christian worship service without congregational singing.

This raises the question: how might we sing well in gathered worship? I offer the following suggestions for consideration: Since singing is a ministry of the Word, then the words should be biblically true, good, and beautiful. If we would not settle for unsound or unclear doctrine in preaching, then why would we settle for unsound or unclear doctrine when singing? Also, everyone must be able to hear the words. The use of any instrumentation—from organs to drums—should enhance human voices rather than drowning out human voices. Otherwise, there is a risk that church music will devolve into indistinct sounds (cf. 1 Cor 14:7–9). Finally, in addition to singing music from every age in church history, we should sing at least some songs from the Bible itself—especially the Psalms. Scholars certainly debate what, exactly, Paul means by "psalms, hymns, and spiritual songs" (Col 3:16),[16] but it borders on incredulity that Paul could have possibly meant, "Sing psalms—except the ones already in Scripture." Local churches do well to cultivate the whole Scripture's centrality in song.

IV. Prayer According to Scripture

Pastors are not apostles; these distinct offices come with some distinct duties (see Eph 4:11). Yet, pastors share some duties in common with the apostles. Namely, the calling to "devote ourselves to prayer and to the ministry of the word" (Acts 6:4). Prayer and

---

16 Peter T. O'Brien, *Colossians-Philemon*, WBC 44 (Grand Rapids: Zondervan, 2000), 209–10.

the ministry of the Word are inseparable from one another in the lives of faithful pastors. They prayerfully prepare in the privacy of study and preach the Word from the pulpit in the public worship gathering. A strong advocate of this two-fold pastoral task, John Owen argues, "To preach the word, and not to follow it with prayer constantly and frequently, is to believe [the Word's] use, neglect [the Word's] end, and cast away all the seed of the gospel at random."[17] Pastors must pray that God will plant his Word in the hearts of our hearers so that it will produce the fruit of faith, repentance, and obedience (see Mark 4:20). After all, this is how Jesus pastored his sheep—especially when praying publicly (see Matt 11:25–27; John 11:41–42; 12:22–29; 17:1–26).

Attentive readers will also notice that the public prayers of pastors in Scripture are heavily dependent on previous Scripture. In other words, pastors in the Bible publicly prayed according to Scripture. Consider the Old Testament prayers of Nehemiah, Solomon, and the Psalmists (1 Kgs 8:12–53; Neh 9:1–38; Ps 111:1–10). By the time of Christ's first coming, Jews had developed the habit of praying according to the Psalms.[18] Most likely, when Acts says that the early Christians "devoted themselves to … the prayers" (Acts 2:42), indicates that they continued this tradition. F.F. Bruce argues that even though "the community's prayers would follow Jewish models … their content would be enriched because of the Christ event."[19] Take, for example, Paul's public prayers as recorded in his letters. They are full of biblical allusions, which find their fulfillment in the person and work of Jesus Christ (see Eph 1:15–23; Col 1:9–12).

---

17 Cited in Charles Bridges, *The Christian Ministry: With an Inquiry into the Causes of its Inefficacy* (Carlisle: The Banner of Truth Trust, 2018), 218.

18 See Jeremy Penner, "Patterns of Prayer in Second Temple Period Judaism" (Ph.D. diss., McMaster University, 2010).

19 F. F. Bruce, *The Book of the Acts: Revised*, NICNT 5 (Grand Rapids: Eerdmans, 1988), 73.

This became the norm throughout church history—especially in the Protestant tradition.[20]

Unfortunately, in the same way that I have attended far too many worship services with far too little public Scripture reading, I have attended far too many worship services with far too little public prayer. Clearly, early Christians prayed together during gathered worship (see 1 Cor 11:1–5; 1 Tim 2:1–3, 8). In the post apostolic church—especially in the West—pastoral leaders oversaw and summed up these prayers with public prayers of their own.[21] Why have so many churches neglected these prudent traditions? It is certainly not because we are spiritually stronger than they were. And so, we need not to pray as much as they did. Robert Murray M'Cheyne once said, "What a man is alone and on his knees before God, that he is, and no more."[22] We might modify this. When we gather to worship God, Jesus Christ is among us (see Matt 18:20). So, would it not be correct to say, what a church is together in prayer before God, that we are, and no more?

Conclusion

Further consideration of other vital aspects of gathered worship, like confessing creeds and partaking of the sacraments, undoubtedly leads to additional support for the centrality of Scripture in gathered worship. Confessing creeds is an aspect of Word ministry. As Marcus Peter Johnson puts it, "When the gospel is properly preached, the sacraments make clear to us visibly what has been

---

20 For excellent examples, consider Arthur Bennett, ed., *The Valley of Vision: A Collection of Puritan Prayers and Devotions* (Carlisle: The Banner of Truth Trust, 1975), or, Jonathan Gibson, *Be Thou My Vision: A Liturgy for Daily Worship* (Wheaton: Crossway, 2021).

21 See Needham, *2000 Years of Christ's Power*, 76.

22 Quoted in D. A. Carson, *Praying with Paul: A Call to Spiritual Reformation*, 2d ed. (Grand Rapids: Baker, 2014), xiii.

offered to us audibly ... the sacraments 'exegete' the preached Word just as the Word 'exegetes' the sacraments—and Christ is offered and received in both."[23] If done rightly, both the confession of creeds and partaking of the sacraments also promote God's glory in salvation through judgment, accomplished by Jesus Christ, then applied by the Holy Spirit.

This brings me back to the story about my grandma. Many pastors would be tempted to consider her positive response to the worship service as confirmation that they had done their job. The truth is, brothers, faithfulness must not be gauged by the response of unbelievers who want their itching ears scratched by pseudo-shepherds (see 2 Tim 4:3). Faithfulness must be gauged by whether or not we have imitated Christ's example of pastoring by the Book. Jesus Christ must be given the first and last word in every aspect of gathered worship. His true sheep must scatter back into the world convinced that God's Word, not our words, is still at work throughout the week (see 1 Thess 2:13). And by God's grace, we can enjoy a bit of rest and relaxation before getting back to our own work on Monday morning. To tweak a well-known quote from Martin Luther, the pastor who has done his job in gathered worship can say with confidence, "I simply [read], preached, and [prayed] God's Word; otherwise, I did nothing. And while I slept or drank ... beer with my friends ... the Word did everything."[24]

---

23 Cited in Michael Reeves and Tim Chester, *Why the Reformation Still Matters* (Wheaton: Crossway, 2016), 158.

24 Cited in Timothy F. Lull, ed., *Martin Luther's Basic Theological Writings*, 2d ed. (Minneapolis: Fortress Press, 2005), 287.

THE PREACHER

8

Chapter ten

Pastoral Preaching

Rich Shadden

Introduction

Several years ago, my wife and I sat under the preaching of Phil Newton for the first time. We were immediately refreshed. Phil aimed to faithfully explain the text and apply it in a manner geared toward edifying the congregation entrusted to his care. That may sound simple enough, but this approach to preaching is not always common in local churches. I eventually learned that Phil referred to his preaching as pastoral preaching.

With the explosion of conferences in the last few decades, pastors often attend conferences with great anticipation to learn more about the topic or theme. While conferences are helpful, one of the unintended consequences is that pastors often return to their congregations and attempt to imitate the preaching just witnessed. The result is more topical sermons or talks. Less emphasis is placed on faithfully working through a book of the Bible.

What I recognized from Phil's approach to preaching in contrast to conference preaching was his sense of an overwhelming responsibility to shepherd the flock; those entrusted to his care through faithful exposition. And he possessed an eye toward shaping a people in the image of Christ. In this chapter I will establish the aim of preaching as a pastor in the context of a local church. I will do so by first answering the question, what is biblical preaching? Second, how does expository preaching ensure we preach biblically faithful sermons? Third, I will define pastoral preaching.

What Is Biblical Preaching?

I preached my first sermon in college. I had no idea what I was doing. I cannot even remember what I preached. I am certain my sermon was lacking in more ways than I would like to admit. Thankfully, prior to my first sermon I listened to faithful preaching for many years in my own local church. However, I had no formal instruction on how to preach. Thus, I did the only thing I knew to do. Pick a passage of Scripture, try to understand its meaning then do the best I could to faithfully proclaim the truth of that text. In its most basic sense, that is the essence of biblical preaching.

In 2 Timothy 4:2, Paul tells Timothy to "preach the word." The word preach is the Greek word *kerusso*. It means to herald or to proclaim. It seems reasonable to think that when Paul wrote these words to Timothy, Paul had the whole counsel of God's Word in mind. Luke records for us Paul's words to the Ephesian elders in Acts 20:26–27. "Therefore, I testify to you this day that I am innocent of the blood of all of you, for I did not shrink from declaring to you the whole counsel of God."

What then is biblical preaching? It is faithfully heralding the whole counsel of God's Word. The goal is not entertainment. It is not proclaiming allegiance to or thankfulness for a city or a country. It is not proclaiming the moral decline of a society. It is not even preaching six steps to a better life. Biblical preaching aims to accurately proclaim the whole counsel of God's Word. This raises an important question. How is this accomplished? It is accomplished via expository preaching.

What Is Expository Preaching?

In his book entitled *The Pastor as Leader: Principles and Practices for Connecting Preaching and Leadership*, John Currie writes regarding preaching, "Preaching is the King's speech! It is through the preaching of his word that Christ the King Himself leads his church into his purposes and mission."[2] I believe this to be true. There is no greater influence in shaping the life of a church than the pulpit. The danger of this reality, however, is that the pulpit can positively or negatively shape a congregation. This truth emphasizes the need for a certain kind of preaching that conforms the church to the image of Christ. What kind of preaching should this be?

Faithful biblical preaching aims to accurately proclaim the whole counsel of God. How is this best accomplished? The answer is through expository preaching. What is expository preaching? Several definitions exist that define expository preaching. Perhaps the most concise and helpful definition is given to us by Mark Dever. "Expositional preaching is preaching in which the main point of the biblical text being considered becomes the main point of the sermon being preached."[3] Let's think about the words expository and preaching.

We have already explored the meaning of the word preach. Preaching means to herald or proclaim. The word exposit means to expound. Thus, *expository* preaching seeks to herald the truth as it is carefully explained from the text of Scripture. Paul gives a clear explanation of expository preaching to his young mentee Timothy in 1 Timothy 4:13, "Until I come, devote yourself to the public reading of Scripture, to exhortation, to teaching."

---

2   John Currie, *The Pastor as Leader: Principles and Practices for Connecting Preaching and Leadership* (Wheaton: Crossway), 129.

3   Mark Dever, *Preach: Theology Meets Practice* (Nashville: B&H Publishing), 2012.

Considering Paul's instruction to Timothy, a faithful expository preacher should read the chosen text, teach the text by explaining its content, and exhort the people of God to live in obedience to the text. With this basic understanding of expository preaching, let's consider the nature of expository preaching.[4]

First, expository preaching is *Text Driven*.

What would happen if you only ate foods that interested you? Or you only ate foods that you craved, but were not necessarily the best for you? Over time your body would become malnourished. If you consistently ate donuts for breakfast, pizza for lunch, and microwavable meals for dinner, you would eventually notice a decline in your health. We know that what you put into your body plays a significant role in how you feel. Thus, it is important to try to eat healthy meals that give us the energy we need to function well. The same is true of preaching. If sermons are driven by topics or ideas rather than the Word of God, then congregations will grow anemic. Therefore, it is essential that the text of Scripture drives preaching.

The expository preacher aims to proclaim the Word of God from any given text. Those who preach expositional sermons hold the conviction that God has spoken, and that His spoken Word is recorded for us in the sixty-six books of the Bible. Thus, the preacher should stay with the text as he preaches, regularly having the congregation look back to the text as he explains it and applies it.

Second, expository preaching is *Canonical*.

Expository preaching generally focuses on a specific text. However, it maintains a conscious awareness of a text's place in the larger story of the Bible. It never loses site of the forest even

---

4   It is important for me to note here that my understanding of expository preaching comes from a collective voice of preachers. While I have tried to work out in my own words the following marks of expository preaching, men like Phil Newton, John Piper, and Mark Dever have greatly influenced my thinking on this subject.

though it may focus on a tree. To preach faithfully, it is essential to study a passage within its immediate context. However, knowing for example how Romans 3:23–25, which speaks of the propitious work of Christ, connects to the Old Testament sacrificial system is critical to faithfully preaching that text.

Although it is essential to understand a text of Scripture's place in the Canon, this does not mean the story of the Bible must be rehearsed in each sermon. But it is necessary to understand how an isolated text of Scripture connects to the entire narrative of redemption. The most helpful structure I have found for putting the Bible together as one story is to study the covenants. For example, the sacrificial system was installed during the Mosaic Covenant but fulfilled in Christ in the New Covenant. This covenant structure is essential for faithful expository preaching.[5]

Third, expository preaching is *Christ-centered*.[6]

As noted above, expository preaching presupposes that all Scripture leads us to the gospel of Jesus Christ. Charles Spurgeon is often quoted for his explanation of the need to preach Christ. Spurgeon declared:

> Preach Jesus Christ, brethren, always and everywhere; and every time you preach be sure to have much of Jesus Christ in the sermon. You remember the story of the old minister who heard a sermon by a young man, and when he was asked by the preacher what he thought of it he was rather slow to answer, but at last he said, 'If I must tell you, I did not like it at all; there was no Christ in your sermon.' 'No,' answered the young man, 'because I did not see that

---

5   Peter J. Gentry, and Steven J. Wellum, *Kingdom Through Covenant* (Wheaton: Crossway, 2012). This book is foundational for understanding how the covenants form the structure for the biblical storyline.

6   I am indebted to Phil Newton for helping me see how the entire Bible leads us to Christ. Multiple conversations with Phil, and his own example of Christ-centered preaching helped me see the glory of Christ in every text.

Christ was in the text.' 'Oh!' said the old minister, 'but do you not know that from every little town and village and tiny hamlet in England there is a road leading to London? Whenever I get hold of a text, I say to myself, 'There is a road from here to Jesus Christ, and I mean to keep on His track till I get to Him.' 'Well,' said the young man, 'but suppose you are preaching from a text that says nothing about Christ?' 'Then I will go over hedge and ditch but what I will get at Him.' So must we do, brethren; we must have Christ in all our discourses, whatever else is in or not in them. There ought to be enough of the gospel in every sermon to save a soul.[7]

This is essential instruction for the expository preacher. However, it is important to realize that some Scripture passages get us to Christ immediately, while other texts walk us to Christ slowly. Therefore, let the text determine how we get to Jesus.

For example, if you are preaching an Old Testament narrative, it may take more time to get to the gospel than if you are preaching a text in the Gospels that explicitly describes the crucifixion of Jesus. In either case, expository preaching lets the text speak for itself while understanding that every text points us to Jesus.

Fourth, expository preaching is *Compelling*.

Perhaps one of the chief misconceptions about expository preaching is that it is a running commentary on the text of Scripture. No doubt, a preacher can easily fall into the trap of simply explaining the meaning of a text and calling it expository preaching. However, we cannot separate the words expository and preaching. The truth that is explained is heralded as the Word of God. Thus, it is compelling in that expository preaching is bold and passionate preaching. Whether in the face of opposition or glad reception, the text is proclaimed as the Word of God. When the text is explained faithfully, the preacher

---

7   Charles H. Spurgeon, "Sermons Likely to Win Souls," in *The Soul Winner*. https://www. thesoulwinner. org/ebooks/The%20Soul%20Winner%20-%20Spurgeon.pdf

is communicating that this is what God is saying to humanity. It is not an academic exercise, but a proclamation of the truth as it is explained. The preacher is not merely a messenger, but a believer in the message.

Expository preaching is compelling in that it is compassionate. Just as Jesus came as the gentle and lowly One in heart, so too the preacher who is the under-shepherd of the Chief Shepherd wants to see God's sheep feed on the green pastures of His Word. The preacher approaches the Scripture text with the understanding that he too is a sheep.

Fifth, expository preaching is *Holy Spirit Dependent*

Paul is clear in his Epistle to the Romans that humanity suppresses the truth about God because of our unrighteousness (see Rom 1:18). This is the fallen condition of every human. Left in this state, we will perish apart from Jesus forever. Pastors must understand this reality. This creates a dependence on God that is essential to faithful expository preaching. Only God can change hearts. Further:

> In 1 Corinthians 2:1–5, Paul says, "And I, when I came to you, brothers, did not come proclaiming to you the testimony of God with lofty speech or wisdom. For I decided to know nothing among you except Jesus Christ and him crucified. And I was with you in weakness and in fear and much trembling, and my speech and my message were not in plausible words of wisdom, but in demonstration of the Spirit and of power, that your faith might not rest in the wisdom of men but in the power of God."

As we preach for both the conversion of unbelievers and the edification of believers, the expository preacher learns to rely on the power of the Holy Spirit to change hearts. No mere human can raise the dead. God must do this work!

How then do we approach
Expository Preaching?

Now that we understand the nature of expository preaching, how do we approach this task? The following steps are designed to give the preacher a plan to faithfully preach the Word of God. The goal is to outline a basic structure for preparing expository sermons.[8]

First, pray to God for help. Praying for God's help as you prepare is crucial to faithful preaching. Getting the meaning of a text right is essential but done without the help of the Holy Spirit will lead to pride and error.

Before you start the work of exegesis, pray over the text. Ask God for divine illumination, help interpretating the text, help with homiletical organization, and for the Word to transform both you and the congregation.

Second, prepare the text. After you have selected a book of the Bible, read it multiple times and organize it into natural divisions. The goal is to understand the author's purpose for writing the book, the main themes, and how to divide it into manageable preaching texts. Once done, then begin reading slowly the first selected section. For example, if you choose Romans, you might select verses one through seven as the opening text. Try to understand Paul's flow of thought.

Now that you understand the flow of thought, create an exegetical outline by organizing the selected text according to its natural logic. Do you see natural points of emphasis in the text? How does the text fit within or continue the flow of thought from the previous text, the larger context of the book, and the larger context of the whole canon of Scripture?

---

8   The following outline is not an exhaustive explanation of how to develop an expository sermon. It is designed to give the preacher the basic steps. Each point needs further study. There are numerous resources to help preachers learn expository preaching.

Third, interpret the text. Now that you understand the logical order of the text, you can interpret its meaning. Paul tells Timothy to "do your best to present yourself to God as one approved, a worker who has no need to be ashamed, rightly handling the word of truth" (2 Tim 2:15). To do this, you must practice exegesis instead of eisegesis. What's the difference between the two? Exegesis reads out of the text what the original author intended to convey. Eisegesis reads into the text what the reader wants it to convey.

If you understand the flow of thought, you can discern the main point, or points of the text. Are there subpoints that support the main point? Once you've done this work, use commentaries to sharpen and check your own understanding of the text.[9]

Fourth, construct the sermon. Once you understand the meaning of the text, putting your work together in an organized outline for communication is crucial. Begin by writing a homiletical outline. This is the basic structure of your sermon built around propositional statements that form the skeleton of your outline. Whether you choose to write a full manuscript or annotated outline, the goal is to write out how you want to communicate each point of your sermon.

+ Work on transitions from one point to the next.
+ Build in illustrations, stories, etc. that help communicate your points. Illustrations should support the point, not distract from the point.
+ Add quotes from helpful sources that support your points.
+ Develop both individual and corporate applications that help the congregation think through how to respond to the text.

---

9   Knowledge of the biblical languages proves extremely helpful during the interpretive process. However, for various reasons, not every pastor has studied the biblical languages. There are numerous resources available today to help preachers understand the meaning of words in their original language.

Fifth, pray over the sermon. Once the work is done, pray over the manuscript. Ask the Lord to use His Word to transform His people. You may think you have two fish and five loaves of bread. But God is pleased to take our feeble efforts to faithfully preach His Word to convert the lost and edify the saint! Ask God to bless His Word.

Having established what biblical preaching is, faithfully heralding the whole counsel of God through expository preaching, let's think more clearly about the distinct nature of pastoral preaching.

What Is Pastoral Preaching?

The foundation for pastoral preaching is laid. So, what is it? Pastoral preaching is faithfully proclaiming the whole counsel of God by preaching expositional sermons with a particular congregation in view. The distinction of pastoral preaching is that the pastor is the shepherd of the flock that God entrusted to his care. He will have to give an account to the Lord for these particular people (see Heb 13:17). A pastor may preach at conferences, retreats, etc., but his primary responsibility is to feed the flock that he knows. This reality shapes various aspects of his preaching.

What then are characteristics of pastoral preaching?

First, pastoral preaching is *faithful exposition*. Without restating all the points above, I think it is important to reiterate that the pastor should not bypass the process explained above. While you know the flock entrusted to your care, and you may be tempted to address issues from the pulpit, pastors cannot force the text to say what you want it to say. This might be a temptation because you know of issues that need addressing. However, we trust the Word to do the work as we faithfully preach the text the way it was intended to be preached.

Having said this, there are other avenues through which issues in the church can be addressed. Members' meetings give an opportunity to address issues. It might be appropriate to do a topical study outside of the weekly corporate worship service to address a theological issue or conflict of some sort. Further, sometimes natural opportunities do arise in the sermon to apply the text in very specific ways. But it should not be forced. Faithful exposition is the best way to ensure we are saying what God has said. So, whatever the text says, aim to preach it faithfully.

Second, pastoral preaching is *wise preaching*. For example, a pastor who is new to a congregation, especially a congregation that does not have a strong theological foundation, would be wise not to select Romans or Leviticus as a first book to preach through. A pastor should select a book of the Bible with an eye toward the congregation's readiness to receive it. Having said this, a pastor who aims to faithfully preach through any book of the Bible is taking on a noble, God-honoring task. I am not suggesting that if a pastor selects Leviticus as his first book that he is in sin or unfaithful. However, is that the best approach? Would it serve the church better to choose a book that lays a clear gospel foundation with fewer contentious theological issues, or one that doesn't require as much Old Testament historical background? I think so.

Choosing a book like Philippians or Colossians might be a good start. Or perhaps preaching through a gospel account having regular interaction with Jesus. There is not a blueprint for what book to choose, but a pastor should pray for wisdom in selecting a book and spend time getting to know the flock so that he can gauge where they are theologically.

I think it is also wise to establish a pattern of preaching through books of the Bible at the church's main worship gathering, rather than preaching through topical series. There are multiple factors that lead me to believe this. I will name two.

One, if a pastor preaches through books of the Bible, he will regularly cover various topics without a forced agenda. In God's providence the church will hear what God has for them each Sunday the way God intended His Word to be heard. Working sequentially through a book of the Bible unfolds God's Word the way He wrote it.

Two, this approach also prevents the pastor from chasing down every topic that arises. So often, we feel overwhelmed with all the cultural issues the church faces. However, if a pastor commits to preaching through books of the Bible, he will always know what text is coming next, and so will the congregation. This creates a church culture that puts the Word at the center of the church's life and not the issues of the day.

Third, pastoral preaching is *tone sensitive*. By tone sensitive, I mean two things. One, the tone of the text should inform the tone of the sermon. A sermon on sin from Romans 1 is going to feel and preach differently than a sermon on praise to God from Psalm 150. Furthermore, the type of literature each text is written in dictates much of the tone of the sermon.

Two, pastoral preaching implies that a pastor is preaching to the congregation he knows. In a similar way that I know my own children and how they respond to my tone, a pastor should be aware of how the congregation might hear him. I realize people hear things differently. I do not mean for a pastor to worry himself over how he thinks his sermon will be received. What I simply mean is, do you love the congregation to whom you are preaching? And if you do, then speak to them that way as you exhort them to obey the Word. Do not "domineer over those in your charge" as Peter says in 1 Peter 5:3. Rather, "teach, reprove, correct, and train" through the Word in love (see 2 Tim 3:16).

Fourth, pastoral preaching is *individually and corporately applied.* Pastoral preaching aims to get the meaning of the text correct but apply it to the members of the church. The Word is applied both to individuals and to the church. Regarding individuals, how does the text apply to single people in their twenties, or single people in their seventies? What about people who work in government, hospitals, businesses, etc.? Or, what about moms, dads, children, or grandparents? Obviously, a pastor should not refer to specific people in the congregation, but he should help individuals in certain seasons of life consider how they might respond to the Word of God.

Regarding corporate application, how does the text encourage us to relate to one another as the body of Christ? How might it encourage us to serve one another? Are there applications that would help us appropriately live out the gospel with a corporate witness? The list is endless, but the point is that pastoral preaching helps the congregation think through how the Word might apply to their lives.

Pastor, you have been called by God to preach the Word. You must work hard to do this faithfully. What a privilege it is to mine the treasures of God's Word and proclaim the truth to those God purchased with the blood of His Son. As you preach, do so faithfully with *the particular congregation in view* the Lord has entrusted to your care. I am thankful for Phil Newton helping me understand the unique nature of pastoral preaching. I pray the Lord will use his example to spur you on to love and serve those under your ministry of the Word.

Chapter eleven

The Roots of South Woods: Ten-Thousand Fruits of Biblical Exposition

J. Matthew Sliger

Introduction

If you seek the essence of this anecdote-laden essay, you will find it in the following thesis: it is impossible to quantify the long-term effects of long–term biblical exposition in a local church.

The Scriptures testify to the veracity of that assertion. For instance, the prophet Isaiah declared that the Word accomplishes every purpose for which the Father sent it (Isa 55:11). The apostle Paul agreed, telling the church at Ephesus that the Word itself is able to build them up (Acts 20:32). To state it simply and briefly: the thesis of this essay is something that can be defended from a theological perspective.

Yet, for a number of reasons, this chapter will *not* attempt to argue for the priority or necessity of biblical exposition from the Scriptures themselves. That case can be found in many other books and other chapters in this book.[1] Instead, over the next few pages, I hope to make plain that the thesis above *also* captures something that can be—and has been—observed. With this festschrift in mind, this chapter intends to spotlight the observable *fruits* of biblical exposition, something the Lord's allowed me to watch unfold in the life and ministry of Phil Newton at South Woods Baptist Church in Memphis, TN.

When my wife and I moved to Memphis in 2007, we were not looking for much in our search for a local church. However, we *were* looking for one that opened the Bible and taught from it. At South Woods, that is precisely what we found.

Soon after we began visiting, Phil began an exposition through the Book of Romans. In the months that followed, week after week we heard the next passage in that majestic letter taught. Romans 1 eventually led to Romans 2. The gospel truths concerning propitiation in Romans 3 prepared the way for understanding Abraham's faith in Romans 4. And though 15-plus years have elapsed since this moment, I have not come close to forgetting when we finally arrived at Romans 8. With the first seven chapters of that epistle expounded, Romans 8:1 landed with such assuring force it was *as if* I had never heard Romans 8:1 before. In those days—as a green seminary student eager to see things I had read about fleshed out—I experienced the benefits of sitting under faithful exposition.

A couple years after we joined, I began serving as one of Phil's many interns. One of the joys of that season was getting to see a little more "under the hood" concerning what went into biblical exposition. While I continued to experience the benefits of that

---

1   Phil A. Newton, *40 Questions About Pastoral Ministry* (Grand Rapids: Kregel, 2021), 119–125; 169–206; John Piper, *Expository Exultation* (Wheaton, Ill.: Crossway, 2018), 51–71; Dennis Johnson, *Him We Proclaim* (Phillipsburg, N. J.: P&R Publishing, 2007); Haddon Robinson, *Biblical Preaching* (Grand Rapids: Baker Academic, 2008).

practice as a church member, I also began to observe more closely what that commitment demanded from a pastor.

After a couple years serving as one of the interns, I then began serving as one of Phil's associate pastors. With that, my exposure escalated. The front row seat to the labor behind biblical exposition went from around five hours a week to five days a week. In the Lord's kindness, that season did not end quickly. For over a decade, multiple times a week, I heard Phil talk about how to preach, teach, and apply the Scriptures.

It would be easy for you to conclude this after the previous paragraphs, but no man has shaped my thinking on biblical preaching more than Phil. In fact, I doubt it is possible for anyone to *ever* supplant him in that way. To put it simply: it is impossible to quantify his effect on me personally.

But not *only* on me. It is impossible to quantify the long-term effects of long-term biblical exposition on the local church I know and love. Because what I observed for merely 15 years at South Woods, Phil did for 35 years.

This chapter will detail—from my perspective—something of a behind-the-scenes view of what the Lord has done through Phil via the faithful exposition of His Word. First, I will describe the faithful exposition I observed. Secondly, I will describe what I believe to be some of the fruit of that faithful exposition.

Faithful Exposition at South Woods

The Scriptures were Preached[2]

In Phil and Rich Shadden's helpful book, *Shepherding the Pastor*, Phil gives this counsel, "Major on preaching the Word.

---

2   Some of this section is slightly adapted from "The Ministry Goal No One Talks About," written for *Southern Equip*: https://equip.sbts.edu/article/ministry-goal-no-one-talks/

God has promised to bless his Word proclaimed and taught to the church."[3] Not unlike ten thousand other sentences he wrote, those are not uncredible words coming from his pen. Said another way, Phil practiced what he preached. Week after week, year after year, he did not succumb to the pressure of standing up and proclaiming something he studied years prior. Nor did he merely preach the easier books or skip the hard passages. Instead, he entered the pulpit and did what he had done seven days before, and the week before that, that is, tackle the *next* text. During his 35 years at South Woods, Phil declared the whole counsel of God, preaching through the entirety of the New Testament as well as many significant books of the Old. The Scriptures were preached.

Further, as he did so, he refused to merely skim along the surface.

The Scriptures were Preached Thoroughly

When Phil finished preaching through the New Testament at South Woods, he did so by considering the ascension of Christ in the final chapter of Luke's Gospel. To walk through that Gospel took around 27 months. Why mention the duration of that particular study? Because it serves as something of a microcosm of the approach Phil took with biblical exposition. While the Book of Romans ought not take 12 years to teach through, neither can it be done justice in 12 weeks. Rather than merely glancing at this or that passage, for decades Phil thoroughly mined the truths of God's Word for the good of God's people.

For 15 years the sermons I heard on Sundays made that evident. As did the process I observed. For example, when I walked into his

---

3   Phil A. Newton and Rich C. Shadden, *Shepherding the Pastor: Help for the Early Years of Ministry* (Greensboro, NC: New Growth Press, 2023), 41.

office on a Tuesday or Wednesday, I would often see his Greek New Testament sitting open. Beside his Greek New Testament would be a piece of paper containing the barely decipherable scribbles of Phil's personal translation. With all his experience teaching the Scriptures, you might think he had would have eventually dialed the intensity of his study back. I never saw it. Instead, he labored over conjunctions and worked through finely tuned arguments in order that he might arrive at sound theological conclusions.

There was evidence of this in that which I observed. There was also evidence in what I had not observed. Having borrowed dozens and dozens of commentaries from him over the years, book after book exposed Phil's previous underlines or his penciled-in exegetical thoughts in the margin. His study was thorough; so were his expositions. The Scriptures were preached; and they were preached thoroughly.

Further, he preached with a particular aim, that is, *to* a particular people.

The Scriptures were Preached with a Congregation in Mind

In his book, *40 Questions About Pastoral Ministry*, Phil wrote, "A preacher can study a biblical text, do superb exegesis, and develop a true-to-the-text homiletical exposition, yet still not preach pastorally."[4] Again, Phil writes what he knows. He did not merely preach to or at people, he pastored them with the Word. More than once, he said that you have not preached the text until you have applied it. As a biblical basis, Phil would often quote Colossians 1:28, noting that the aim in preaching Christ is to "present everyone mature."[5] Not unlike the Apostle Paul, Phil labored with that goal in mind. In the Lord's mercy,

---

4   Newton, *40 Questions About Pastoral Ministry*, 169.
5   Newton and Shadden, *Shepherding the Pastor*, 53.

his teaching helped to form a people, from Romans 6, in Ecclesiastes 11, in Acts 20, in Genesis 50, and so on.

He preached the Scriptures. He preached thorough expositions. Further, those expositions were prepared with a particular congregation in mind, a congregation Phil lived among and loved for a long time.

The Fruits of Faithful Exposition at South Woods

That local church—which meets in a beautiful, wooded setting—appropriately bears the name South Woods. Right outside Phil's office window stood a massive oak. That tree's greenery greeted everyone entering to worship at South Woods for decades. And the biblical imagery concerning trees has been part of this body's story too. In fact, at South Woods' initial dedication service in the late 80s, the front cover of the bulletin included a picture of an oak. Underneath that image they printed Psalm 1:1, words about fruit that accompanies one who meditates upon and delights in the Word, words about the wind driving away those that do not. The point is: while the Lord used Phil to plant this body of believers called South Woods, from the beginning it was clear that biblical exposition would root it.

I mentioned in the introduction that a couple years after joining South Woods I became an intern and then a couple years later began serving as Phil's Associate Pastor. What I did not mention is that after 15 years of sitting under Phil's preaching, I am now in the unenviable role of following him as the primary preacher at South Woods. To be clear, it is not unenviable in *every* way. On the one hand, following a man with his pedigree, experience, and sterling reputation is not for the faint of heart. However, on the other hand, I've found the foundation laid through him via biblical exposition to be quite sturdy. Or, to mix metaphors, that which was planted is firmly rooted.

To explain, if one of the central ways we might evaluate a leader's influence is by what he leaves behind, there is more to commend than this chapter, or even this *book*, would allow. Because South Woods was planted in gospel soil, rooted in biblical exposition, and watered by years and years of the Spirit's kind work, the fruits are in the tens of thousands.

Having described characteristics of this faithful exposition above, I will now lay out what I believe to be some—though not all—of those fruits, or effects.

Transformation

The first sentence of this chapter, "It is impossible to quantify the long-term effects of long-term biblical exposition in a local church," is a sentence I have said to a number of people. The context for the statement, at least originally, was to encourage a number of pastor friends in their first five to ten years of ministry. Inevitably, they would share with me particular difficulties they faced, whether experiences with immature believers, conflict over inconsequential matters, or maybe just the endless minutiae of so-called "ministry" that often seems far from the emphases of the New Testament. Though I did not always do this, sometimes when my friends shared those challenges, I would reply with *that* sentence concerning the long-term effects of biblical exposition. The impetus for doing so was the hope that they would once again commit themselves to just teaching the next text.

The next text would not solve all the church's problems, of course. That is a pressure some in pastoral ministry put on themselves that is quite foreign to the New Testament. In the case of South Woods, it is doubtful that any particular week—or any particular sermon—did the job of reformation on its own. However, what I had observed in the wake of another's faithful ministry is that the accumulation of biblical teaching in the life of a church grows, matures, and transforms the body.

How can I say that with such confidence? Primarily because the Scriptures declare it. But it is not irrelevant that those fruits have been observed. Over decades, the Lord has used His Word at South Woods to transform a people, bringing about renewal and gospel-driven repentance. The Lord has used His Word to spur believers on to love and good deeds. He has used His Word to enable those inherently selfish to prefer one another above themselves. He has used His Word to promote others-centered unity. The Lord has used His Word at South Woods to encourage His people to forgive as they've been forgiven, even when they have not wanted to. His Word has strengthened those caring for aging parents. It has guided those wearied by the challenges of raising children. God has used His Word to repair marriages on the brink of ruin. He has used His Word to reprove, rebuke, and exhort over and over again. He has comforted those walking through deep affliction by His Word. His Word has assured His people of things unseen. It has helped them live as if He is truly the rewarder of those who seek Him. The Lord has used His Word at South Woods to embolden believers to share gospel truths with co-workers, neighbors, and family members. He has used His Word to encourage kingdom-minded sharing of resources. The Lord has used His Word to lead men and women to sell possessions and go to the nations. This paragraph could easily go on and on listing fruit after fruit. But, in short, the Lord has used His Word at South Woods to mold a people into the image of His Son.

To you, each of those sentences above might sound like vague assertions or hyperbole. For me, for my fellow elders, and for Phil, each assertion has *at least* one face, and in most cases, *more* than one. For decades, the Lord has used the Scriptures preached to steady, edify, and direct a people. The Scriptures declare the Word to be living and active (Heb 4:12). At South Woods, the Scriptures declared have brought about gospel transformation.

And that kind of transformation changes desires.

A Desire to Study the Word

Not too long ago, while I was preaching through Hebrews, we arrived at one of the more fascinating characters in all the Scriptures: mysterious Melchizedek. If you know Hebrews 7, you know that not *only* is the character of Melchizedek mysterious, but the logic of the passage itself is dense. At one point, while talking about how Levi *both* received tithes and also—somehow—*paid* tithes through his ancestor Abraham, I looked out at the congregation and saw something startling. Though the analogy is unlike *anything* in our Western culture, and though I was boring *myself* attempting to communicate it, I looked out and saw a congregation on the edge of their seats.

Then, after the service, and in the days ahead, church member after church member asked thoughtful questions about Melchizedek, his better priesthood, and the argument of Hebrews 7. While I thought I was dragging a congregation against their will through the weeds of my study, they were locked in. Why point this out? Because that desire for the meat of the Word did not come about overnight. Further, I personally had little to do with it. I was four years old when South Woods was planted. I was not even a Christian when this foundation was being laid. I merely inherited a body eager for the thoughtful study of the Scriptures.

And eager they are. In fact, as we approached the end of that study, I jokingly told a gathering of church members that I enjoyed Hebrews so much I was considering finishing chapter 13 and then beginning right back at Hebrews 1. Though I was not *close* to serious, those that heard me pitch the idea did not bristle. In fact, one or two of them said to me, "Maybe you could do ten weeks or so on it?" What is the point of that anecdote? They wanted *more*.

Which leads to the final fruit of biblical exposition I will mention.

An Appetite for the Word

Because Phil preached the Word, so faithfully and thoroughly, I did not have to attempt to follow *him*—his multiple doctorates, the sonorous timbre of his bass voice, his 40-plus years of experience teaching the Bible. Instead, he handed me the baton of picking up where he left off, building on the same foundation the Lord used him and others to lay.

In fact, on my first Sunday as Phil's "successor," not a syllable was said about it being my first Sunday in that role. It was the Lord's Day. Further, on that Lord's Day I preached Acts 21:27–40. It might be worth putting this chapter down and skimming that passage. That pericope details a crowd being stirred up in Jerusalem, subsequently dragging Paul out of the temple, followed by a brief conversation between the commander of a Roman cohort and Paul about whether he was the Egyptian who had previously stirred up a revolt of assassins. Why detail that? Because I strongly doubt you would choose *that* text for your first Sunday as the Senior Pastor at any church. I doubt anyone would, in fact. So why did I preach that particular passage on that particular Sunday? Because it was the next text. And *that* is what the congregation expected. The baton Phil handed me was the Word preached.

Because of decades of faithful ministry, watered by the Lord's kind mercies, South Woods Baptist Church is a local church with an appetite for the Word and a desire to study it thoughtfully so that they might continue to be transformed by it.

As this essay began, it is impossible to quantify the long-term effects of long-term biblical exposition in a local church. But the effects can be described. They can be experienced. And the long-term effects of God's Word on a people can be rejoiced in.

Chapter twelve

Prizing and Proclaiming: The Preeminence of Christ in the Canon[1]

Jordan Thomas

Introduction

I love Phil Newton and am humbled to have the opportunity to offer this essay in his honor. I would be a fabulously blessed man if the Lord would grant me a double portion of his spirit! I met Phil in 1998 when I was a twenty-year-old summer student at the *Stephen Olford Center for Expository Preaching* in Memphis, TN. Our small cohort nearly doubled the modest crowd at South Woods Baptist Church on a Wednesday evening when we joined the saints there for worship. Little did I know how God would use that evening as a massive inflection-point in my heart, life, and ministry.

Upon the modest crowd a holy hush settled as Pastor Phil's baritone-voice sweetly exalted Jesus from the pages of Acts. *'I want to do that!'* was the visceral reaction of my heart upon hearing him unfold the beauty of Christ from God's Word. Since then, Phil has become one of my dearest friends in pastoral ministry. He has loved me well! For over twenty years he has prayed for me, patiently

---

1   All Scripture referenced from NASB95 unless otherwise noted.

endured much self-righteousness in me and relentlessly encouraged me to feed upon Christ and to feed Christ to His people.

Lest anyone suppose I am teetering on venerating Phil, let me begin by admitting he often got it wrong. He would be the first to tell you, with a broken heart, that the earliest years of his preaching too often failed to *explicitly* accentuate the beauty of Christ. Like me and many other pastors, Phil has lamented and repented from the many times we have attempted "to be faithful to a biblical text" while failing to preach Christ *from that text*.

By surveying the Christ-revealing, Christ-exalting, divine intention of seven selected redemptive epochs of the Old Covenant, part of my hope is to expose Christ-less preaching as wasted breath.[2] Or worse than wasted, it is *detrimental* breath. By drawing attention to Scripture's witness that every epoch of God's Book is saturated with the glory of Christ and His gospel labors, my greater hope is to buttress your conviction to "know nothing … except Jesus Christ, and Him crucified" (1 Cor 2:2). The centrality of Christ in our preaching does not ignore the Old Testament, the Law of God, or the Bible's multiplied imperatives for obedience. Instead, these inspired riches have "become our tutor to lead us to Christ, so that we may be justified by faith" (Gal 3:24).

This prayer-soaked essay hopes to reorient the hearts of Bible-heralds to a Christ-centered conviction in our expositional exultation.[3] Phil, myself, and millions of other Christians have

---

2   The seven epochs of the Old Testament we will consider are the eras of eternity past, and the epochs of Creation, Adam, Abraham, Moses, David, and the Prophets.

3   John Piper, *Expository Exultation: Christian Preaching as Worship* (Wheaton: Crossway, 2018), 16, argues for the terminology of "Expository exultation" as an appropriate descriptor for Christian preaching. He wrote, "[Preaching] is intended to communicate that this unique form of communication is both a rigorous intellectual clarification of the reality revealed through the words of Scripture and a worshipful embodiment of the value of that reality in the preacher's exultation over the word he is clarifying."

(often, slowly and painfully!) come to see that Jesus and His saving labors are the True North of all of Scripture. Deviate from Christ's all-supremacy and all-sufficiency as the guide-needle of Scripture's compass to your own peril. Not only will your teaching be lost, so will the souls of your hearers. Jesus pronounced a damnable "woe" to those who travel far and wide to make proselytes who are "twice as much a son of hell as yourself" (Matt 23:15). If any man wields the Bible with Christ-less content and application, "… it would have been good for that man if he had not been born" (Matt 26:24).

To proclaim *any* biblical text faithfully is to major on "Christ the power of God" (1 Cor 1:24). But that does not imply to speak about Jesus in the exact same way in every sermon is gospel preaching. On one hand it is better to insert a "canned gospel presentation" into any sermon than to have no gospel at all. But Phil is a model example of not only embracing a commitment to preach Christ in every sermon but to do so *from the text*. Especially the Old Testament texts—in a way that does not lull a regenerate hearer to sleep. Graeme Goldsworthy described mechanical approaches to gospel preaching the way many feel but are too embarrassed to say: "Ho hum! now here comes the Jesus bit."[4]

Scripture: A Treasure-Trove of the Glory and Gospel of Jesus

When we agree with the risen Jesus that the entire Old Testament is an inspired repository of Who He is and what He accomplished; then we too, will have a full appreciation of preaching Christ from the entire Bible. Based on the pages of the Old Testament, we will agree with Jesus that the Old Testament authors wrote about

---

4   Graeme Goldsworthy, *Preaching the Whole Bible as Christian Scripture: The Application of Biblical Theology to Expository Preaching* (Leicester: Inter-Varsity Press, 2003), xi.

the glorious person of our Savior—"the Christ." And we will be amazed at the wonder of His gospel accomplishments—"it was ... necessary ... [for Him to] ... suffer these things and to enter into His glory" (Luke 24:26). Embracing the Bible's testimony about the Christocentricity of the Old Testament will not only show up in our preaching but will affect the way the saint's disciple their children. The rocking chairs of the grandmothers in our congregations will become pulpits. There Leviticus and Habakkuk will be employed to teach their grandsons "from childhood ... the sacred writings which are able to give ... wisdom that leads to salvation through faith which is in Christ Jesus" (2 Tim 3:15). The only saving gospel that exists is the good news that "Christ died for our sins *according to the Scriptures*, and that He was buried, and that He was raised on the third day *according to the Scriptures*" (1 Cor 15:3–4; emphasis added).

What I especially love about Phil Newton is his evident Christ-ward humility. That is, an engagement with the canon that continually embraces Christ in its pages. Such humility has led to an increasing maturity *including repentance* from preaching "synagogue sermons." That is, a big God theology that is divorced from the gospel. Oh, how I pray this essay might nudge other servants of the Lord forward on the pathway of beholding Christ and "being transformed into the same image from glory to glory" (2 Cor 3:18). All who gaze upon God's Word Incarnate through God's Word written have our breath taken away as did Sheba's Queen before Solomon (cf. 1 Kgs 10:5). Indeed, "something greater than Solomon is here" (Matt 12:42). Has *the glory of Jesus* stunned and staggered you from the opening paragraph of 1 Kings 10? If so, like Jesus, you will be ruined if you make Solomon the hero of that passage. Demons can explain the Bible, but Christians alone exult in Christ through its pages (cf.

Jas 2:19)! Rather than a cut-and-paste gospel presentation that is irrelevant to the sermon text, Phil's maturity in Christ led him to ask, "'Did the sermon show how the text testifies to Christ?'"[5]

To engage our theme of the Christ-centeredness of the entire canon, we will trace the story of the Old Testament with a Christ-centered lens. Our effort and aim do not intend to end with hermeneutics, but homiletics. The question is: How will we faithfully "preach Christ crucified" from every portion of Scripture (1 Cor 1:23)? Yes, we must see the Christ of Scripture, in Scripture, by the Spirit's illuminating power. But we also desperately need the Spirit's help as preachers to say what we see "so that the cross of Christ would not be made void" (1 Cor 1:17). From beginning to end, we want our engagement with, and exposition of, God's book to be founded upon the conviction that the Bible exists *for Jesus*. Yes, you read that correctly. As Dr. Jason Derouchie asked himself rhetorically, "As a Christian, did my hermeneutical approach and ministry practice align with the truth that God created all things (including the Old Testament) by the Son, through the Son, and for the Son (Col 1:16)?"[6] Phil Newton, myself, you, our churches, the Bible, *our sermons*, and everything else exists for Jesus. Oh, may our preaching and teaching ministries evidently agree!

We will begin with a biblical view of the Lord Jesus, reckon with His declaration about Scripture, then skip across the mountaintops of seven epochs of God's redemption story, adding some application for our preaching throughout. Let's begin with a biblical view of Jesus.

---

5   Goldsworthy, *Preaching the Whole Bible*, 138.

6   Jason Shane DeRouchie, *Delighting in the Old Testament: Through Christ and for Christ* (Wheaton, IL: Crossway, 2024), xxii.

The Preeminent One

God knows everything. "His understanding is *infinite*" (Ps 147:5). Is there anything, though, God does not know? Yes. He does not know any other "god" besides Himself. "Is there any other God besides Me ... I know of none" (Isa 44:8). God doesn't know something that does not exist. In the vastness of His all-knowingness, God is ignorant of any other god besides Himself. Do you know this one True God (John 17:3)? Jesus taught that *no one* knows God unless "the Son wills to reveal Him" (Matt 11:27). In other words, unless we know God in, and through, and by Jesus, we do not know Him at all. So, who is Jesus?

Jesus is preeminent. He holds "first place in everything." This exalted position is most clearly seen and enjoyed on earth in the context of "His body, the church." This is where Christ's Person and work hold the place of highest honor (Col 1:18). As His voice is heard, His sheep hear and follow Him (cf. John 10:27). God is glorified to the degree that Jesus is prized. In the end, when all persons affirm "Jesus Christ is Lord" this will be "to the glory of God the Father" (Phil 2:11). Now, and forevermore, Jesus of Nazareth is exalted "far above all rule and authority and power and dominion, and every name that is named, not only in this age but also in the one to come" (Eph 1:21).

Put simply, Jesus is "above all" (John 3:31). "He is exalted above the heavens" (Heb 7:26). His immanence seamlessly intermingles with His transcendence. At once Jesus is "God with us" and the Lord who is simultaneously "ascended far above all the heavens" (Matt 1:23; Eph 4:10). Jesus effortlessly radiates the glory of God *because* He possesses the nature of God (Heb 1:3). To see Him is to see the Father (John 14:9). To behold Jesus is to see "the Light of the knowledge of the glory of God" in His face (2 Cor 4:6). By the decree of God the Father, God the Son is the only proper object of all angelic praise (Heb 1:6). The Father is glorified in subjecting all things to the Son (1 Cor 15:27–28).

The Bible is a bottomless and brimless treasure-trove of the gospel of the glory of Christ. From all eternity the Father has beheld the reflection of His glory in the face of His Son by the Spirit's power. Scripture is the window through which we may enjoy the same experience. There, we find Him as the object of faith and the satisfying fascination of our heart. *This is the One* who "made purification for our sins and sat down at the right hand of the Majesty on high" (cf. Heb 1:3). Let us "fix our eyes on Him" (Heb 12:2).

Come, let us behold Him! And let us proclaim "the unfathomable riches of Christ" that our churches may "know the love of Christ which surpasses knowledge" (Eph 3:8, 18). If you run out of ideas for preaching the beauty of Jesus, just turn to another page of Scripture for more material than you will ever be able to exhaust!

Proclaiming the Glory of Christ from Eternity Past

Many false religions suppose that Jesus fits nicely within their doctrinal constructs. They assert admiration for Him as a good man, or good teacher, or faith-healer, or prophet. And insist they are honoring Him. But their notions are deluded altogether, and their doctrine will prove damnable. Any Christology that denies the eternality of Jesus of Nazareth is heretical. If He is not *from forever*, He cannot *save forever*. He cannot export what He does not possess. Adding Him to a compilation of other deities is hell-deserving. Supposing to appreciate Him while rejecting His substitutionary sacrifice as the sole basis of faith is cause for condemnation. He saves forever precisely because he hails from forever. And our preaching must surpass time, dipping into the oceans of His eternal existence. If anyone wants to be saved by Jesus, they will want to grow in knowing the Jesus who does the saving.

"Eternal life," according to Jesus, is knowing "the only true God and Jesus Christ whom He has sent" (John 17:3). Sent from *where?* Our Savior can save eternally because He came to us from the portals of eternity (cf. Isa 57:15). Jesus is qualified to provide "eternal life" to "whosever believes in Him" *because He is eternal* (John 3:16; 8:28).

The hope that lies before us as Christians is that we will enjoy, with Jesus, that which Jesus has forever enjoyed. Knowing something of His infinitude in eternity past gives us a foretaste of the eternal home He has prepared for us. Our joy *in the coming eternity* will be a partaking with Jesus in the joy He has enjoyed *from eternity*. There, then, in the coming ages, we will delight in God, with God. Just as He has eternally and exuberantly enjoyed it. The Savior born in Bethlehem came from the days of eternity (cf. Mic 5:2).

Seeing the uncreated, self-existing, never-beginning, *eternal* Jesus is motivation for our worship. The living *creatures* and *created* angelic beings are worshipping Jesus now. They are presently extolling Him "who was and is and who is to come" (Rev 4:8). The contemplation of Christ's infinitude provokes their ceaseless praise.

Homiletical Applications of the "Epoch" of Christ's Eternality

The applications of Christ's eternality to our preaching and teaching ministry are … *eternal*. As we "proclaim Christ" let us labor to have heavy hints of His "unfathomable-ness" and "incomprehensible-ness" and "unsearchable-ness" *purposefully* wafting from our words (cf. Col 1:28; Rom 11:33). If we are not explicit our hearer's may infer a time-bound "Jesus." If so, they conceive in their minds one other than the Jesus of Scripture. One of the gravest dangers to our souls is the supposition that God is "just like you" (Ps 50:21).

The "lamb of God who takes away the sin of the world" whom John the Baptist *proclaimed* was simultaneously his *younger cousin* who "He existed before" him (John 1:15, 30). As we prepare to herald the Jesus of Scripture, let us be careful to soak our sermon notes into the reservoirs of His endlessness.

The gospel we preach centers on the bloody death and bodily resurrection of Jesus. And *that Jesus* "who loves us and released us from our sins by His blood" is "the Alpha and the Omega ... who is and who was and who is to come" (Rev 1:5, 8). Therefore, our gospel preaching should be perfumed with the myrrh of Him who stepped out of the heavenlies to hunt the cross. There is no other gospel, for there is no other grace. As Paul proclaimed, "... you know *the grace of our Lord Jesus Christ*, that though He was rich, yet for your sake He became poor, so that you through His poverty might become rich" (2 Cor 8:9). This is a reference to *eternal* riches purchased in time by our *timeless* Jesus. He is the I AM who is "before Abraham" (John 8:58). Therefore, in our preaching of Jesus, let us seek to showcase the One who "is able to save forever" because "He always lives to make intercession" (Heb 7:25).

Proclaiming the Glory of Christ as Creator

The "God" who "in the beginning created the heavens and the earth" is Triune (Gen 1:1). In the very first verse of the Bible the deity we meet is One seamless, unified, plural.[7] The *one God* held conference in His triune Personhood, delightfully affirming; "let *Us* make man in *Our* image" (v. 27).

---

7   אֱלֹהִים (*elohim*) is the plural form of the name for "God" in Genesis 1:1.

Even so, the further we read in Scripture the more apparent it becomes that the agent through Whom God brought about all of creation was Christ, the Son. The New Testament is clear about this fact: "All things came into being through Him, and apart from Him nothing came into being that has come into being." The "Him" is undoubtedly a reference to "the Word" who "became flesh and dwelt among us" (John 1:3; cf. vv. 1, 14). The "Him" in Paul's creation account assertion that "*by Him* all things were created … all things have been created *by Him* …" is the Father's "beloved Son" (Col 1:16; cf. v. 13). As astonishing as it is and mind-boggling to conceive—Jesus made His own mother. Jesus was immaculately conceived by the Holy Spirit in Mary's womb which was conceived and sustained by Him Who inhabited it.

In the final analysis, it is irrelevant if people doubt that Jesus created everything that exists. Because God the Father shamelessly asserts that He did. Speaking *to the Son*, God the Father rejoiced that "… You, Lord, in the beginning laid the foundation of the earth, And the heavens are the works of Your hands" (Heb 1:10). The Jesus of the Bible, whom we are to proclaim, is the "one Lord, Jesus Christ, by whom are all things, and we exist through Him" (1 Cor 8:6).

Homiletical Applications of Christ as Creator

All *biblical* preaching about the Creator must accentuate the omniscient genius and omnipotent ability of God the Son. Seeing the role of Christ as Creator enables Christian's be awe struck and understand His role in salvation and the coming new creation. In both its macro and micro aspects, the creation is dumbfounding and stupefying. But nothing in all creation compares to Christ's power in making us "a new creation" (Gal 6:14). Therefore, let us seek to Scripturally stun our hearers with the wonder of God's creative power and precision. And, above all, let us seek to help them see *that Creator* suspended on the cross for our salvation. He made the tree that germinated the seeds into one from which the wood of His crossbeams would be hewn. His hands formed the hillside into which His borrowed tomb would be hewn. The design of creation is to magnify its Maker (cf. Ps 19:1). The Scripture declares: "For since the creation of the world His invisible attributes, His eternal power and divine nature, have been clearly seen, being understood through what has been made, so that they are without excuse" (Rom 1:20). If carnal man is excuse-less before our Creator how much more preachers who herald His Book in a Christ-less fashion? "How will they hear without a preacher" (Rom 10:14)?

Our goal in proclaiming Christ as Creator is not to entertain crowds. But we ought to induce the content of the canon into the consciences of our congregation by casting before them Christ their Creator. We are aiming at conversion and the preeminence of Christ in His church! Paul makes the connection between Christ as Creator and Savior clear:

> He is the image of the invisible God, the firstborn of all creation. *For by Him all things were created*, both in the heavens and on earth, visible and invisible, whether thrones or dominions or rulers or authorities—all things have been created through Him and for Him. He is before all things, and in Him all things hold together. He is also head of the body, the church; and He is the beginning, the firstborn from the dead, so that He Himself will come to have first place in everything. For it was the Father's good pleasure for all the fullness to dwell in Him, and through Him to reconcile all things to Himself, *having made peace through the blood of His cross*; through Him, I say, whether things on earth or things in heaven (Col 1:15–20; emphasis added).

Let us, in our proclamation of Christ be equally clear that the One who "made peace through the blood of His cross" is the same One through whom all things were made and are sustained (cf. vv. 20, 16–17). The truth that Christ is Creator requires and inspires Christ-centered worship. The *reason* the twenty-four elders of Revelation ceaselessly "worship Him who lives forever and ever" is *because* He made everything. Let us lead our listeners to join this heavenly chorus to Christ: "Worthy are You, our Lord and our God, to receive glory and honor and power; for You created all things, and because of Your will they existed, and were created" (Rev 4:11).

Proclaiming the Glory of Christ from the Adamic Epoch

The days of our first parents are rife with accentuations of, and allusions to Christ. In the meta narrative of Scripture, Jesus is posited at the "last Adam," the true Man (1 Cor 15:45). The first Adam was "a type of Him who was to come," namely Jesus (Rom 5:14).

As we preach the truthfulness of Adam's headship of humanity, we establish the biblical framework for the federal headship of Jesus by faith. "But the free gift is not like the transgression. For if by the transgression of the one the many died, much more did the grace of God and the gift by the grace of the one Man, Jesus Christ, abound to the many" (Rom 5:15). Paul was riveted to the associations and disassociations between Adam and Christ in his longest diatribe about the gospel.[8]

---

8   A diatribe is an argument with an imaginary opponent. In Romans 1–11 Paul lays out his most thorough articulation of the gospel. At every point he anticipates and over-whelmingly and persuasively argues against anti-gospel logic, questions and refutations that may arise in the minds of his readers.

> For if by the transgression of the one, death reigned through the one, much more those who receive the abundance of grace and of the gift of righteousness will reign in life through the One, Jesus Christ. So then as through one transgression there resulted condemnation to all men, even so through one act of righteousness there resulted justification of life to all men. For as through the one man's disobedience the many were made sinners, even so through the obedience of the One the many will be made righteous (Rom 5:17–19).

If we lose Adamic anthropology, we lose biblical soteriology. Without Adam we have no basis for mankind to be God's image bearers or image defenders. And, worse, without biblical human origins we are incapable of receiving the image of Christ as the reversal of the curse of Genesis 3 (cf. Rom 8:29). The good news of the gospel—put biblically—is being "in Christ" and therefore becoming "a new creature" (2 Cor 5:17).

Homiletical Applications of Christ in Comparison with Adam

The failure of Adam and the triumph of Christ are paralleled in their respective temptation narratives.[9] The New Testament presents Jesus as "tempted in all things as we are, yet without sin" (Heb 4:15). Therefore, in our proclamation of Christ Jesus, let us seek to show how He flourished where the first Adam failed. As such, Jesus is the only adequate Priest for us in God's presence (cf. Heb 4:14).

It was owing to Jesus "becoming obedient to the point of death, even death on a cross" that "God highly exalted Him and bestowed on Him the name which is above every name" (Phil 2:8–9). While "Adam, the son of God" became infected with sin

---

9   cf. Genesis 3:1–12 and Matthew 4:1–11.

and contaminated the entire human race with his guilt, "[Jesus] was [God's] Son who learned obedience from the things which He suffered" (Luke 3:38; Heb 5:8).

In Adam, let us preach the dignity of every single human being as God's image bearer (Gen 1:28). And let us clearly declare the depravity and death with which all people are infected due to Adam's original crime (1 Cor 15:22). Then, let us be careful to point to Jesus in whom "the fulness of Deity dwells in bodily form" (Col 2:9). Also let us exult in and exalt the incarnate Christ, "Immanuel ... God with us" (Matt 1:23). This one alone brings us to the final, whole-earth Eden, where the redeemed by His blood will walk with Christ forever (cf. Rev 21–22).

Proclaiming the Glory of Christ from the Patriarchal Epoch (~2000 B.C.)

The Christian faith-father is Abraham. He was not the first to believe in the promised Messiah. But God identified Abraham as the exemplar of His family in a redemptive-historical fashion. This means, in God's providence that Abraham becomes the template for all who are in God's family. Abraham is the proto-typical "believer" to whom "Scripture ... preached the gospel" (Gal 3:9). The Bible is not ambiguous about how Abraham received God's righteousness. Like him, we too, must be justified by faith in the Lord Jesus. Righteousness was "reckoned to him" upon "believing" (Gen 15:6). Therefore, anyone to whom the righteousness of God will be applied must believe upon the same object of faith in whom Abraham believed.

Does the Bible make clear that Abraham believed in *Jesus*? Yes! Abundantly so. "And if you *belong to Christ*, then you are Abraham's descendants, heirs according to promise" (Gal 3:29). God is unwilling to leave us wondering about the meaning of "the blessing of Abraham." His Name is "Christ Jesus" (cf. Gal 3:14). According to Paul, "Christ" is the "seed" to whom God's promises were spoken as Abraham dropped the dagger from his hand atop Moriah (cf. Gal 3:16; Gen 22:18).

Homiletical Applications of Christ Revealed in the Abrahamic Epoch

Let Paul's logic lacerate your soul and layer itself into all our Bible teaching and preaching. As the Scripture says:

> What then shall we say that Abraham, our forefather according to the flesh, has found? For if Abraham was justified by works, he has something to boast about, but not before God. For what does the Scripture say? "Abraham believed God, and it was credited to him as righteousness." Now to the one who works, his wage is not credited as a favor, but as what is due. But to the one who does not work, but believes in Him who justifies the ungodly, his faith is credited as righteousness (Rom 4:1–5).

In this argument, Paul dismantles works-righteousness. Either right standing with God comes to us by faith or not at all. But then, Paul presses the issue again. Leaning into Genesis 15:6, Paul picks up this argument for the imputation of Christ's righteousness to all who believe the gospel (cf. v. 9–13). That portion ends with the "righteousness of faith" (v. 13). But, like a master surgeon, Paul's scalpel cuts deeper still.

In Romans 4:16–25 Paul uses Abraham's trust in God's promises to move from Sarah's barren womb to Christ's empty tomb. And the common denominator in Paul's argument is whether a person will "waver in unbelief" or "grow strong in faith, giving glory to God" (v. 20). Then, again—for the *eighth* time in this chapter—Paul hearkens back to Genesis 15 to argue that "all who believe"

(v. 22) are, like Abraham, "credited … righteousness" (v. 22). That is not enough for Paul. No. *Two more times*, Paul used the "crediting" of righteousness to believers as a crescendo to his argument (cf. vv. 23–25). Here, the Christ-centered focus finally becomes explicit:

> Now not for his sake only was it written that it was credited to him, but for our sake also, to whom it will be credited, as *those who believe in Him who raised Jesus our Lord from the dead, He who was delivered over because of our transgressions, and was raised because of our justification.* (Rom 4:23–25; emphasis added)

The culmination of Paul's gospel presentation in Romans chapter four culminates by showing that Abraham like faith is Jesus trusting faith.

Proclaiming the Glory of Christ from the Mosaic Epoch (~1500 B.C)

Moses' faith was stabilized because his eyes were on Jesus as he fled Egypt. The Scripture declares, "He left Egypt, not fearing the wrath of the king; for he endured, as seeing Him who is unseen" (Heb 11:27). For Moses, *the Messiah* was of greater value than all the riches of Egypt. Even the scorn and suffering that accompanied being with Jesus was more valuable to Moses than all the gold of North Africa. He considered "the reproach of Christ greater riches than the treasures of Egypt" (v. 26). If we are to understand and proclaim the life, faith, writings, and ministry of Moses; we must see the centrality of Christ Jesus in it all.

All of Moses' writings are about Jesus (cf. John 5:39–47). More specifically, the books of Moses are about "the sufferings of Christ and the glories to follow" (Luke 24:26). Philip understood and taught that "Jesus of Nazareth, the son of Joseph" was the point Moses wrote about in the Law (cf. John 1:45). The sacred writings of Moses are "able to give you the wisdom that leads to salvation through faith which is in Jesus Christ" (2 Tim 3:15).

The Deity whom Moses met in the burning bush is Jesus, the I AM.[1] This Jesus is also the Lawgiver who etched His commands in the stone tablets. Then, the same Lawgiver Moses encountered on the mountain humbly came to earth as incarnate God to ascend another mountain to preach that same Law![2] The entire sacrificial system of the Law, including its tabernacle are direct foreshadowing of "Christ our Passover" sacrifice (John 1:14; 1 Cor 5:7).

Homiletical Applications of Christ Revealed in the Mosaic Epoch

Through Scripture, and by the Spirit's illuminating power—as Peter, James, and John experienced in the first century—we are also invited to the mount of transfiguration. In the Scripture we are given a window to see the glory of Jesus that Moses and Elijah also beheld on that mountain (cf. Luke 9:28–36). And in the Scripture, we are enabled to see that Jesus leads a greater "exodus" for God's people by His death.[3] Indeed, Jesus is the true deliverer, the Greater Moses. This is why Stephen's final sermon majored on the reality that Jesus is the Prophet like unto Moses to whom we must listen (Acts 7:37).

In our preaching of the Mosaic epoch of redemptive history, and all its biblical material, our hearers should be drawn to see and

---

1   John was careful to connect the Jesus of his Gospel to the identity of the very God Moses encountered in the burning bush of Exodus 3. Cf. John 6:35, 48; 8:12, 58; 10:7, 11; 11:25; 14:6.

2   Matthew 5–7, The Sermon on the Mount.

3   The word "departure" in Luke 9:31 is the Greek word ἔξοδον (pronounced 'exodus').

trust Christ. As our Lord put it, "For if you believed Moses, you would believe Me, for he wrote about Me." Amen!

Proclaiming the Glory of Christ from the Davidic Epoch

Matthew is careful to begin and end his Gospel with a connection to Christ as David's Son, our eternal King. In Matthew 1:1 "Jesus the Messiah" is "the son of David." In Matthew 28:18, this *risen* Jesus possesses "all authority." As we consider the Davidic epoch of redemptive history through a Christ-centered lens, for the biblical material is replete with connections to His glory and gospel labors.

To begin, Jesus insisted twice that His resurrection in David's biblical writings is about Him.[4] While enduring the agony of the cross, Jesus cited Psalm 22 as a description of what He was enduring (cf. Mark 15:44). The writer of Hebrews cannot cease to make connections to Christ from the Old Testament writings of David.[5] Jesus silenced His interrogators by inferring that He is the Lord of Psalm 110 (cf. Matt 22:22–46). He is David's forever-enthroned Son (cf. Acts 2:30).

Homiletical Applications of Christ Revealed in the Davidic Epoch

If we are faithfully proclaiming *how* God brought David into a saving relationship with Himself, then we must proclaim the same Christ that David proclaimed. Consider that Psalm 16 was written by David but is not about David. This inspired song—written roughly a millennia before Jesus was born—"Looked ahead and

---

4   Luke 24:27 — "He explained to them the things concerning Himself in all the Scriptures." Luke 24:44 —"... all the things which are written about Me in ... the Psalms ..."

5   cf. Hebrews 1:5–13; 2:6–9, 12–13; 3:7–11; 5:5–9; 7:21; 10:5–14.

spoke of the resurrection of Christ" (Acts 2:31). *This risen Jesus*, then, must be our message if we are to accurately understand, proclaim, and apply Psalm 16 today. The One God promised to send in the Old Testament is "His Son, who was born of a descendant of David according to the flesh, who was declared the Son of God with power by the resurrection from the dead ..." (Rom 1:2–4).

The only reason David could sing, "How blessed is he whose transgression is forgiven, whose sin is covered" is because he had "kissed the Son" and taken "refuge in Him" (Ps 32:1; 2:11–12). Jesus is the blessed Man who meditates on God's Word in Psalm 1 and the worshipping Man who lives for God's glory in Psalm 2–150. Like the physical eyes of Bartimaeus, our spiritual eyes and those in our churches, will be opened, as we cry out: "Son of David, have mercy on me!" (Luke 18:39). In turn, this will lead to "following Jesus, glorifying God" (Luke 18:43).

Proclaiming the Glory of Christ from the Prophetic Epoch (~1000–500 B.C.)

The prophetic era of the Old Testament covers much ground and was written in various places by multiple authors. But the one common thread is that all the prophets are the material Jesus employed to "explain the things concerning Himself" (Luke 24:27). The Lord Jesus rebuked the "foolish men and slow of heart to believe in all that the prophets have spoken" for not connecting *the writings of the prophets* to *His sufferings and glory* (Luke 24:25–26). Hopefully we make those connections.

Portions of Jonah are well known bible stories among many children. Jesus insisted that people understand Jonah's message so that we might marvel at Him, the true Risen Prophet! As we preach the Prophets, our primary take-away should be that "something greater than Jonah is here" (cf. Matt 12:41).

Isaiah's encounter with the Lord of glory, surrounded by angelic hosts, and being undone by mankind's pervasive sinfulness is another well-known passage (cf. Isa 6:1–9). But the three-fold anthem, "Holy, holy, holy" is owing—according to John's Gospel—to Isaiah's vision of ... the enthroned Jesus (cf. John 12:41). The eunuch's conversion was predicated on the Spirit using Philip's preaching to preach Christ beginning from Isaiah 53 (cf. Acts 8:25–31).

Oh, may we realize that "among those born of women there has not arisen [a prophet] greater than John the Baptist!" But John lived in an overlap of the ages between the Old and New Covenants. John was privileged to see the Savior with his own eyes all the other prophets proclaimed. But he did not live long enough to witness the events of the gospel after Resurrection Sunday. Jesus declared concerning John, "Yet, the one who is least in the kingdom of heaven is greater than he" (Matt 11:11, cf. verse 9 to confirm that Jesus is referring to John as the greatest prophet). That's us! We have the full gospel story fulfilled.

Homiletical Applications of Christ Revealed in the Prophetic Epoch

If we are to preach the prophetic books in a way that pleases Christ, then we must unashamedly declare: "... of Him *all the prophets bear witness* that through His name everyone who believes in Him receives forgiveness of sins" (Acts 10:43; emphasis added). Instead of making up our own use of the prophetic material of Scripture, let us employ Peter's hermeneutic; namely, that "God announced beforehand by the mouth of *all the prophets*, that His Christ would suffer, He has thus fulfilled" (Acts 3:18; emphasis added).

Perhaps you have never preached or taught from Isaiah to Malachi. But if you do, please bear in mind: if you "state nothing but what the Prophets … said was going to take place," then your entire message would major on this fact: "[T]hat the Christ was to suffer, and that by reason of His resurrection from the dead He would be the first to proclaim light both to the Jewish people and to the Gentiles" (Acts 26:23).

Peter labored to explain that the Old Testament prophets "prophesied of the grace that would come to you" (1 Pet 1:10). And it was "the Spirit of Christ within them" who was predicting "the sufferings of Christ and the glories to follow" (1 Pet 1:11). According to Peter, whenever we preach "the gospel" of Christ's death, burial, and resurrection as our only means of reconciliation with God; we are simply asserting the same truth the Old Testament Prophets were declaring (1 Pet 1:12).

According to Jesus, if we are persecuted or falsely accused and have evil things said about us "because of [Jesus]," then we are in good company and should "rejoice and be glad." Why so? "For your reward in heaven is great; for in the same way, they persecuted the prophets who were before you" (Matt 5:11–12). Oh, may we proclaim that Jesus is the One whom the Old Testament Prophetic books exist to accentuate!

Conclusion

Goldsworthy supplies a fitting conclusion, declaring,

As Jesus speaks to the larger group of disciples and opens their minds to understand the Scriptures, it would appear that Luke intends us to understand the centrality of his suffering and resurrection for our hermeneutics (Luke 24:45–47). This point cannot be emphasized enough for it signifies that the meaning of all the Scriptures is unlocked by the death and resurrection of Jesus.[6]

May more and more preachers embrace the reality, as Phil Newton increasingly has and does, that "all of the Scriptures" are "unlocked by the death and resurrection of Jesus."

---

6   Goldsworthy, *Preaching the Whole Bible*, 54.

Chapter thirteen

Preaching Christ from the Old Testament

Mitch Kimbrell

In the fall of 2016, I headed from Memphis, Tennessee, where I was a PhD student and adjunct professor at Mid-America Baptist Theological Seminary, to Hughes, Arkansas. There I was to provide pulpit supply at First Baptist Church. I had decided that I would preach an overview of the Noah narrative from Genesis 6–9. I would give special attention to how those chapters typologically foreshadow the life and work of the Lord Jesus Christ. Noah is a type of salvation rest in Christ (Noah's name in Hebrew, *nōaḥ*, meaning "relief," "comfort," or "rest"). Noah and his family's salvation from the judgment of floodwaters resolves in Christ's salvation of His people through the judgment of the cross, and so on.

I remember hoping that a particular theology professor at my seminary would not come across a recording of that sermon. He had instructed me not to regard anything in the OT[1] as typological of Christ without specific NT warrant. I believed the Noah account obviously prophesied Christ's person and work that I risked drawing his ire for the sake of helping that congregation to see how the OT spoke of Christ.

---

1   "OT" is Old Testament throughout, "NT" is New Testament throughout.

A couple of months later, my wife and our two baby girls began attending South Woods Baptist Church where Phil Newton was pastor. And we began to hear preaching like that represented in this excerpt from Phil's sermon on Genesis 37:

> This entire picture in Genesis 37 points us to something much greater. How amazing that God would synergize (work together) with what was intended for evil to accomplish good in delivering the children of Israel from famine and giving them the best of Egypt's land! But that pales in comparison to what God has done through Jesus Christ.[2]

What Phil said about Genesis 37, the story of Joseph's brothers selling him into slavery in Egypt, rang true to me. When we began to attend South Woods, it seemed to my soul like going from drinking from a muddy river with a straw with a hole in it to drinking the sweetest nectar directly from a firehose. Before I had previously only seen and approached Christocentric[3] Bible reading and preaching with fear and trembling. Now, someone I admired and respected was saying how the Joseph narrative pointed beyond itself to the life, death, resurrection, and exaltation of Jesus Christ, even without explicit NT warrant to do so.

---

2   Phil Newton, "Behind a Frowning Providence" (sermon, South Woods Baptist Church, Memphis, delivered September 28, 2013, manuscript accessed June 4, 2024, https://cdn.subsplash.com/documents/JF89ZG/_ source/c7052f57-6999-4fc4-a378-f84dfb-64c50b/document.pdf).

3   "Christocentric" is the agreed-upon term for the hermeneutical method I advocate in this essay. I also quite like the term "Christotelic," from the Greek word telos meaning "goal," "aim," or "end" and referring to an OT hermeneutic that regards Christ's Person and work as the telos of the whole Bible. For an articulation of what I mean by "Christocentric," see Jason DeRouchie, "Redemptive-Historical, Christocentric Approach," in *Five Views of Christ in the Old Testament*, eds. Brian J. Tabb and Andrew M. King (Grand Rapids: Zondervan Academic, 2002), 181–211.

In this essay, it is my aim to commend a particular approach to Bible interpretation for the Bible reader and preacher. This method regards Christ's person and work as the Holy Spirit-intended *telos* of the whole of the OT. To accomplish this, I will survey some of the most relevant NT passages that will compel the preacher to preach Christ from the OT. Then, I will advocate for a method of Christocentric preaching that takes seriously both a passage's historical-grammatical and redemptive-historical contexts while providing guardrails that avoid subjective allegorizing. Finally, I will provide a short case study in my own understanding of preaching Christ from the OT.

It should be noted that while I credit Phil with being among the first to demonstrate to me preaching Christ from the OT, this essay is not an attempt to articulate Phil's specific hermeneutic and should not be interpreted to represent his hermeneutic.

NT Warrant for OT Christocentric Preaching

In Luke 24, Luke recorded Jesus' walking with two of His disciples on the first Easter Sunday: Cleopas and another unnamed follower of the Lord. Those two disciples gloomily recounted to Jesus, who was yet unidentified to them, what had transpired over the past few days in Jerusalem (Luke 24:17). Specifically, they rehearsed how Jesus had been delivered up by the Jewish religious leaders to the Romans for crucifixion. After they finished recounting the weekend's events they lamented: "But we had hoped that he was the one to redeem Israel. Yes, and besides all this, it is now the third day since these things happened" (24:21).[4]

---

4   Unless otherwise noted, all Scripture quotations come from *The Holy Bible: English Standard Version* (Wheaton, IL: Crossway Bibles, 2016).

Jesus' reaction in 24:25–26 seems a bit harsh: "O foolish ones, and slow of heart to believe all that the prophets have spoken! Was it not necessary that the Christ should suffer these things and enter his glory?" Then, "beginning with Moses and all the Prophets, [Jesus] interpreted to them in all the Scriptures the things concerning himself" (24:27).

The Lord upbraided these followers of His for not having read their OT correctly. They were to have read it in a way that would have had them anticipating His resurrection three days after His death—not glumly mourning it. According to Jesus, the OT prophets taught that the redeemer of Israel necessarily had to suffer before entering His glory.

Later in Luke 24, when Jesus appeared to the other eleven disciples with Cleopas and his companion, Jesus further elucidated the OT's Christocentricity. In 24:44, the risen Lord declared, "These are my words that I spoke to you while I was still with you, that everything written about me in the Law of Moses and the Prophets and the Psalms must be fulfilled." The Hebrew people divided their Bible (our OT) into three big sections: the Law, the Prophets, and the Writings (of which Psalms is the biggest part). Jesus asserted that the entire OT prophesied of Him.

More specifically, the Lord said in 24:46 that the OT prophesies of the Christ's suffering and resurrection from the dead on the third day. No wonder He rebuked the Emmaus-bound disciples for acknowledging that three days had passed since Jesus' death but without anticipating His resurrection.

Taken together, Luke 24:25–27 and 24:44–47 teach that the OT in all its parts—the Pentateuch, the Prophets, and the Writings—prophesy of the death and third-day resurrection of Jesus Christ. What is more, reading the OT Christocentrically will cause the hearts of those who love Jesus to burn within them too. In seeing Christ in the people, events, and institutions in the OT, Christians see the one whom their soul loves (Song of Solomon 3:4).

Luke 24 is not the only place the NT gives the preacher warrant to interpret the OT Christocentrically. Jesus said to His Jewish opponents in John 5:46, "If you believed Moses, you would believe me; for he wrote of me."

Where does Moses write about Jesus? Jesus told us of at least one place, in the Lord's nighttime conversation with Nicodemus in John 3. Jesus declared the account of the bronze serpent in Numbers 21 as a prophecy of His being lifted up to die for the salvation of any who would look on Him in faith. Peter, in Acts 3, authoritatively interpreted the prophet Moses speaks of in Deuteronomy 18 to have been a prophecy concerning the Lord Jesus Christ.

To the Corinthians Paul said, "that Christ died for our sins in accordance with the Scriptures, that he was buried, that he was raised on the third day in accordance with the Scriptures" (1 Cor 15:3b–4). When Paul referred to "the Scriptures" there, what could he have meant other than the OT? As a result, Paul said to the Corinthians that the OT teaches that Christ would die for our sins, be buried, and be raised on the third day.

It is a fair to ask: "Where does the OT say that Jesus would be raised on the third day?" Paul said as much in 1 Corinthians 15 and Jesus appeared to say the same thing in Luke 24:46. Obviously, one such place is found in Jonah. Jesus said to the scribes and pharisees in Matthew 12 that: Jonah "in the belly of the great fish" for three days and three nights prophesied of the Son of Man's being three days and three nights in the heart of the earth. Is Jonah the only place where a three-day resurrection from the dead is found in the OT? Certainly not.

On what day is Isaac, the miraculously born, beloved son of Abraham received back from the dead (Hebrews 11:19)? Genesis 22:4 tells us when Abraham, Isaac, and their servants reached the top of Moriah: "on the third day." When did Queen Esther experience her kind of resurrection from the dead, being welcomed into the king's presence though she came in unbidden, risking her death? Esther 5:1 tells us: "on the third day." When did Hosea the prophet say that the LORD will "raise us up"? Hosea 6:2: "on the third day."

Luke 24, John 5, and 1 Corinthians 15 are not an exhaustive list of NT passages that could be adduced in an argument for Christocentric OT preaching, but they are a sufficient list.

A Method of Christocentric Interpretation

Even among those who advocate preaching Christ from the OT, approaches differ. Those differences usually involve two considerations. The *first* is authorial intent. Related to this is both a commitment to a historical-grammatical interpretation of the OT and an avoidance of mistreatment of the Scriptures through fanciful allegory.

The *second* consideration is the apostles' treatment of the OT. Do the apostles give us a hermeneutic to learn and employ? Do we regard their Christocentric interpretation as something they, in their Spirit-inspired writing, had unique warrant to do? Or do they say to those who come after them, "Don't try this at home"?[5]

The method advocated below is based on the belief that the apostles did not employ a hermeneutic they regarded as only for

---

5   Space considerations preclude my interacting with those who would argue that we should not adopt the apostles' hermeneutic in our OT reading and preaching. For a thorough articulation of this perspective, see three works by Richard N. Longenecker: "Can We Reproduce the Exegesis of the New Testament?," *Tyndale Bulletin* 21 (1970): 3–38. "'Who Is the Prophet Talking About?' Some Reflections on the New Testament's Use of the Old," *Themelios* 13, no. 1 (September 1997): 4–8. *Biblical Exegesis in the Apostolic Period*, 2nd ed. (Grand Rapids: Eerdmans, 1999).

themselves. Rather, I contend that the apostles were teaching their audiences (present and future) how to read the OT Christocentrically. Peter Leithart's sentiment strikes a chord here: "I want to read the Old Testament and the New as a disciple of Jesus, and that means following in the footsteps of the disciples' methods of reading."[6]

As regards an approach to carefully respecting an OT text's historical-grammatical context while also faithfully seeing how the text resolves in the person and work of Christ, I have not found anything superior to the approach made famous by Edmund P. Clowney. A couple of Clowney's former students have taken his work and developed it into a system.[7] The seminal work where Clowney's hermeneutical method can be seen is his *Preaching and Biblical Theology* published in 1961.

The best-known and longest-lasting contribution from Clowney's work is his typological triangle, reproduced here:[8]

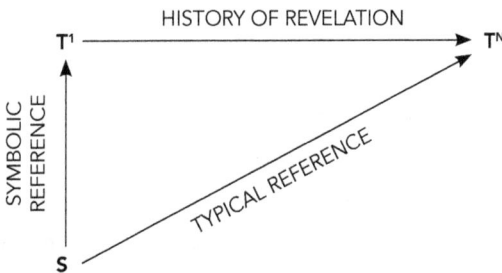

---

6   Peter J. Leithart, *Deep Exegesis: The Mystery of Reading Scripture* (Waco, TX: Baylor University Press, 2009), viii as quoted in Mitchell L. Chase, *40 Questions about Typology and Allegory*, 40 Questions, ed. Benjamin L. Merkle (Grand Rapids: Kregel Academic, 2020), 51.

7   See Dennis E. Johnson, *Him We Proclaim: Preaching Christ from All the Scriptures* (Phillipsburg, NJ: P&R Publishing, 2007); Vern S. Poythress, *Biblical Typology: How the Old Testament Points to Christ, His Church, and the Consummation* (Wheaton, IL: Crossway, 2024).

8   Edmund P. Clowney, *Preaching and Biblical Theology* (Phillipsburg, NJ: P&R Publishing, 1961), 110.

Clowney's method, as represented by his triangle, will be employed here. The Passover lamb from Exodus 12 fits well. Because the Passover lamb; though physical and historical, possessed symbolic significance to Israel; can be represented here by S.

The truth that the Passover lamb symbolized—that one will be rescued from the plague of death only by the offering of the blood of an unblemished lamb in his place—is represented here by T^1. Some criticize Christocentric preaching as running roughshod over the OT passage's historical-grammatical context. This is done to get to Christ very quickly. Both S and T^1 have thus far dealt only with what lay on the surface in Exodus 12.

It is only after the Bible reader or preacher has done the work represented in S and T^1 that he "connects this earlier revelation with T^n, the fullness of that truth revealed in Christ."[9] In this instance, the truth symbolized by the Passover lamb reaches its apex in the exclamation from John the Baptist in John 1:29, "Behold, the Lamb of God, who takes away the sin of the world!"

The NT reveals that the Passover lamb's spotlessness and its bloody substitutionary death for the sparing of the one for whom the lamb died resolves in the death of the sinless Son of God. Paul comments on the theology in 1 Corinthians 5:7, "Christ, our Passover Lamb." Christ's blood-offering on the cross rescues from eternal and spiritual death all for whom Christ died and to whom His blood is applied by faith.

Clowney's method and his triangle put up guardrails so that rank allegory is less apt to be employed in OT interpretation. Poythress recalled when someone told him that the three gifts given to the Christ-child in Matthew 2—gold, frankincense, and myrrh—correspond to God the Father, God the Son, and God the Holy

---

9 Clowney, *Preaching and Biblical Theology*, 110.

Spirit.[10] Would the use of Clowney's triangle help one avoid coming to such a fanciful and unsubstantiated conclusion? In a word, "yes."

S in Clowney's triangle requires that we first locate the meaning of S in the text itself. In our work concerning the Passover lamb above, what we said about this in T^1 is what any well-instructed Israelite would have known about the lamb. Christocentric Bible reading and preaching does not—indeed, *must not*—insert truths that were never related to the first meaning of a text. Such a textual mishandling can lead to a person surmising that the gifts of the magi corresponded to the Trinity. No, instead Christocentric interpretation takes an OT passage's first meaning and declares, "That passage means this, and what's more, it additionally means *this*."

In that way, then, faithful Christocentric interpretation is not adding to a text a meaning God never intended. Instead, it uses reliable hermeneutical tools to arrive at the fuller, Christocentric meaning that God meant for a particular OT text all along.

An age-old illustration can be helpful. Imagine a living room with couches, tables, lamps, a piano, and bookshelves where all the lights are off. Or there is a light controlled by a dimmer switch on its lowest setting. As the dimmer switch goes from off to entirely on, everything in the living room can be clearly seen—*but nothing was there that was not already there*. Just because the person walking into the dark living room cannot see all the furniture does not mean that the furniture has not all been there in the same place all along.

Likewise, when I advocate for Christocentric interpretation of the OT employing Clowney's method, I do not see anything about an OT text that was never there. Rather, I am arguing that the coming of Christ and the NT writings of the apostles have shed

---

10 Poythress, *Biblical Typology*, 128.

additional light on the redemptive-historical living room that is the
OT. In reading and preaching the OT Christocentrically, the aim is
to do nothing except identify what the entire sense of the meaning
of an OT passage is. This is accomplished by the will of the Holy
Spirit. Hopefully, how that passage resolves and points to the person
and work of the Lord Jesus Christ.

A Case Study in Christocentric Interpretation

The first OT book I preached through was Genesis. As a case study
in this interpretive method let us consider Genesis 24:1–67. This
text contains the narrative concerning Abraham's servant finding
Rebekah as Isaac's bride. Here is how I employed Clowney's method
to preach Christ in my sermon from that passage.

First, I offered a brief apologetic for searching for a
Christocentric "fuller sense" (*sensus plenior*) in the text:

> "Now, Genesis 24:1–67 doesn't mean anything less than what I've just
> preached to you. It is a marvelous story, masterfully told, of God providen-
> tially orchestrating events so that His covenant promises to Abraham will not
> fail. And it is a fairly good love story to boot. But is it more than that? Oh
> yes, it is much more. It's a story that resolves, ultimately, in the One to Whom
> Isaac points, the Lord Jesus Christ, and His love for His bride, the church."

Since the construction from the sermon manuscript echoes the
kind of Christ-centered, OT preaching I heard from Phil Newton
it is not by accident.

The opening verse of the NT calls Jesus Christ "the son
of Abraham." It logically follows, therefore, that the promised,
miraculously born son of Abraham in the first instance, Isaac,
would typologically point to Christ. As a result, I connected in my

sermon the search for Isaac's bride with the quest for the bride for the greater-than-Isaac, Jesus Christ. "Our text heralds the LORD will stop at nothing to make sure the promised son of Abraham will have his bride. If that is true of the type—Isaac and Rebekah—it's even more gloriously true of the fulfillment: Christ and the church."[11]

In what ways does Genesis 24:1–67 prophesy of Christ and the church? By my reckoning, in at least three ways.

First, like Isaac, the Lord Jesus receives His bride as a gift from His Father. It was Isaac's father who made his servant swear an oath and sent his servant with extremely specific instructions about a bride for his son.

Likewise, the bride of God's (and Abraham's) son Jesus is a gift from His Father. Over and over, Jesus refers to His people as a gift to Him from the Father. In John 6:37, Jesus relates how, "All that the Father *gives* me will come to me, and whoever comes to me I will never cast out." Again, in John 6:39, "And this is the will of him who sent me, that I should lose nothing of all that he has *given* me but raise it up on the last day."

In John 17, hours before the cross, Jesus prays for His people. As our great high priest, he beseeches His Father, "glorify your son that the son may glorify you, since you have given him authority over all flesh, to give eternal life to all whom you have *given* him." And again, in John 17:9, Jesus prays to the Father, "I am praying for them. I am not praying for the world but for those whom you have *given* me, for they are yours."

Abraham's servant swore an oath with God as his witness that he would not indiscriminately take a bride for Isaac. She had to be from among his father's people. Likewise, Jesus' bride does not consist of the entirety of humanity indiscriminately. Jesus' bride—the ones

---

11   Kimbrell, "The Promised Son Receives His Bride."

for whom He prayed in John 17, the ones for whom He died—He tells His Father, "I am not praying for the world but for those whom you have given me."

Now, even though the church was a gift to the Son from His Father, Jesus does not play the passive role that Isaac played. The servant did all the legwork for Isaac's bride. Not so with the bride of the true and better son of Abraham. The hymnwriter rightly declared, "From heav'n he came and sought her to be his holy bride; with his own blood he bought her, and for her life he died."[12]

Jesus did not wait for His bride to come to Him. And He did not even meet her (us) halfway. He came from heaven to earth, came all the way to us, clothed Himself in our flesh, in our humanity. So that we could be His beloved bride, He died for us. And,

> Surely, he has born our grief and carried our sorrows, yet we considered him stricken, smitten by God and afflicted. But he was pierced for our transgressions. He was crushed four our iniquities. Upon him was the chastisement that brought us peace. And with his wounds, we are healed. All we like sheep have gone astray. We have turned, everyone, to his own way. And the Lord has laid on him the iniquity of us all (Isa 53:4–6).

The bride-price he paid for us was not some jewelry and garments as with Rebekah. The bride-price for the church was Christ Himself. It was the entire offering of His own body and the pouring out of His own blood. It was the willing absorption of all the Father's righteous wrath toward all the sins of all His people as he suffered on the cross. This was the only way for us to be made right with God, for our sins to be forgiven, for us to have eternal life. There is no passivity from our heavenly bridegroom. Our

---

12   Samuel S. Wesley, Samuel J. Stone, "The Church's One Foundation," 1866.

bridegroom receives us as a gift to Himself from His Father. But he also pays for us, His bride, with His spotless body and blood.

Second, the passage in view for this case study prophesies of Christ and the church by highlighting Isaac's abundant love for his bride. Genesis 24:67 says in beautiful simplicity that Isaac "loved her." He loved his bride, Rebekah. She was not just a convenient incubator so that he could produce some offspring to keep the promise going. She was his beloved bride.

In Song of Solomon 4:9–10, Solomon says to his beloved:

> You have captivated my heart, my sister, my bride; you have captivated my heart with one glance of your eyes, with one jewel of your necklace. How beautiful is your love, my sister, my bride! How much better is your love than wine, and the fragrance of your oils than any spice!

Consider those words on the heart of the greater Son of David, Jesus Christ, as He thinks and speaks even more lovingly of His bride who is the church.

To this bride the Savior says, "You have captivated my heart." As you think about how your Savior thinks of the church, how we would hear Him speak of us if we could hear Him? Is this what comes to mind? It ought to be because this is what is true. This is God's word concerning how the Son loves His bride.

When Paul wanted to tell husbands how to treat their wives, what did say in Ephesians 5? "Husbands, love your wives, as Christ loved the church and gave himself up for her" (v. 25). The hymn writer declares this love right well: "Could we with ink the ocean fill and were the skies of parchment made, were ev'ry stalk on earth a quill and every man a scribe by trade, to write the love of God above would drain the ocean dry, nor could the scroll contain the whole though stretched from sky to sky."[13]

The promised, beloved son of Abraham loved his bride. And the promised, beloved son of Abraham and Son of God loved and loves His bride.

Third, the blessedness Isaac experienced, he shared with Rebekah. By the time Abraham died, he had become extraordinarily rich indeed. And Genesis 25:5 declares that "Abraham gave all he had to Isaac." That which Isaac received Rebekah received as well. She benefitted from her union with Abraham's son.

What was true in the type is even more fully and glorious true in its fulfillment. The bride of Christ benefits from her union with the Father's son. What he inherits we also inherit. And what has he inherited? Through His perfect obedience, death, and resurrection; he has inherited everything. Revelation 11 declares: "The kingdom of the world has become the kingdom of our Lord and of his Christ, and he shall reign forever and ever."

And we have inherited it with and from Him. We share in His universal and all-encompassing blessedness. Jesus confessed in Matthew 25 that He will say to His people on the last day, "Come, you who are blessed by my Father, inherit the kingdom prepared for you from the foundation of the world."

Paul also wrote to the Romans in Chapter 8, "The Spirit himself bears witness with our spirit that we are children of God, and if children, then heirs—heirs of God and fellow heirs with Christ, provided we suffer with him in order that we may also be glorified with him." Again, Jesus tenderly reaffirmed it in Luke's Gospel: "Fear not, little flock, for it is your Father's good pleasure to give you the kingdom."

13   Frederick M. Lehman, "The Love of God," 1917.

Christ's blessedness is our blessedness too. His inheritance from His Father as the Father's only begotten, beloved Son is our inheritance too. He gets the kingdom and so do we. We will rule as His vice-regents over a restored universe wherein dwells only righteousness.

Christ's bride has fixed a sure and certain hope on inheriting a universe where "death shall be no more, neither shall there be mourning, nor crying, nor pain anymore, for the former things have passed away" (Rev 21:4). And all this in a resurrection body free from sin and all its cursed, devilish entanglements. Face-to-face with God in Christ, with all the saints, in paradise, forever, ruling under Christ. That is the church's inheritance. Surely, we can confess, therefore, that all is well.

There is at least three ways Genesis 24:1–67 prophesies of the true and better son of Abraham's love relationship with His bride— the church. *First*, the Lord Jesus has received His bride as a gift from his Father. *Second*, Christ profoundly loves and delights in His bride. And *third*, the Son is our bridegroom who willingly shares with us His blessed and measureless inheritance from the Father. This story is about Isaac and Rebekah in the first instance. But Moses would say to us today, "This story is profound, and I am saying that it refers to Christ and the church" (Eph 5:32).

Conclusion

Entire monographs, theological conference sessions, and series in academic journals have had as their focus whether and how to preach Christ from the OT. So, this brief essay cannot necessarily interact with all the questions and issues that pertain to this topic.

It will suffice to commend to the reader the absolute necessity of understanding that Jesus Christ is the center and *telos* of the entire OT. D. A. Carson is right, what Jesus says in John 5:39—"You search the Scriptures because you think that in them you have eternal life; and it is they that bear witness about me"—serves as the "comprehensive hermeneutical key" to the whole OT. This "is understood to point to Christ, his ministry, his teaching, his death and resurrection."[14]

To read and preach the OT Christocentrically is to see Christ there. Paul wrote to the Galatians, "It was before your eyes that Jesus Christ was publicly portrayed as crucified" (Gal 3:1). How could Paul say that? Had the Galatians been in Jerusalem when Jesus was crucified? Unlikely. Paul is teaching that the preaching of the cross from the Scriptures is, as it were, to have Christ's cross manifestly fill one's gaze.

Likewise, to read and preach the OT Christocentrically is to hear Christ. The apostle writes to the Romans in 10:17, "So faith comes from hearing, and hearing through the word of Christ." The Scriptures are the word of Christ. Jesus says in John 10:27, "My sheep hear my voice, and I know them, and they follow me." To hear the Scriptures preached with Christ as their center and aim is to hear the word of Christ, to hear the voice of the Good Shepherd.

To see His death for sinners and to hear His voice as He is preached from all the Scriptures is to see the one whom your soul loves. And it is the unique way—until we see Him no longer as through a mirror dimly (1 Cor 13:12)—to have your heart to burn within you. That was the effect Phil Newton's preaching of the Lord Jesus Christ had on me to my eternal good.

---

14   D. A. Carson, *The Gospel according to John*, *The Pillar New Testament Commentary* (Leicester, England; Grand Rapids, MI: Inter-Varsity Press; W.B. Eerdmans, 1991), 263.

Chapter fourteen

John A. Broadus and Phil A. Newton — Both Cut from Aristotle's Rhetorical Cloth

Roger D. Duke

Introduction [1]

It was my best understanding at the time that I was led of the Lord to do graduate work in the field of Classical Rhetoric and Communication Theory. I must confess to thoroughly enjoying every minute of it. Most students who go on to do graduate work study a particular person, event, or theory. Conversely, when one studies rhetoric, a method is considered rather than a particular content. Since that time, I have become what some would refer to as a "rhetorical snob." That is, I have been on a crusade to save the word "rhetoric" from all its pejorative usage. I long to see it once again established amongst its lost but most honorable place in the Trivium of Classical Education, which consists of grammar, logic, and rhetoric. Today one hears such trite sayings as the "rhetoric of the Democrats," "the rhetoric of the Republicans," or "governmental rhetoric." Mostly this is heard in political talk or by those who comment about politics like the multiple news media. But many

---

1   This paper has been edited for usage in this volume.

have no idea what rhetoric is, or where it originated, or how it can be used for the good. And hence, rhetoric has taken on a negative connotation. This is one reason for this monograph—to make an apology for the proper study and usage of rhetoric—especially as a homiletical tool.

The second and more pertinent reason, is to honor my long-time colleague Dr. Phil Newton. He has been my friend and acquaintance for nearly forty years, my pastor and confidant, and my cowriter of a volume on John Bunyan—*Venture All on God: The Piety of John Bunyan*. Having seen him in various venues, I can say with full assurance that Phil Newton is the same godly man in the pulpit as he is out of the pulpit.

Both reasons come together in Phil's preaching and pulpit ministry. I asked him once, after hearing him preach, if he had ever read Aristotle or studied rhetoric. He answered in the negative, that he had not studied to teach like Rev. Jim Carnes or like me in a formal venue. Carnes was one of Phil's fellow elders at the South Woods Baptist Church at the time. He taught rhetoric at a classical Christian school for many years, and I taught communication and rhetoric at the collegiate level for several years. To our astonishment, much that Carnes and I taught in a formal setting Phil exhibited in his pulpit oratory. Even though he had not studied the art and craft of rhetoric academically, he has a command of much that Aristotle taught. So, I dedicate this reading to Dr. Phil Newton. One who has moved well beyond being just a rhetor to one who employs rhetorical eloquence to his pulpit ministry. He may not have studied Aristotle's treatise or Broadus's homiletical handbook in detail. But he has surely mastered the rhetorical techniques of both. In what follows, please consider Broadus's

approach to preaching as a fitting description of the skill charac-
teristic of Phil Newton's pulpit ministry.

Broadus's Use of the *Canons of Rhetoric*

Aristotle "systematized" the *Canons of Rhetoric* by the end of the
fourth century B. C. E. His system would forever serve as a rhetorical
paradigm. It came to be "fleshed out" later by Cicero and Quintilian.[2]
Aristotle's system simply stated what rhetoric should entail:

> [T]he *classical system* of rhetoric [where] there are three principal kinds
> of public speech: the *legal speech*, which takes place in the courtroom and
> concerns judgment about a *past action*; the *political speech* in the legislative
> assembly, concerned with moving people to *future* actions; the *ceremonial
> speech* in a public forum, intended to strengthen shared beliefs about the
> *present* state of affairs. In the classical system, these three situations constitute
> the entire domain of rhetoric (emphasis added).[3]

Broadus understood well that rhetoric could be adapted for
preaching. This was an undeniable focus in his early study of Greek
and Latin, modern foreign languages, and contemporary sermons.
Most contemporary sermons were built upon a learned "eloquence"
or rhetoric as it was then known in the 19th century.[4]

Studying the *Canons of Rhetoric* was considered essential to
become an effective orator in those times. Everyone who trained
in public address knew "classical rhetoric divides the process of

---

2   Patricia Bizzell and Bruce Herzberg, eds., *The Rhetorical Tradition: Readings from Classical
    Times to the Present* (Boston: Bedford Books of St. Martin's Press, 1991), 3.

3   Bizzell and Herzberg, *The Rhetorical Tradition*, 3.

4   See: Broadus's *On the Preparation and Delivery of Sermons*, 20ff, for a fuller discussion of
    the "Nature of Eloquence" and the synonymous usage of eloquence with rhetoric.

preparing a persuasive speech into five stages."[5] These are the five canons of rhetoric:

1. *Invention*, the search for persuasive ways to present the information and formulate arguments,

2. *Arrangement*, the organization of the parts of a speech to ensure that all the means of persuasion are present and properly disposed,

3. *Style*, the use of correct, appropriate, and striking language throughout the speech,

4. *Memory*, the use of mnemonics and practice,

5. *Delivery*, presenting the speech with effective gestures and vocal modulation.

This five-part composing process remains a cornerstone of the study of rhetoric.[6]

Rhetoric in its classical iterations had a sustained impact on all of Broadus's preaching and teaching praxis. It was because of this influence that he organized his *Treatise*[7] around these canons, as Paul Hubert writes, "The textbook written by Broadus reflects both his interest in and knowledge of public speaking ... . Aware that memory is no longer considered in the traditional classical sense, he does not discuss it separately, but only in reference to delivery."[8]

---

5   Bizzell and Herzberg, *The Rhetorical Tradition*, 3.

6   Bizzell and Herzberg, *The Rhetorical Tradition*, 3–4.

7   *A Treatise on the Preparation and Delivery of Sermons* is Broadus's magnum opus on Homiletics.

8   Paul Huber, "A Study of the Rhetorical Theories of John A. Broadus" (Ph.D. diss., University of Michigan, 1956), 3.

Broadus on *Invention*

The ancient rhetor selected elements from personal education as well as experience to craft the speech for each occasion. For Aristotle, this was at the heart of the persuasive process and event. Aristotle observed, "Let rhetoric be [defined as] an ability, in each [particular] case, to see the available means of persuasion."[9] At the center of these observations was the canon of *invention*. George Kennedy also affirmed Aristotle, explaining, "Invention is commonly defined as the process of determining what to say in a discourse. This process includes both *the choice of a subject* and *the accumulation of materials* which will enable a speaker to transform the subject into a living speech" (emphasis added).[10] This was the essence of Broadus as he prepared any address.

Broadus did not have to "invent" his means of persuasion. He possessed these in abundance from the Holy Scriptures, formal education, wide reading, and life experiences. All of these served as sources of invention for him. He asserted, "The chief materials of a sermon are in the great mass of cases not really *invented* at the time of preparation; they are the results of previous acquisition and reflection."[11] All that a minister possessed was his intellectual library for preparation in Broadus's schemata.

Broadus had no personal affection or affinity for rules of invention *per se*. However, he did quote Daniel P. Kidder, who "mentions some ... practical suggestions in reference to *invention* in the form of rules:

---

9   George A. Kennedy, trans., *Aristotle: On Rhetoric; A Theory of Civic Discourse* (New York: Oxford University Press, 1991), 36.

10 Huber, "A Study of the Rhetorical Theories of John A. Broadus," 10.

11 Broadus, *Treatise*, 118–119.

(1) Address your mind to the *invention* of thoughts, not words. Words may be employed, but only as auxiliaries ...

(2) Pursue *invention* in every variety of circumstance, in the study and out of it ... .

(3) Make an early selection of subjects in order to secure the advantages of the repeated and incidental action of the *inventive* powers ... .

(4) Use former studies and preparations as helps to *invention* rather than as substitutes for it."[12]

Broadus's use of the Bible as his primary source kept him from having to employ invention in the classical sense. Scripture was his ready "textbook for invention."

Broadus drew his invented materials from another source as well, the discipline of Systematic Theology. Here his love and passion were particularly observable. He writes,

> "*Systematic Theology* is of unspeakable importance to the preacher, indispensable if he would be in the best sense instructive and exert an abiding influence over his hearers ... . Exegesis and Systematic Theology properly go hand in hand. Neither is complete, neither is really safe, without the other."[13]

The Bible and Systematic Theology were symbiotic for the preacher's task in Broadus's rhetorical construct.

All these sources taken together; a working knowledge of the Scriptures, an education informed by personal experience and wide readings, and a working knowledge of Systematic Theology served

---

12 Daniel P. Kidder, *A Treatise on Homiletics* (New York: Phillips & Hunt), 152; quoted in Dargan & Broadus, 119–121.

13 Broadus, *Treatise*, 122–123.

Broadus as his means of invention. He used the Bible for his content and rhetorical invention as his method while both were underwritten by formal education, current events, and life experiences. The integration of exegesis and interpretation of Scripture intersected with his rhetorical method of invention.

Broadus on *Arrangement*

Broadus's oratorical acumen proved the necessity and importance of the canon of arrangement. He did not treat arrangement as meticulously as other canons such of invention, style, or delivery. He used an eclectic approach as he drew upon the ancient principles for his modern-day iterations needed to teach homiletics.[14] He drew from two classic rhetorical treatises: *De Inventione* by Cicero and *Institutio Oratoria* by Qunitilian. Huber notes in his *Treatise*, "[Broadus] says far less on arrangement than is found in either of these classical works."[15] Here Broadus more closely aligned with his contemporaries' use of rhetorical theory. Broadus gleaned what met his needs. Concerning this eclecticism, Huber further observed, "The influences he reflects originate from both classical and modern sources, but in giving his [*Treatise*] readers the ideas of others he not only reveals selectivity in his choices, but also offers many conclusions that appear to be based upon his own thinking and experiences."[16]

Broadus borrowed from a contemporary orator's understanding of how arrangement should be understood. He knew that any composition should have order for the discourse to hold together. To vindicate his theory, he cited Vinet's use of Pascal.

---

14 Huber, "A Study of the Rhetorical Theories of John A. Broadus," 45.

15 Huber, "A Study of the Rhetorical Theories of John A. Broadus," 45.

16 Huber, "A Study of the Rhetorical Theories of John A. Broadus," 45.

"'Good thoughts,' says Pascal, 'are abundant … .' I will not go so far as to say that a discourse without order can produce no effect … . But we may affirm … the power of discourse is proportional to the order in which [arrangement] reigns in it."[17]

Although Broadus did not give prevalence to arrangement, he nonetheless gave some extended comments about its appropriation. He demonstrated, "(1) Arrangement is of great importance *to the speaker himself* … . (2) Still more important is good arrangement as regards the *effect on the audience* … . And finally, it causes the discourse to be *more easily remembered*."[18] As Broadus closed his discussion on arrangement in the *Treatise*, he summarized by utilizing another contemporary colleague, commenting, "Coquerel says that the lack of [the arrangement] method is the most common fault of preaching, and the most inexcusable, because [it is] usually the result of insufficient labor. 'A man cannot give himself all the qualities of the orator; but by taking the necessary pains, he can connect his ideas, and proceed with order in the composition of discourse.'"[19]

Broadus on *Style*

Broadus took greater pains concerning his discussions about rhetorical style. This was somewhat juxtaposed to his rather short treatment of arrangement. When he began the discussion of style in the *Treatise*, he was greatly concerned with its nature, value, and improvement for the apprentice orator. The three perceived characteristics most important for style were *perspicuity*, *energy*, and *elegance*. Here, his *Treatise* demonstrated its extremely pedagogical

---

17 Adolphe Vinet, *Homiletics*, Thomas Skinner, trans. (New York: Ivison & Phinney, 1855), 264–265; quoted in Broadus, *Treatise*, 242.

18 Broadus, *Treatise*, 243–247.

19 Coquerel, Observ. sur la Pred., 163; quoted in Broadus, *Treatise*, 245.

nature. It was broken down into minute detail with many examples to serve the reader.[20] Broadus's classical education emerged prominently in this canon.

Broadus understood invention and style as necessary tools for the young or experienced minister as well. The novice should know them both in their classical sense and apply them to contemporary circumstances. Broadus left the young minister the right and privilege to develop his own style through learning, experiences, and personal interests. He reasoned that "the most important property of style is perspicuity. Style is excellent when, like the atmosphere, it shows the thought, but itself is not seen."[21]

What then was this perspicuity? Broadus again borrowed from a contemporary protégé for insights. William T. G. Shedd's, *Homiletics and Pastoral Theology*, shined light on the subject:

> The thoughts which the religious teacher presents to the common mind should go straight to the understanding. Everything that covers up and envelops the truth should be stripped off from it, so that the bare reality may be seen … . When the style is *plain* … the hearer experiences the sensation of being touched: and this sensation is always impressive. … The preacher should toil after this property of *style*, as he would toil after virtue.[22]

Broadus shared a homespun anecdote in the *Treatise* that illustrated well how this energy of style should be delivered. He recounted, "There is a homely story of a preacher who suggested to a sleepy hearer that snuff might keep him awake [during his sermon],

---

20 Huber, "A Study of the Rhetorical Theories of John A. Broadus," 78.

21 Broadus, *Treatise*, 339.

22 William T. G. Shedd, *Homiletics and Pastoral Theology* (New York: Charles Scribner's Sons, 1898), 63–69; quoted in Broadus, *Treatise*, 340.

and was asked in return, 'Couldn't you put a little snuff into your sermons.'"[23]

His descriptions of style were quite a departure from the sermons of his day. Dignity was the hallmark of the age. Animation, force, or passion that evoked any sort of emotional feeling was not very well known among the contemporary pulpit orators. His use of these three ideals of energy was balanced. He argued that "the chief requisite to an energetic style is an energetic nature. There must be vigorous thinking, earnest if not passionate feeling, and the determined purpose to accomplish some object, or the man's style will have no truly exalted energy."[24] This "truly exalted energy" was best understood by Broadus as God's Holy Spirit applying the preacher's message to the hearts of the hearers. Perspicuity then, was the main thing for Broadus. The preacher had to think clearly to preach clearly. It was an absolute must!

Rhetorical style, therefore, consisted at its core foci of perspicuity, energy, and elegance. It was only one of the paramount dynamics that made the pulpit come alive. For Broadus, all the *Canons of Rhetoric*, *inventio* (invention), *dispositio* (arrangement), *elocutio* (elocution or style), *pronuntiatio* (delivery), and *memoria*,[25] each had its unique place in his "puzzle of rhetoric." None of the canons, however, was more important to Broadus than was the canon of delivery.

Broadus on *Delivery*

Broadus left his lengthy discussion of delivery until last in the *Treatise*. He presented three chapters explaining factors involved in

---

23 Broadus, *Treatise*, 340.

24 Broadus, *Treatise*—Dargan rev., 381.

25 See Kennedy's *Aristotle: On Rhetoric and Bissell & Herzberg's The Rhetorical Tradition* for an in-depth discussion of the classical Canons of Rhetoric.

the delivery of speeches and sermons. As he delineated this canon, he jettisoned the Aristotelian tradition.

For Broadus, "everything old was new again." His adaptation of an address or sermon to a particular audience's need was not innovative. This technique had been employed down through the rhetorical tradition. This is also a major focus for communications theorists today. This theory is presently known as *audience analysis.* A rhetor's audience analysis explores all that can possibly be known about the people he is "*talking to or will be talking to so that* [he] *can adapt material to their interests, needs, attitudes, fund of knowledge, beliefs, values, and backgrounds.*"[26] Kenneth Burke, in his *Rhetoric of Moves,* offers another take, expounding, "[A speaker] persuade[s] a man only insofar as [he] can talk his language by speech, gesture, tonality, order, image, attitude, idea, identifying ways with his."[27] This was Broadus's method and he regularly employed it throughout his preaching and teaching career.

Broadus coupled audience analysis with listener receptivity in his delivery. They were both of utmost concern to him, quite crucial to his thinking. He reminded his readers of their collective dual responsibility. He exhorted,

> We are willing to grant ... that there is not much good preaching; but we beg leave to remark that the proportion of good preachers is quite as great as the proportion of good listeners ... . One great point of excellence in a preacher, especially to the restless hearers of the present day, will be that he is easy to listen to ... . Let all preachers strive to be so clear, so sprightly, so earnest and magnetic, that men may hear with ease and pleasure and profit; nay, let them

26 Larry A. Samovar, *Oral Communication: Speaking Across Cultures,* 11th ed. (Los Angeles: Roxbury Publishing Company, 2000), 67.

27 Kenneth Burke, *Rhetoric of Motives*; quoted in Samovar, 67.

solemnly strive so to speak, in love of their hearers and in the fear of God, that men cannot choose but hear.[28]

There was "anointed" hearing as well as "anointed" preaching in Broadus's understanding.

In the *Treatise*, Broadus discussed the differing views on the major types of delivery. "Reading, reciting, extemporaneous speaking—which is the best method of preaching?"[29] His response was: "It is a question affecting not only one's manner of delivery, but his whole method of preparation, and in fact all his habits of thought and expression."[30] Method affects the manner.

Broadus as Extemporaneous Preacher

Broadus set about in his *Treatise* to show an extemporaneous model for preaching. In his preface to the first edition, he gave one specific rationale for this chosen style. He declared that special pains were taken, at the proper points of the *Treatise* to give practical suggestions for extemporaneous speaking.[31] He referred to this model of oratory as "free speaking."[32] He felt compelled to explain further exactly what he meant by his new idea.

> The technical meaning of this expression requires to be *defined*. Primarily, of course, it denotes speaking without preparation, simply from the promptings of the moment. The colloquial expression for this is "off hand," the image being

28 John A. Broadus, "One Responsibility of Hearers—Good Listening," Western Recorder (March 1888). http://www.bereabaptistchurch.org/articles/BroadusJohnA/OneResponsibility.html.

29 Broadus, *Treatise*, 406.

30 Broadus, *Treatise*, 406.

31 Broadus, *Treatise*—Dargan rev., Author's Preface to the First Edition, n.p.

32 John A. Broadus, *On the Preparation and Delivery of Sermons*, rev. ed. (New York: Harper & Brothers, 1944), 325.

that of shooting without a rest .... This popular phraseology is suggestive .... [W]e insist that *free speaking*, after the discourse has been written in full as preparation, but without any effort to repeat the language of the manuscript, shall be called *extemporaneous speaking*.[33]

Throughout his long and distinguished career, Broadus became known for this favored method.

Broadus advocated this very strongly, urging, "Consider then, the advantages [of extempore]:"[34]

The extemporary method enabled a person to think more quickly than would be possible if the manuscript was fully written. In a context where time was of the essence the speaker was able to spend his strength on more difficult parts of the address. This method also had the advantage in that the most-noble thoughts came to the speaker while he was engaged in the task of speaking. New thoughts might come illuminating the whole of the prepared material in the mind of the speaker as he preached. There might even be a level of inspiration that might come "in the moment" of the spoken word. And in addition to all of this, the preacher could watch for the effect of the message on the face of the audience.[35]

Broadus honed his extempore skills throughout his life. During the Civil War he served as a combination missionary and chaplain to General Lee's Armies of Northern Virginia. Broadus recounted that, "For three months of that summer [1863] I preached as a missionary in General Lee's army."[36] He reflected that "it was the

---

33   Broadus, *On the Preparation*, 326.

34   Broadus, *Treatise*–Dargan rev., 458.

35   Broadus, *Treatise*–Dargan rev., 458–462.

36   J. W. Jones, "Seminary Magazine," April 1895; quoted in Archibald Thomas Robertson, *The Life and Letters of John A. Broadus*, repr. (Harrisburg, VA: Gano Books Sprinkle Publications, 2003), 198.

most interesting and thoroughly delightful preaching I was ever engaged in."[37] With all the goings and comings he scarcely had time to prepare or study. Broadus remembered that "it is very difficult here to think up an unfamiliar discourse."[38]

Broadus exhibited a certain remiss of preparation time in a letter addressed to his wife on Monday July 6th. It concerned him greatly that he was forced to use old material. His heart was no doubt discouraged due to the great loss just suffered at Gettysburg. He confessed to her that,

> "I haven't got use to the tent, and am constantly making acquaintances. A good many soldiers in attendance both times [I preached] yesterday … . You [may] perceive that I am taking my old sermons … . The sermons were not particularly good or particularly bad. God grant that they may do some good."[39]

He had taken his text from Proverbs 3:17, "Her ways are ways of pleasantness."[40] Dr. J. Wm. Jones later recalled that he employed that particular text on various other occasions.[41]

Broadus also possessed a natural ability to bring to the preaching event the rhetorical mode of *pathos*. He was swept away by personal emotion like unto Jesus Himself when He said, "O, Jerusalem, Jerusalem … I would have gathered thy children together …" (Matt 23:37 KJV). Pathos may have been Broadus's greatest natural trait. Fant and Pinson observed:

---

37   Jones, "Seminary Magazine," 198.

38   Robertson, *The Life and Letters*, 200.

40   Robertson, *The Life and Letters*, 200.

41   Jones, Seminary Magazine, April 1895; quoted in Robertson, *The Life and Letters*, 208–10.

> The qualities displayed by Broadus will serve any preacher well; *kindness,*
> *urbanity, understanding,* and *sympathy* abounded in this Virginia gentleman.
> He once said. "If I were asked what is the first thing in effective preaching, I
> should say *sympathy*; and what is the second thing [sic], I should say *sympathy*;
> and what is the third thing, I should say *sympathy.*" His deep awareness of
> the needs of people led him to meet the immediate, personal needs of others
> (emphasis added).[42]

Even before communication theory appeared as an academic discipline Broadus employed audience analysis to his addresses.[43] He possessed a gift for the extempore and was received well by all who heard him. His freedom from the contemporary use of manuscripts allowed him to look directly at his audience and establish eye contact.[44] Stanfield observed that "he assiduously cultivated this habit and developed the ability to make each person in the audience feel that he was talking directly to him."[45]

As a description characterizing Phil Newton's preaching, this is the one place where he diverges from Broadus concerning delivery. Phil follows the nineteenth century model of sermon preparation and delivery—that of the written manuscript. My wife and I have sat under the pastoral preaching of Phil for more than a decade. During that time, he has always preached from a manuscript. He is not, however, a slave to its practice. He prefers it this way because he desires to express the right thing, in the right way, at the right

---

42 Robertson, *The Life and Letters*, 353–54; quoted in Clyde E. Fant, Jr. and William M. Pinson, Jr., 20 Centuries of Great Preaching, vol, 5 of *An Encyclopedia of Preaching* (Waco, TX: Word Books Publisher, 1971), 51.

43 For a fuller discussion of Audience Analysis see, Larry A. Samovar, *Oral Communication: Speaking Across Cultures,* 11th ed. (Los Angeles: Roxbury Publishing Company, 2000).

44 Vernon Latrelle Stanfield, *Favorite Sermons of John A. Broadus* (New York: Harper Bros. Pub., 1959), 12.

45 Stanfield, *Favorite Sermons,* 12.

time. This should be true of any preacher who desires to be a pulpit craftsman. The one who desires to see the Word of God proclaimed and lodge in the hearts of the hearers.

Having made mention of that, let me also testify, many-a-time Phil has left his manuscript and ventured off into an area where it was apparent the Holy Spirit was leading him. Each time this occurred, he lapsed into that zone of "free speaking" to which Broadus referred. And it was done so flawlessly and effortlessly, the congregant would never know that Phil was preaching from a manuscript, much less that he left it, unless following along. Newton is so well-polished at reading his text, a visitor could hardly tell he was reading the sermon. Phil's reading even has an air of Broadus's "free speaking" dynamic about it.

In addition to this controversial mode, Broadus developed a conversational manner. His preaching was a "conversation" with the people. He also encouraged his students to "talk like folks talk."[46] He perfected this even to the point where his sermons were referred to as "enlarged conversations."[47] In his quiet delivery he used very few hand gestures. His voice was not terribly strong. Broadus could balance between the conversational style on the one hand and being loud enough to be heard on the other. Stanfield further observed, "It [Broadus's voice] was marked by a soft richness, fine flexibility, and often expressed deep *pathos*. He articulated carefully and there was a good distribution of emphasis (emphasis added)."[48]

Perhaps Broadus's method of delivery was most appreciated by the congregations that were blessed to hear him. Audiences have always delighted in preachers who looked at them in the eye and

---

46   Stanfield, *Favorite Sermons*, 12.

47   Stanfield, *Favorite Sermons*, 12.

48   Stanfield, *Favorite Sermons*, 12.

spoke to them directly.[49] This new method was even accepted by the academe of the day. "His Lyman Beecher Lectures on Preaching, which were delivered in this manner, were enthusiastically received by the students and faculty at Yale University."[50] Since this unique method of preparing and delivering sermons gained wide acceptance from the unlearned soldier to the scholar, "it must be listed as an important element of strength in his preaching."[51]

Many other preachers and orators have been men of renown. But Stanfield declared, "It was, however, the total impact of *man* and *message* that made John A. Broadus such a tremendously popular preacher to his own generation (emphasis added)."[52] Broadus's audience sensed a "reality"[53] that had not been experienced before. Perhaps it is best sensed by "One listener [who] summarized and made articulate what many felt about Broadus's [method of] preaching."[54] He observed: "It was not so much what he said. It did seem that almost anyone might have said what he was saying. But it was the man behind the message. He spoke with the authority of one who tested and knew the truth."[55]

Gleaned Observations from Broadus

In his critique of the electronic media, *Amusing Ourselves to Death*, Neil Postman cited "Marshall McLuhan's [often quoted] aphorism

---

49 Stanfield, *Favorite Sermons*, 13.

50 Stanfield, *Favorite Sermons*, 13. For a more in-depth discussion of the Lyman Beecher Lectures see Robertson, *The Life and Letters*, 375–80 or Mark M. Overstreet, "The 1889 Lyman Beecher Lectures and the Recovery of the Late Homiletic of John A. Broadus (1827–1985)" (Ph. D. diss., The Southern Baptist Theological Seminary, 2005).

51 Stanfield, *Favorite Sermons*, 13.

52 Stanfield, *Favorite Sermons*, 13.

53 Stanfield, *Favorite Sermons*, 13.

54 Stanfield, *Favorite Sermons*, 13.

55 Claude W. Duke, "Memorial Address of Dr. John A. Broadus," in *Review and Expositor* (April 1927): 172; quoted in Stanfield, Favorite Sermons, 13.

'the medium is the message.'"[56] Vernon L. Stanfield, longtime professor of preaching at New Orleans Baptist Theological Seminary, also observed: "Gradually, an art or science evolved to assist in the publication of the Christian message. That science came to be called homiletics."[57] Broadus embodied both of these communication truths and skills. To have known Broadus was to experience a genuine preacher in manner, in mode, in deportment, in character, and in speech. He elevated this science of homiletics to a new height of artistic oratory for his era and following generations.

For the succeeding generations who would not have the blessing of hearing him, Broadus left a rich literary legacy: *A Treatise on the Preparation and Delivery of Sermons* with all its iterations and succeeding revisions. His *Treatise* was his classical gift to Southern Baptists as well as the church-at-large. A strong case can be made that the effectiveness of the church rises or falls on the strength of her pulpits. Broadus certainly contributed to the pulpit's lasting efficacy. Stanfield articulated this quite strongly when he stated,

> Perhaps no book on homiletics has been able to achieve the comprehensiveness, the timelessness, and the simplicity of *On the Preparation and Delivery of Sermons*. Based on solid principles and tested procedures, and drawing upon the very best literature related to the art of sermon preparation ... [all its revisions and] edition[s] will be indispensable tool[s] for ... [every] new generation of preachers. Christian history has shown that the strength of the church is directly related to the strength of the pulpit. When the message from the pulpit was uncertain and faltering, the church was weak; when the

---

56 Marshall McLuhan, "The Medium is the Message," http://www.marshallmcluhan.com/main.html (19 August 2006); quoted in Neil Postman, *Amusing Ourselves to Death* (New York: Viking Penguin Books, Ltd., 1985), 8–9.

57 John A. Broadus, *On the Preparation and Delivery of Sermons*, 4th ed., rev. Vernon L. Stanfield (San Francisco: Harper & Row Publishers, 1979), 9.

pulpit was given a positive, declarative message, the church has been strong. The need for effective preaching has never been greater.[58]

This comment was almost prophetically germane for the twenty-first century. Broadus's life and work has left a powerful legacy for that of effective preaching. It is my belief that Dr. Phil Newton fulfills all these theories of Broadus as well as any Southern Baptist minister alive. But then again I might be just the least bit biased!

---

58   Broadus, *On the Preparation*. These are introductory comments in the front dust cover.

Chapter fifteen

Dogma and Declamation: Orthodoxy as Hermeneutical Principle in Preaching

Tom J. Nettles

Declamation is the art, the effective practice, of speaking publicly. Sometimes it describes outrageous bombast, but in itself, without the perversion, the word relates to the purposefully developed skill of persuasive and informative speaking. Dogma refers to received truths. Dogmatic theology is a system of necessary truth, doctrines structured by argument and tested by history. The preacher is called by God to declamation of dogma. The church is called to embrace, live according to, and witness to the world that which it has received as dogma.

One of the powerful traits of Phil Newton's preaching is its doctrinal content. He has at his disposal the whole range of exegetical confessional theology as an aid to his exposition, declamation, and application. His instruction to believers and his evangelistic calls to sinners arise from and depend upon carefully synthesized biblical truth. As an aid in discerning the clearest and most pertinent presentation of biblical truth, Phil has placed confidence in the revelatory status and inspiration of Scripture. Because it is God-given and for the instruction of sinners and the salvation of the elect, the message is clear. As of being from God, it is deep and its clarity increases in intensity with the expanding and deepening study of the text of the entire canon. By its self-proclamation, sound teaching and a body of faith may be derived from it.

The minister of the gospel must "hold firm to the trustworthy word as taught, so that he may be able to give instruction in sound doctrine and also to rebuke those who contradict it" (Titus 1:9). Paul not only instructed others in this calling of teaching the trustworthy word, but he practiced it with every fiber of his being. In every providential opportunity, in duress or in security, he could say, "I would remind you of the gospel I preached to you, which you received, and in which you stand, and by which you are being saved, if you hold fast to the word I preached to you" (1 Cor 15:1). [1] Paul never entertained a doubt about the eternal verity of his message. In believing it with the heart and confessing it with the mouth, salvation would be manifest in the believer.

Phil Newton promotes the earnest and urgent declamation of dogma as an unexceptionable privilege and duty of the gospel minister. The safety of the church, the salvation of sinners, and the purity and clarity of witness to the world depend on it. Taking as his text Jude 3–4, Phil set forth an Athanasian urgency in the matter of "contend[ing] for the Faith once for all delivered to the saints." After the council of Nicaea, Athanasius was installed as Bishop at Alexandria and spent 17 of the next 45 years in exile due to his refusal to compromise on the deity of Christ, a vital aspect of the revealed truth, the faith delivered to the saints. Neither pretentious nor contentious, Athanasius knew that the glory of God, the safety of the Church, and the salvation of sinners was at stake in the undiluted assertion and belief of this truth. Phil exhorts not only pastors, but church members to see such contending for the faith as their

---

1   All citations of Scripture are from the New King James Version (NKJV) unless otherwise noted.

stewardship. "Contending for the faith is everyone's responsibility in the church." Without being contentious or poisonous in language and posture, the Christian must nevertheless recognize that a revealed body of truth has been once-for-all delivered—yes, to God-called proclaimers of this word—but with just as intentional urgency, to the saints—the churches formed and continually informed by the gospel and its sanctifying truth and power.

This reality means that saints must listen while preachers proclaim the fullness of the truth—composed by all the individual truths—of the Bible. Central to our stewardship of God's condescending love is the declamation of dogma. As Phil Newton points out, "Long before Athanasius stood against the world for the truth of heaven, Jude, the half-brother of Jesus and leader in the early church, had already laid groundwork for the work of Athanasius." Observing the intrusion of false teaching and corrupt living, "Jude felt an urgency to call for them to contend for the faith." Taught and led by pastors of deep and spiritual moral conscience arising from a firm and deep grasp of biblical dogma, "The local community of believers in every generation must embrace the necessity of contending for the faith once for all delivered to the saints." Instead of hearing only, church members must also be doers. "We must learn," Pastor Newton instructs, "to be contenders for the faith. … Contending for the faith is everyone's responsibility in the church."[2]

The Burden of Declamation

What does such declamation involve? There is a great burden on those who are called to proclaim God's oracle (Zeph 9:1; Mal 1:1). Those who claim the burden, or oracle, but speak falsely are under the anger of God (Jer 23:33–38). For faithful declamation of dogma,

---

2   Phil Newton, Sermon on Jude 3–4.

we must consider it from several perspectives. Proclaiming dogma assumes that objectively revealed truth presides as the perpetual arbiter of personal and corporate experience. It arises from the oracle of God and has the certainty of God's own trustworthiness. Dogma rises above human intuition, human opinion, and even the most controlled and disciplined aspects of human observation. Paul paraphrases Isaiah 64:4 in saying, "Eye has not seen, nor ear heard, nor have entered into the heart of man the things which God has prepared for those who love Him" (1 Cor 2:9). Instead of empirical experimentation or philosophical ratiocination, "God has revealed them to us through his Spirit" (1 Cor 2:10).

The Spirit does this, for the Spirit Himself is God knowing the "deep things of God." This work of the Spirit arises from His eternal participation in the covenantal love and decrees resident within God for all eternity. Thus, all that God wants His image-bearers to know about His character and eternal purpose must come from truth provided from deep within the Godhead, set in understandable terms of human language, and communicated through chosen messengers. Sometimes the truths they spoke transcended their understanding, but they still spoke them. These mysteries would yield their meaning through future revelation (1 Pet 1:10–12). Paul wrote of the mystery "which in other ages was not made known to the sons of men, as it has now been revealed by the Spirit to His holy apostles and prophets" (Eph 3:5). Dogma presses on the conscience as a heavy responsibility to be delivered accurately, faithfully, and urgently.

The Whole Bible

Dogmatic declamation always has the whole Bible for its text. This kind of preaching recognizes the specific meaning of individual texts but derives that meaning from a comparison with the whole.

Small spheres of interpretation include the range of meaning for individual words, the peculiar meaning that word has in a sentence, the meaning of the sentence in a paragraph, and the purpose of the paragraph in a narrative. The kind of literature that constitutes the narrative gives a further layer of meaning to words, sentences, and the consequent narrative. Is it history, is it poetry, is it a parable, is it lament, is it sarcasm, is it rebuke, is it internal interpretation of other texts, is it doctrinal argumentation?

How should such individual biblical statements as these be set in the context of dogma? "Man has no advantage over animals for all is vanity" (Eccl 3:19). "For an empty-headed man will be wise, when a wild donkey's colt is born a man. ... The wicked man writhes with pain all his days, and the number of years is hidden from the oppressor" (Job 11:12; 15:20). "Praise the Lord! For it is good to sing praises to our God; for it is pleasant and praise is becoming" (Ps 147:1 NASB). "I saw the Lord sitting on a throne" (Isa 6:1 NASB). "No one has seen God at any time" (1 John 4:12 NASB). "In the beginning was the Word, and the Word was with God, and the Word was God" (John 1:1 NASB). "He who has seen me has seen the Father. ... The Father is greater than I" (John 14:9, 28 NASB). "You foolish Galatians, who has bewitched you, before whose eyes Jesus Christ was publicly portrayed as crucified?" (Gal 3:1 NASB). "And though you have not seen him, you love Him, and though you do not see him now, but believe in him, you greatly rejoice with joy inexpressible and full of glory" (1 Pet 1:8).

Each of these passages forms part of an argument that is understood within the larger framework of its context. That contextual meaning, then, is given a richer relevance by its place and purpose within the whole canon. The argument of Ecclesiastes gains its vibrancy and true profundity only after the whole story is in. The speeches of Job and his friends must be evaluated in light of the progress of God's revelatory purpose at that point and each speech must be seen in light of the other speeches and God's final appearance and reprimands. John's opening Christological salvo gains even more power when seen in terms of all that has preceded it concerning the power of the Word in creation, revelation, and redemption. Seeing or not seeing God and grasping the radically distinct dimensions of the person of Christ must be sorted out with careful and reverent biblical synthesis of apostolic eyewitness, manifestations of heavenly glory, and saving spiritual perception. Paul's enraged sarcasm is only one element of his ferocious defense of his status as an apostle in service of the exclusive power-to-save of the gospel he preached. His letter served a congregation in danger of doctrinal dereliction while Peter wrote tenderly to a church in the throes of physical persecution. From the combination of different genres, text-types, layering of revelatory propositions, and isolation of central recurring themes, we synthesize doctrine, the certain dogmatic truths that churches are under divine mandate to believe and proclaim.

Historic Christian Witness

The declamation of dogma takes seriously the historic Christian witness to distinctive Christian truth expressed in the confessions. Trying to come to grips with Jesus (Christological questions) and God (trinitarian dogma) dwarfs all other questions in mystery and importance. All other doctrines depend on getting this right. What may be accurately denominated as universal orthodoxy developed under the details of biblical data over a span of four and one-half centuries, and on it goes. Taking their cues from the pastoral defenders of the faith in the ante-Nicene era (such as Clement, Ignatius, Polycarp, Justin, Tertullian, Cyprian), pastor-theologians emerged in the 125 years from Nicaea (325) to Chalcedon (451) to achieve both verbal and doctrinal clarity on the Trinity and person of Christ. During these years four ecumenical councils discussed several theological issues with a major emphasis on Christology intermixed also with rejection of Pelagian views of human sinfulness and divine grace. Nicaea and Constantinople (381) asserted trinitarian truth in these words:

> One Lord Jesus Christ, the only-begotten Son of God, begotten from the Father before all time, Light from Light, True God from True God, begotten not created, of the same essence as the Father, through whom all things came into being, who for us men and because of our salvation came down from heaven, and was incarnate by the Holy Spirit and the Virgin Mary and became human. ... And in the Holy Spirit, the Lord and life-giver, Who proceeds from the Father, Who is worshipped and glorified together with the Father and Son, Who spoke through the prophets.[3]

In the recension of the creed developed in the West, the procession of the Holy Spirit was affirmed as "from the Father and the Son." This extra phrase, known as the *filioque* ["and the Son" in Latin] gave rise to a generous amount of theological interaction, but did not affect a common commitment to full trinitarianism.

Still unsettled in both language and perception concerning the mystery of the Incarnation—"the Word was made flesh and dwelt among us"—the church needed unambiguous expression of the singularity of Christ's person without compromising either His full humanity or His eternal essential deity. The Council of Chalcedon set forth a succinct formula using single words that Albert Outler

---

3   John H. Leith, Ed. *Creeds of the Churches*, "*The Constantinopolitan Creed*," Rev. ed. (Richmond: John Knox Press, 1973), 33.

has translated by using several words for each to give a full expression of the verbal intensity involved.

> [We also teach] that we apprehend [*gnoridzomenon*] this one and only Christ-Son, Lord, only-begotten—in two natures [*duo physesin*]; [and we do this] without confusing the two natures [*asunkutos*], without transmuting one nature into the other [*atreptos*], without dividing them into two separate categories [*adiaretos*], without contrasting them according to area or function [*achoristos*]. The distinctiveness of each nature is not nullified by the union. Instead, the "properties" [*idiotetos*] of each nature are conserved and both natures concur [*suntrechouses*] in one person [*prosopon*].[4]

These carefully deduced summaries will be part of the content and the hermeneutical practice of the Christian preacher. "The Father is greater than I," "emptied Himself," (Phil 2:7 NASB), "He Himself was tempted" (Heb 2:18 NASB), "having been made perfect" (Heb 5:9 NASB), "I lay down my life" (John 10:17 NASB) and many others will not become texts that imply the ontological inferiority of Jesus. Instead, they will form discreet elements of revelatory truth that help define the true Incarnation of the Son of God, the unity of His person, and the pilgrimage that established His fitness as a true substitute in both obedience and death for His people. As Nicaea stated in 325, "who, on account of us men and on account of our salvation came down and was enfleshed and embraced full manhood," and Constantinople summarized, "who for us men and for our salvation, came down from heaven, and was made flesh from the Holy Spirit and the virgin Mary and was made man,"[5] so the Outler translation of Chalcedon amplified,

---

4   Leith, *Creeds*, 36.

5   My translation of the text in Philip Schaff, *Creeds of Christendom*, 3 vols (Grand Rapids: Baker Book House, nd [previous copyrights 1877, 1905, 1919 Harper and Bros]), 2:57, 60.

> "Before time began [*pro aionon*] he was begotten of the Father in respect of his deity, and now in these 'last days' for us and on behalf of our salvation, this selfsame one was born of Mary the virgin, who is 'God-bearer' [*theotokos*] in respect of his human-ness [*anthropoteta*]."[636]

These principles are true summaries of pervasive biblical truth; one cannot be a minister of the Christian gospel who ignores, changes, or minimizes the governing power of these truths. This is essential to faithful declamation of dogma.

Other dogma embraced within the Reformed evangelical confessional historical development could be summarized as the five Reformation *solas*: *sola, scriptura, sola fide, sola gratia, solo christo, soli deo gloria*. Protestant Confessions from Augsburg (1530) to the *Baptist Faith and Message* (2000) emphasize those evangelical doctrines of grace and the cross. At least three of these *solas* are stated and the others implied in this brief statement on justification from the *Augsburg Confession*:

> It is also taught among us that we cannot obtain forgiveness of sin and righteousness before God by our own merits, works, or satisfactions, but that we receive forgiveness of sin and become righteous before God by grace, for Christ's sake, through faith, when we believe that Christ suffered for us and that for his sake our sin is forgiven and righteousness and eternal life are given to us. For God will regard and reckon this faith as righteousness, as Paul says in Romans 3:21–26 and 4:5.[7]

Here we see that faith alone without any meritorious works from us constitutes our entry into salvation. We see also a clear

---

6   Leith, *Creeds*, 36.
7   Leith, *Creeds*, 69.

statement that only by what Christ has done and suffered are forgiveness and righteousness obtained. All of this is arranged in the wisdom of God "by grace." All of it must be commended "before God" and its sum of effectuality comes with the words "for God will regard and reckon." The whole tightly stated exposition arises, not from councils or tradition or papal decrees but from Scripture.

The Westminster Confession of Faith (1646) gives powerful undiluted witness to the Reformation principles. *Sola scriptura* is asserted in paragraph 6 of chapter 1:

> "The whole counsel of God, concerning all things necessary for his own glory, man's salvation, faith, and life, is either expressly set down in Scripture, or by good and necessary consequence may be deduced from Scripture; unto which nothing at any time is to be added, whether by new revelations of the Spirit, or traditions of men."

In its discussion of saving faith, the confession says, "By this faith a Christian believeth to be true whatsoever is revealed in the Word, for the authority of God himself speaking therein."[8]

Sola fide, stated or implied in many places finds unwavering expression in these words of chapter 11, paragraph 2:

> "Faith, thus receiving and resting on Christ and his righteousness, is the alone instrument of justification; yet it is not alone in the person justified, but is ever accompanied with all other saving graces, and is no dead faith, but worketh by love."[9]

---

8   Leith, *Creeds*, 195, 209.

9   Leith, *Creeds*, 207.

Solo Christo saturates the confession with power and beauty exquisitely in chapter 8 "Of Christ the Mediator" and also in this sentence in chapter 11, paragraph 1:

> "Those whom God effectually calleth he also freely justifieth; not by infusing righteousness into them, but by pardoning their sins, and by accounting and accepting their persons as righteous: not for any thing wrought in them or done by them, but for Christ's sake alone."

Again, under the doctrine of "Saving Faith," the confession reads, "The principal acts of saving faith are accepting, receiving, and resting upon Christ alone for justification, sanctification, and eternal life, by virtue of the covenant of grace."[10]

As with the others, the principle of *sola gratia* flows in mighty rushing waters as well as through small rivulets in this confession. We find that all the actions and motives of predestination are done "to the praise of his glorious grace." Under the topic of "Free Will" the confession says, "When God converts a sinner, and translates him into the state of grace, he freeth him from his natural bondage under sin, and by his grace alone enables him freely to will and to do that which is spiritually good." Similarly, under effectual calling, God's elect "come most freely, being made willing by his grace."[11]

That all the decrees of the covenants and the works of creation, providence, revelation and redemption are done to the glory of God alone—*soli deo gloria*—permeates the confession. "The whole counsel of God, concerning all things necessary for his own glory" is found in Scripture. God's very being infinite in all moral perfection, incomprehensible in being, eternal in duration, omnipotent in all

---

10   Leith, *Creeds*, 207, 209.
11   Leith, *Creeds*, 198, 205, 206.

his actions, pure and utterly whole in act and extension, "most wise, most holy, most free, most absolute, [works] all things according to the counsel of his own immutable and most righteous will, for his own glory." Concerning the decrees of God, the confession affirms in chapter 3, paragraph 3, "By the decree of God, for the manifestation of his glory, some men and angels are predestined unto everlasting life, and others foreordained to everlasting death." All works of providence are done "to the praise of the glory of his wisdom, power, justice, goodness, and mercy." In the final chapter entitled "On the Final Judgment," the writers acknowledge that "the end of God's appointing this day is for the manifestation of the glory of his mercy in the eternal salvation of the elect; and of his justice in the damnation of the reprobate, who are wicked and disobedient."[12]

Soli deo gloria along with the other *solas* must be considered as dogma, settled truths pervasively shaping the whole biblical narrative, to be declared and declaimed within the church by God-qualified and God-called preachers of truth.

We will not extend this discussion, but one could identify settled and biblically coherent truths that define distinctive Baptist theology. The baptism of believers only, regenerate church membership, liberty of conscience, the qualifications for the teaching office of the church and a few other distinctive doctrines must be maintained. Because these are biblical doctrines and concern the purity and earthly witness of the bride of Christ, these doctrines should not be considered as of inferior importance for faithfulness to a full biblical witness.

---

12 Leith, *Creeds*, 195, 197, 198, 200, 229.

In the Interest of Eternity

Declamation of dogma serves the interests of eternity. This kind of preaching says, "Do not labor for the food that perishes, but for the food which endures to everlasting life, which the Son of Man will give you" (John 6:27). He sees what the Preacher saw when he observed, "All the labor of man is for his mouth, and yet the soul is not satisfied" (Eccl 6:7). The minister of dogma sets in urgent context the "dust will return to the earth as it was, and the spirit will return to God who gave it." And then, no matter what one's status has been in society, how one fared in the realm of human justice, whether oppressed or oppressor, "God will bring every work into judgment, including every secret thing, whether good or evil" (Eccl 11:7, 14). All labors, accolades, humors, and pleasures invested merely in temporal interest without an awareness and intention toward the glory of God will wither under the heat of divine judgment.

Christians must learn to contextualize the alluring appeal of the Social Gospel. Many of the calls of the Social Gospel have compelling plausibility for the Christian who would like to see the social implications of redemptive truth permeate the entire social order. While redeemed persons work, earn, and speak honestly, seek to live justly and generously, live as salt and light in a corrupt and dark world, they do not reinterpret the work of Christ in temporal terms. In defending his views on social redemption to the minimization of eternal redemption, Walter Rauschenbusch wrote:

> Western theology saw salvation mainly as forgiveness of guilt and freedom from punishment. It interpreted the work of Christ accordingly, and laid stress on the death and atonement. If the Kingdom of God was the guiding idea and chief end of Jesus—as we now know it was—we may be sure that every step in His life, including his death, was related to that aim and its

realization, and when the idea of the Kingdom of God takes its due place in theology, the work of Christ will have to be interpreted afresh.[13]

Rauschenbusch set aside "the legal fiction of imputation" as explanatory of either sin, or atonement, or justification. All elements of forensic salvation he rejected as outdated and morally indefensible. Rauschenbusch gave a strange turn to the relation of Jesus' death to His relation to the Father. He looks at Christ's death as a refusal to capitulate to the sinful power of society and thus His "supreme act, also, of obedience to God, to which he was moved by love to God and loyalty to his kingdom." This show of courage, loyalty, and love enhanced "his power to assimilate others to his God-consciousness and to gather a new humanity."[14]

No ontological deity of Christ does Rauschenbusch require, and so no Trinity; no imputation or substitution are necessary, and thus there is no assurance that the "blood of Jesus Christ His Son cleanses us from all sin" (1 John 1:7). Dogma is dead and so are sinners. Rauschenbusch and a host of his fellow modernist deniers of dogma have led much of the church into the haunted uncertainties that confront mortals: "It is appointed unto man once to die, and after this the judgment." Dismal the darkness for they have substituted the temporal for the infinitely larger reality of the eternal. They have substituted a sense of temporal well-being and stability for the joyful hope, "So Christ was offered once to bear the sins of many. To those who eagerly wait for him He will appear a second time, apart from sin, for salvation" (Heb 9:27–28).

---

13   Walter Rauschenbusch, *A Theology for the Social Gospel* (New York: the Macmillan Company, 1922), 144.

14   Rauschenbusch, *A Theology*, 240–248, 266.

Doctrinal Preaching Is Always Christological

Faithful declamation of dogma is unexceptionally Christ-centered. The goal of the preacher should be the goal of God, "the summing up of all things in Christ, things in heaven and things on the earth" (Eph 1:10 NASB). One should always ask, "How does the Spirit, in this text, lead me to Christ?" From creation ("For by Him all things were created, … He is before all things, and in Him all things consist" [Col 1:16–17 NASB]) to consummation ("'Yes, I am coming quickly.' Amen. Come Lord Jesus. The grace of the Lord Jesus be with all. Amen" [Rev 22:20–21 NASB]) the Scripture unfolds His story. He is the seed promised in Genesis 3:15; he is the seed through whom Abraham would be a blessing to all nations and the one who gives substance to the "everlasting covenant" (Gen 17:7); he holds the scepter of Judah (Genesis 49:10); he is the one in whom the throne of David will be established forever (2 Sam 7:16). He is the one through whom the "everlasting covenant" and the "faithful mercies shown to David" gain substance (Isa 55:3). He is the "Sun of righteousness … with healing in his wings" (Mal 4:2). The New Testament begins, "The book of the genealogy of Jesus Christ, the Son of David, the Son of Abraham" (Matt 1:1); Mark opens with the announcement, "The beginning of the gospel of Jesus Christ, the Son of God" (Mark 1:1). Luke engages his reader with a carefully arranged narrative leading to the angelic announcement to Mary, "And behold you will conceive in your womb and bring forth a Son, and shall call his name Jesus. He will be great, and will be called the Son of the Highest; and the Lord God will give Him the throne of His father David. And He will reign over the house of Jacob forever, and of His kingdom there will be no end" (Luke 1:31–33). John reaches into eternity past, "In the beginning was the Word, and the Word was with God, and the Word was God. He was in the beginning with God" (John 1:1, 2).

Jesus claimed God as His Father making Himself "equal with God" and told His alarmed resisters, "If you believed Moses, you would believe me; for he wrote about Me" (John 5:18, 46). After His resurrection, Jesus gave a lesson in right biblical interpretation to some confused and slightly bewildered followers, "O foolish ones, and slow of heart to believe in all that the prophets have spoken! Ought not the Christ to have suffered these things and to enter into His glory?" Knowing that the claim needed illumination to their cloudy minds, Jesus began at "Moses and all the prophets [and] expounded to them in all the Scripture the things concerning Himself" (Luke 24:25–27). Hebrews 3:1 admonishes those who share together in a heavenly calling to give intense mental reflection toward Jesus, the Apostle and High Priest of their confession. Their *confession* is the propositional content of revealed truth (See also 1 Tim 6:12–13). Jesus is its Apostle, meaning that he is the one who is sent with the message that all the promises, types, and ceremonies are fulfilled. Jesus also is its High Priest. He is the One who has executed the final sacrifice that constitutes the perfect fulfillment of God's eternal purpose of revelation and grace. Our preaching must be just as Christ-centered as the intent of God in Scripture.

In 1881, Charles Spurgeon was greatly energized by biblical critics of the nineteenth century seeking to tame the itinerant prophet claiming to be the Son of God, the atonement for sin, and the way, the truth, and the life. They wanted him "rectified and squared," a good moral teacher that matched the interests of modern thought. In preaching, they wanted elegant, logical, rational, advice bypassing all the outdated palaver about sin and depravity, repentance and faith, substitution and wrath, and a Savior from sin to be the most urgent and greatest need of humanity. Spurgeon countered, "A sermon without Christ as its beginning, middle, and end is a mistake in conception and a crime in execution." No matter how grand the language or the contemporaneity of its thought, it is "merely much-ado-about-nothing if Christ be not there." And he made it clear that he was not speaking about Christ as an example or his teaching of ethical precepts, but "his atoning blood, his wondrous satisfaction made for human sin … If justification by faith be not set in the very forefront in the full blaze of light, nothing can be accomplished."

So many writing in the "Life of Christ" genre know little to nothing about the meaning and urgent mission of Jesus but they seek "to rectify certain of his dogmas, especially such as justification by faith, or atonement, or the doctrine of election." As for Spurgeon, "We must preach the gospel for Christ has revealed it." Those who do "not acknowledge Christ to be all" have "virtually left him out, and are without him."[15] In this same year, 1881, Lord Shaftesbury observed and wrote to Spurgeon, "Signal as are the talents that God has bestowed upon you, they would without preaching Christ in all his majestic simplicity have availed you nothing to comfort and instruct the hearts of thousands."[16]

Neither the person of Jesus nor the dogmas surrounding His work need to be rectified. Our task is that unashamed declamation of dogmatic truth be the constant output of our teaching ministry. Phil Newton has made the point that an important part of our common task as Christians is to build one another up doctrinally. We are to contend earnestly "for the once-for-all-handed-down-faith." Pastor Newton, like Spurgeon, points to *the truths that we*

---

15   Charles Spurgeon, "Without Christ—Nothing," in Metropolitan Tabernacle Pulpit, 1881 (London: The Banner of Truth Trust, 1971), 598, 599.

16   Richard Ellsworth Day, *The Shadow of the Broad Brim* (Philadelphia: The Judson Press, 1934), 227.

know as the gospel of Jesus Christ. It's the truth that we stand upon and live in as Christ's followers." We cannot talk about the gospel "without talking doctrinally." When some may suggest that "we don't need doctrine; we just need Jesus," Phil asked, "What Jesus do we need? Do we need the Jesus of Arianism that is not God? Or do we need the Jesus of the Bible who is fully God and fully man? To speak in these terms is to speak doctrinally."[17] The declamation of dogma is vital to Newton's ongoing ministry.

Dogma Is Always a Servant of Grace

Declamation of dogma, because relentlessly Christological, always infuses the reality of grace in its proclamations and exhortations. "Of His fullness we have all received, and grace for grace" (John 1:16). The fullness of Christ involves His eternal pre-existence, His eternal Sonship, His covenantal relations, His Incarnation, His human life of perfect obedience, His voluntary, substitutionary death, His resurrection, His ascension, His present session and intercession, and His promise to return, to receive us to Himself, to transform us into the perfection of His human holiness, and His giving us the joy and glory of His own relationship with the Father through the fullness of the presence of the Spirit. His fullness is the fountain from which all grace flows, from which every expansion of God's gracious dealing with His elect develops—grace upon grace. Christian conversion, knowledge, and growth arises from expanding spheres of grace that permeate God's purpose.

In Romans 4:16, Paul says that "It is of faith that it may be according to grace." As our declamation includes all that is meant by "faith" both objective as a revelation and subjectively embraced as a grace (2 Tim 4:7; Jude 3, 20; Rom 5:1; Eph 2:8; 1 Tim 1:19

---

17 Phil Newton, *Sermon,* "A Pattern for Christian Living," Jude 17–23.

[both subjective and objective]) so the preaching of faith flows with grace. Thus, it is by faith that it may be by grace. The word "faith" refers both to the objective deposit of revelation and the receptivity of mind and heart in order to seal the truth that everything revealed must be believed. By faith one recognizes that God performs the work of salvation from its inception to its culmination (1 Cor 1:26–31). God has chosen all who receive, and Christ has become all that they need to receive.

To preach about eternity must involve God's purpose and grace before the ages began and redound "to the praise of the glory of his grace" (2 Tim 1:9; Eph 1:6). To preach about creation must involve the conviction that, in this, God sets in motion His decrees of grace ("All things were created through Him and for Him" [Col 1:16]). To preach about revelation announces God's voluntary condescension in gracious disclosure ("the dispensation of the grace of God which was given to me for you, how that by revelation He made known to me the mystery" [Eph 3:2–3]). The entire Christ event as unfolded in history will be the subject of constant and increasing delight in heaven. We will be made exponentially cognizant of "the exceeding riches of His grace in His kindness toward us in Christ Jesus, for by grace you have been saved through faith" (Eph 2:7–8). Nothing about which God's ministers are called to preach subsists apart from grace or outside the circumference of grace.

Conclusion

The gospel preacher does not deal in uncertainties. He communicates from divine revelation truths that are clear and consistently framed throughout the biblical corpus. He does not have options about what to include and what to omit. Spurgeon's preface to the 1861 *Metropolitan Tabernacle Pulpit*, the year in which the congregation entered the newly constructed place of worship and ministry, sounded this certainty with typical Spurgeonic conviction:

> In the matter of gospel doctrine, we trust no reader will perceive any variation. No new gospel have we aimed to declare. More faith is needed, but not a new creed; a firmer confidence, but not a better covenant; a stronger trust, but not a more solid foundation. Developments, discoveries, and theorizings, we are content to leave to those who, having never tasted the old wine, are naturally thirsty for the new. Our colours are nailed to the mast, and in doctrine we take for our motto, *"semper idem."*[18]

The whole Bible about a whole Christ who operates out of the provisions of a grace-permeated covenant is the constant authoritative source for the God-called steward of revealed truth. Phil Newton enters the pulpit with a deep and fascinated sense of biblical authority. Considering the very presence of apostles and the call to remember their spoken words, Phil reminded his congregation, that even if "Peter or John or Paul had visited with them and spoken the word to them," we should find amazement "in that the apostolic message—the New Testament—has been handed down to us in written form." While first-century Christians were admonished to "remember the words *'spoken beforehand*,'" we may do essentially the same thing since "we have the apostolic words in the twenty-seven books of the New Testament."[19]

This is the unvarying content of declamation. The gospel minister must not be embarrassed to be dogmatic in this sense. He should find the freedom of declamation to be the delightful burden and great privilege of his calling.

---

18   Charles H. Spurgeon, *The Metropolitan Tabernacle Pulpit, 1861* (Pasadena, TX: Pilgrim Publications, 1973), v. The Latin means "always the same.

19   Phil Newton, "A Pattern for Christian Living," Jude 17–23.

Appendix of Appreciation
for Dr. Phil Newton

From Michael Dirrim:

Dear Pastor Phil,

Thank you for your generous, constructive and hopeful investment in my life. I am the pastor I am today because of those formative days in which you played such a pivotal role. Even though our time together was brief, just a couple of years, you gave me a great deal of your time. You maximized our conversations for my good. You compelled me to serve in ways I had not considered myself capable.

I will always remember your exhortations to love the people, to "rare back and preach!" and to always preach Christ. Your humble encouragements have stuck with me all these years. When a young man interrupts me for help, as I train men to teach and preach, each time I lead an elders meeting, I think of you and your warm and generous approach. Thank you for giving me opportunities to preach and teach and taking time to critique, counsel, and commend.

You were very patient with me in my ignorance. You were salutatory towards me in groups of men far my betters. You were passionate in defense of the gospel when under attack. You depended on your fellow elders for wisdom and encouragement. You were sometimes weary, sometimes invigorated, sometimes sorrowful, sometimes joyous. I saw you as a pastor in these contexts, as my pastor, because you invited me in and let me understand a taste of what was to come in my ministry.

Thank you for preaching full and forthright messages. Thank you for the continued prayers, support and encouragement over the years. Thank you for being there the day my wife gave birth to our first child. Thank you for answering the phone and praying with me when my mother died. Thank you for recommending me to my first pastorate. Thank you for leading my ordination council. God conveyed so much grace through you to me in such a short time. Praise be to God! I thank Him upon every remembrance of you.

I have many memories of you as my pastor, but I will close my letter with my favorite. On the last hymn before a sermon that I was to preach, I was instructed to be up on stage next to you. As we sang together, I was vitally encouraged by the gusto of your hymn singing. It has been my favorite hymn ever since. I can still hear your voice sounding forth:

> *Lo! th'incarnate God ascended,*
> *Pleads the merit of His blood;*
> *Venture on Him, venture wholly,*
> *Let no other trust intrude:*
> > *None but Jesus*
> > *None but Jesus*
> > *None but Jesus*
> *Can do helpless sinners good.*

Grace and Peace,

Michael Dirrim

Pastor, Sunnyside Baptist Church

Oklahoma City, OK

From Randy McLendon:

It would be hard to express my gratitude for the love shown to me and my family by Phil Newton and South Woods Baptist Church. After serving as a pastor for some 12 years, I often reflect on how beneficial it was for me to prepare for ministry under Phil. He, the elders at South Woods, and the congregation as a whole invested heavily in me, and by God's grace, the fruit of that investment is reaping fruit for the Kingdom.

My family and I arrived at South Woods sometime around the year 2000. We were immediately drawn to this church because of its worship service, which displayed their commitment to the Word of God. I had begun to have a desire for ministry years earlier and had plans to attend seminary soon, which I eventually did. But in time, Phil helped me understand that the training ground for ministry was the local church. Seminary could be helpful; some might even say necessary. But it cannot replace what the local church does in the way of preparation for pastoral ministry.

How did Phil and South Woods help prepare me? First, as we regularly attended worship gatherings, Phil's faithful verse-by-verse exposition of Scripture became a model for me. There are many, many books on how to preach, and many of them are quite helpful. But nothing can substitute time under a faithful expositor. Phil was certainly this, and more. I would eventually be asked to participate in a pastoral internship, where Phil directed me to several good books I would read, along with some writing assignments. There were also many helpful "hands-on" sessions where we discussed many of the ins and outs of preaching. His kind but fair critiques along the way were of great assistance to a young preacher trying to learn the ropes. Phil allowed me to preach some, putting into practice everything I was learning under his gracious, guiding hand.

I would eventually be asked to serve South Woods as one of their elders. Phil oversaw our monthly elder's meetings, and it was here that another valuable aspect of leadership was observed. It was in these meetings that we prayed for the church and discussed all the various matters that come up in congregational life. I soon learned that pastoring was much more than preaching. I knew preaching was central to the ministry, but Phil also taught and modeled the importance of prayer, exercising godly wisdom, and working together as elders. Phil's continual display of love for Christ and His church will have an unceasing impact on me. I'm so thankful to the Lord for my time serving under him and alongside him.

Shepherding together,
Randy McLendon
Pastor, Trinity Reformed Baptist Church
Memphis, TN

From Jason Murphy:

I am probably the least qualified to write about Dr. Phil Newton. I have only known him for approximately four years. During those four years, there has been limited personal interaction. Yet, Dr. Newton has positively influenced and impacted my life and ministry. The fact that our interactions have been limited and yet he has impacted the ministry speaks to his character and leadership.

When I hear his name or think about, Dr. Phil Newton, several things come to mind about his character. The first thing that comes to mind is that he is a Christian gentleman. He treats everyone with kindness and respect. The second thing that comes to mind is that he is genuine. There is no pretense in him. He is comfortable being who he is and who God shaped and molded him to be. The third thing that comes to mind is that he is committed.

He is committed to the Lord. He is committed to the Scripture. He is committed to his wife and family. He is committed to the church. He is committed to the ministry. He is committed to faithfully preaching the Word of God. He is committed to serving. He serves his family, church family, fellow ministers, and those preparing for the ministry. The afore mentioned list was not an exhaustive list. Hopefully, it was enough to show that Dr. Newton is a man of Christian character.

When I hear the name or think about, Dr. Phil Newton, several other things come to mind concerning his leadership. The first thing that comes to mind about his leadership is that it is recognizable. Those fortunate enough to spend time around him naturally recognize his leadership. The second thing that comes to mind is that he is wise. Wisdom seems to flow from him. The third thing that comes to mind is he is approachable. He is available for you to approach him about various issues and scenarios related to ministry. When you approach him, he is ready to answer your questions, calm your concerns, or help you think through the complexities of ministry situations by pointing you to Scripture and exalting Christ. The fourth thing that comes to mind is his example. Dr. Newton practices what he preaches. His example is a leadership lesson in and of itself.

Dr. Newton's character and leadership positively impacted my ministry. It caused me to evaluate my ministry philosophy and purpose. It caused me to reflect on what it means to be a pastor. On that note, Dr. Newton's book, *40 Questions About Pastoral Ministry*, is a worthy addition to any pastor's library. Lastly, Dr. Phil Newton influenced and impacted my ministry by simply persevering. He is a living example of what it looks like to persevere in the Christian life and ministry. His example inspires me to persevere in the face of hardship and to "fight the good fight of faith" (1 Tim 6:12 ESV).

Servant of the King,
Dr. Jason Murphy
Pastor, Grace Chapel
Collierville, TN

From Bill Murray:

When I first met Phil Newton in the mid-80s, he was a freshly minted Doctor of Ministry grad from Fuller. He came to Memphis to be the founding pastor of a new church plant. The young church soon moved to a building given the nickname "The Alamo" due to its exterior walls being covered in large stones. We had some longtime friends who were part of that church start up, and so we had an "inside line" on the church's growth and ministry.

I was able to see Phil's dedication and the challenges he faced as he determined to serve the Lord there. He "kept the faith" and plowed ahead, determined to do his best to honor our Lord. The Lord blessed, and the church grew. However, some trying times were on the horizon. As it seems with all church plants, the newness soon wore off; and the church began to struggle. Yet, Phil remained dedicated to "the Word" and the God's Word.

When some folk with "itching ears" began to stir, Phil stuck with preaching the word as he was learning from our Lord and growing in his own faith. The Lord used the challenges to strengthen and to grow Phil for the days ahead. I was watching all this while I was serving in my first pastorate just across Mississippi state line and doing doctoral work. Little did I know that some difficult times lay ahead for me as well. I saw some troubling things with men in the ministry and became quite disenchanted with the idea of continuing.

This caused me to spend some time with Elijah in the cave. Even so, I still had an eye on Phil and saw his perseverance during his trials. This, along with some wise council from a mentor, reminded me that, as Paul said, "We must through much tribulation enter into the kingdom of God."

Some years after graduation and searching for a place to serve, the Lord led us to join with Phil and the now ten-year-old church (approx.) where we served joyfully for a number of years by teaching Sunday School, Biblical doctrine, church history, and doing missions. This allowed me to get "up close and personal" with Phil. I saw how the Lord can and will use one who stays on the path with Him, no matter the trials, no matter the cost. Our Lord later opened a place of ministry for me as a professor in a fine, small liberal arts university in the hills of South Carolina. But again, difficulties lay ahead.

Phil was diagnosed with a rare form of cancer, and his future looked quite dim. However, true to his character (and our Lord's who worked through him), he did not give up. He "attacked" M. D. Anderson hospital, and all of us who knew the situation "attacked" our Lord with prayer. The rest of the story is known to all who know Phil. He still carries on with vigor in serving our Lord, though both he and I are adding on the years. And so, the Lord has used him to encourage me and to bless me by reminding me that our lives are in the palm of His hand. He has called us to remain faithful and to persevere to the end. Phil has shown me this; may I follow his example.

Bill W. Murray, PhD
Professor, College of Christian Studies
North Greenville University
Greenville, SC

From Nathaniel Perry:

I want to make a few remarks concerning what Pastor Phil Newton means to me. First, he invited me to be a pastoral intern at South Woods as I was beginning my studies in seminary. For the first time in my life, I had a pastor to invest his time in me. His exposition of Scripture in his preaching was the bulk of my education but his help with looking at different ministry issues was also beneficial. He was patient with me as I began to learn from him as an intern. I felt way behind in my theological development, but Pastor Phil certainly helped me to exercise discipline to focus and study.

Phil helped me in sharing his ministry experiences in dealing with weddings, conducting funerals, and preaching. The Lord has gifted Pastor Phil to help young men in their calling to pursue the pulpit. He always encouraged me as I made progress in my preaching. The central focus of a sermon should be the gospel of Christ and Pastor Phil helped me to do that from different books of the Bible.

He also enabled me with to focus on a text of Scripture and how to rightly interpret it with biblical hermeneutics. I also learned that if a church needs change and reform, then a pastor will have to be there for the long haul. I was just glad that I could receive help from a local church so that I could be better prepared to later serve as a pastor.

I currently glean from Pastor Phil as I deal with complex issues in my church now and he is always prompt in responding. I learned from him that most churches that are in need of change are simply not ready, even if they would be healthy and helpful changes.

A pastor's job is to help his church to think more biblically concerning both method and doctrine. At South Woods I got to see both as Pastor Phil's goal was to keep the church biblically focused on the centrality of Christ.

Phil's approach to explain Scripture with the desire to see the believer mature, brought help to me in the current situations of my life. His application of Scripture was uplifting and encouraging. My favorite sermon was his review of the 11 chapters of Romans. It provided encouragement and a drive to press on in the gospel ministry.

Due to my exposure of Romans from his preaching, I think about the many doctrines that have sunk deep in my heart, namely the glory of Christ in saving sinners by faith. He helped to shape how I think about God, the church, and doing the work of ministry. When I first came to him, he had his arms wide open to me. And I was in dire need of direction and focus. I was prepared well through Pastor Phil's preaching and care. He is still a significant help to me today. He shepherds the flock well.

Nathan Perry
Pastor, Lexa Baptist Church
Lexa, AR

From Zane G. Pratt:

16 September 2024

Dear Phil,

You and I have known each other for almost three decades, and you have been a blessing to me and my family that entire time. I remember meeting you at an annual meeting of the Southern Baptist Convention. I had recently returned to the United States on furlough after my first four-year term overseas, and I was in massive reverse culture shock. You were one of a small group of pastors and friends who helped me keep my bearings that week! You and your church subsequently adopted my family and our work in Central Asia. I remember with great fondness times you visited us on the field, and every trip back to the States had to include a visit to Memphis to spend time with you. Your church showered kindness on us during our years overseas. My kids still remember Uncle Phil and Aunt Karen and the great memories they have of you. You guys blessed us more than you will ever know.

When I think of you and your ministry, several things stand out. At the top of the list is your wonderful combination of kindness and conviction. You know what you believe, and I happen to think you are right in those beliefs! You have thought through your theological convictions with depth and skill, and you articulate them well. At the same time, you never come across as harsh or demeaning toward those who disagree with you, but the fruit of the Spirit of kindness and gentleness characterize your interactions with others. You are the consummate pastor, which is why your current role with Pillar Network is a perfect fit for you. Your writing is clear and deep, and many have been helped by the books you have penned.

I was sad when you announced your retirement from the church you pastored for so many years, but it gave me joy when you embraced your current role. As a member of a Pillar Network church, I am very glad that you are pastoring other pastors in a church movement I believe in deeply. I look forward to many more years of fruitful ministry for you, and of fellowship between you and me. Thank you for your faithfulness to our Savior!

In His grace,

Zane G. Pratt

Vice President, Training,

International Mission Board, SBC

Associate Professor of Christian Mission, SBTS

From Nathan Sawyer:

When asked to write a letter of encouragement as a friend of Phil Newton, it was an easy "yes." I have known Phil for nearly 20 years and despite the demands associated with pastoring a church along with the opportunities he was given to speak and write, his friendship was always personal. You mattered to Phil.

I want to thank God for this dear brother through three brief vignettes.

First: Encouragement and example to a young pastor

Our church was planted in the same city as South Woods and one of our earliest conversations was with Phil and the elders of South Woods. I am not sure of all we discussed that evening. This I do remember. When we shared the location for where we were going to gather as a church, he looked at his fellow pastors to inquire of a family visiting their church that was near the neighborhood we were planting. He suggested they encourage this family to consider visiting our church since we were closer to them. I was 28 at the time, had grown up in a church culture where it was common for people to jump from one church to the next and where it was common to attempt to make your church more appealing than other churches in the same area. This was the first example I had seen where the kingdom of God was more important than one pastors church. He cared about other churches.

Second: Reaching out to pray when my sister passed

Phil was on sabbatical when my sister suddenly passed away a couple of years ago. The morning of her service I was up early both grieving and preparing. An email shot in my inbox. It was Phil offering sorrow and prayers. He was on sabbatical and took the time early in the morning to convey his love and prayers for my grief. When I replied to thank him for reaching out on his sabbatical he kindly sent, "You can contact me anytime. Sabbatical is not a barrier for a beloved brother."

Third: Joy

This is less of an event and more of what Phil embodies (Gal 5:22). He is marked with joy in the Lord. In the face of church challenges, cancer and just the complexities and hardships that accompany life Phil's joy in Jesus has remained steadfast (1 Cor 15:58).

I thank the Lord for this dear brother and count it a blessing to know him as a friend and faithful servant of our Lord Jesus.

Nathan Sawyer
Elder, Grace Church Memphis
Memphis, TN

From Bryan Smith:

Sunday, August 18, 2024

Dear Phil,

I am immensely thankful for the Lord's kindness to myself and fellow pastors in Memphis through your life of preaching, pastoral ministry, and friendship.

My life, for one, has been impacted by your many years of faithful labors, especially in the pulpit. Your humble transformation into more gospel-centered Christ-exalting preaching has served as both an example and comfort to my own soul and ministry. Your careful treatment of each biblical text and pastoral heart bleed through in your sermons.

Pastorally, God has used you to both train and pastor local pastors. Not many pastors in the Memphis-area have escaped your good pastoral influence. I have personally benefited from the phone calls and conversations over the years where you have gently imparted both instruction and wisdom. I'll never forget the three young pastors of Grace Church just starting out in the church planting endeavor receiving sound advice back in 2006. I have always felt supported and encouraged by your words in each interaction.

Perhaps most encouraging is your friendship. Your good influence and brotherly love has been evident in every context we have crossed paths. You have been marked by the aroma of Christ, not only in church settings, but also in secular settings like basketball gymnasiums, restaurants, or weddings. You are dependable, gracious, and warm, and I am happy to call you, my friend.

Brother, my sincere hope is that the Lord will continue to use you for His glory in Memphis for the remainder of your days on earth until you are able to see Jesus' face to face. You are loved!

Your partner in the gospel,
Bryan Smith
Elder, Grace Church Memphis
Memphis, TN

From James Tarrance:

Two challenges lay before me: 1) to adequately detail my appreciation for Phil Newton's impact on my life, my family, and my ministry in only 500 words, and 2) to do so with Phil's voice in my mind instructing me not to make much of man, but to give all honor to "the LORD God and His Christ!" I met Phil in 2011 on our first Lord's Day visit to South Woods Baptist Church in Memphis. From that day forward, he has modeled a ministry firmly bound to the Scriptures and resolutely fixated on the glory of Christ Jesus.

Phil impressed upon me the paramount need for careful biblical exposition through his pulpit ministry and weekly discipleship at pastoral internship meetings. Through faithful teaching and living, he showed me the preciousness of the local church, unfolding before me a healthy ecclesiology. He showed me how to minister the Bible to families in hospital by doing so for my wife and me at the birth of our second child. He coached me in preaching true hope in Christ at my first funeral. His book *Conducting Gospel-Centered Funerals* laid a foundation for my bereavement care. He exemplified compassion, love, and confidence in God through trials.

I found my own soul invigorated by his trust and faith in King Jesus in the face of his personal health disaster. His zeal for the lost globally and leadership in missions opened my eyes to how a local congregation can effectively engage in long-term international mission work. He helped me think scripturally when evaluating fads in American church life. He challenged me by his academic rigor, rolling up his sleeves and preparing for all manner of ministry opportunities with relentless study. Phil is a machine! I once explained to him how dreadfully busy my schedule was with full-time work, full-time seminary studies, and a growing family. Instead of giving me sympathy and well wishes for an easier load, he shocked me, saying, "Good! I am glad to hear it. It is good for you." I have not gotten over how productive the man is and the pace at which he blazes ahead. Yet, Phil is not too busy for the small things that often matter most. He learned my children's names and interests, encouraged my wife in the daily grind of motherhood and homeschool challenges, and remembered the spiritual needs of my distant family members he never knew.

Phil continued to mentor me even after we moved away. When the Lord opened the opportunity to enter pastoral ministry, Phil guided me through the candidate process. He has been a trusted counsellor in difficult pastoral moments, all the while applying the Word, fighting for the health of my marriage and family, and championing Christ's Bride who needs faithful, long-term shepherds. Most recently he has guided me in preparing for an imposing sermon series. When I read Hebrews 13:7, Phil Newton comes to mind. I appreciate you, dear brother! SDG.

James Tarrance
North Hills Church
West Monroe, LA

From Don Whitney:

Lord's Day
September 22, 2024
Kansas City, MO

It is an honor and joy to write words of appreciation for my friend, Phil Newton.

At this writing, I have known Phil for more than forty years. He is, in the words of one of Spurgeon's best-known writings for pastors, a man with an *All-Round Ministry*. He is a pastor, a preacher, a counselor, a writer, a teacher, a witness, a disciple-maker, and much more. Few ministers are skilled in all these aspects of ministry, but Phil is.

Phil has always been a man of God; a Christ-centered man in all respects. He is a man of the Word—he loves the Word of God, believes it implicitly, lives under its supreme authority in all areas of life, and preaches it faithfully and unflinchingly. He is a man of the Reformation, rejoicing in all five *Solas*.

Phil is a faithful man—faithful to his wife and family, to his calling as a minister of the gospel, and to his word. He is appropriately serious-minded about all things related to his Lord, yet I have never seen him anything but cheerful and friendly around others. His joy is contagious.

It seems that all those whom God has used greatly have been called to suffer greatly. Phil is no exception. But he has been exceptional in the way he has suffered with faithfulness, patience, perseverance, and joy.

All the above has resulted in Phil rightly becoming a pastor to pastors. In many ways this began many years ago, but since then this ministry has increased in extent and intensified in fruitfulness. I have rejoiced in watching this, for it is the result of a life of faithfulness, consistency, character, and Christlikeness.

May the Lord give many more years of fruitful ministry to my friend and brother, Phil Newton.

By His grace and for His glory,
Donald S. Whitney
Professor of Biblical Spirituality
John H. Powell Professor of Pastoral Ministry
Midwestern Baptist Theological Seminary

From Chris Wilbanks:

In July of 2001, my expectant wife and I moved to Memphis, Tennessee, so I could attend a local seminary. We were trusting the good hand of God to direct our paths, confident that time in this modest city would bring us a few steps closer to our long-term plans of serving Jesus far away from Grizzlies and Graceland. Little did we understand that a local church tucked away in the southeast corner of Shelby County would become a marvelous, long-term detour from our overseas strategy. The sovereignty I would learn so much about through that very church's teaching and preaching was the very sovereignty directing our clumsy steps. We have been astonished by the cords of kindness our Father has shown to us through the years as members of South Woods Baptist Church. He has drawn us near, protects us from our best laid plans, and continues to pursue us in love. All our lines have fallen in pleasant places, indeed.

One feature of this new fellowship that immediately drew us in was the careful exposition of God's word. Though familiar to our spiritual appetites, expository preaching remained foreign to our church experiences. During those initial Sundays we felt like our son, who would jump inside my wife's womb at the sound of this new voice thundering the gospel of grace. Here it was! No frills. No frivolity. No oral flourishes meant to woo or wow. Just the simplicity of opening a text, getting the sense of it, while featuring Scripture's central figurehead—the crucified and risen Christ! Of course, the slightly southern, *Alabamian* accent declaring such riches was none other than the person to whom this work is dedicated.

In time, that voice would become more than just the sound of one of the best preachers I have known in my 48 years of inhaling and exhaling God's unending provisions. Behind that voice was a faithful pastor and a steady friend, always there through my own deepest sorrows and highest joys.

The contents of this festschrift have set out to suitably honor the life and ministry of Phil Newton. Because I have spent countless hours with Phil in difficult trenches and joyful mountaintops, I have confidence that he will suitably (and not so subtly) honor his Lord as he holds in his large, yet gentle hands, this compiled effort from the brotherhood. *"The fear of the LORD is instruction in wisdom, and humility comes before honor"* (Prov 15:33).

Chris Wilbanks
Elder/Minister, South Woods Baptist Church
Memphis, TN

From Jeremy Wright:

As a beneficiary of Phil's ministry, I am immensely grateful to see him honored with this volume of essays. His life and ministry have impacted countless lives through local church ministry; his writing, teaching in conferences and seminary classrooms, and his work encouraging pastors through networks, associations, and denominational life. When Paul encourages the Philippian church to "honor such men" speaking of Timothy and Epaphroditus, I cannot help but think of faithful servants like Phil who have modeled Timothy's pastoral heart for decades: "For I have no one like him, who will be genuinely concerned for your welfare" (Phil 2:20). Phil's ministry impact is born out of that genuine concern to see Christ glorified in the welfare of his saints and that impact is echoing out now through multiple generations of pastors who have been recipients of his wisdom and care.

For years I have benefited from Phil's contagious hope, an optimism formed by the gospel that Christ will build His church for His glory. His hope was evident in conversations over difficult member-care situations, in his walk-through cancer treatments and recovery, and in his eagerness to serve the next generation of pastors. I have been able to watch firsthand as Phil's deeply rooted conviction that Christ and His church are worth serving and strengthening has made an impact on the city that we serve and now with an even wider arena of influence through his work at the Pillar Network. The Lord has used Phil's hopefulness time and again to encourage me in difficult seasons of ministry and his example is one I want to emulate now and, in the years ahead.

In my experience one key ingredient of Phil's contagious hope is a Christ honoring humility that is eager to serve without craving the spotlight. A few years ago, I asked if he would be interested in starting a podcast to encourage pastors: take one issue and discuss it for 10–15 minutes with the aim of serving less experienced pastors. The podcast, Pastors & Pastoring, was relatively short-lived and lasted for about a year, but it made an impact and had a significant following. Behind the scenes it was just Phil and a microphone, carving out time to address issues in pastoral ministry and send them out in the hope of strengthening the church. It was something that succeeded almost despite our efforts, as someone close to him told me when he heard about the idea of a podcast: "he's the least self-promoting person I know." He was faithful and had a wealth of experience and wisdom to share, and he carried it out in a quiet and Christ-exalting way, never seeking the main stage or attention.

I know that my love for Jesus and ministry in the church are infused with more hope on account of Phil's example and his ministry over the years and I praise God for his tremendous impact for the sake of the gospel.

Jeremy Wright
Pastoral Care and Administrator
Restoration Fellowship
Memphis, TN

Publisher's Note

I am thankful for Phil and Karen Newton. They have invested their lives to help encourage the next generation of pastors and their wives. Phil has written numerous volumes and continues to publish biblically sound works that will be beneficial for Christ's bride. It has been a privilege to be able to work with the "Spurgeon of the South." May the Lord continue to bless his ministry!

Evan Knies
April 2025

www.ingramcontent.com/pod-product-compliance
Lightning Source LLC
Chambersburg PA
CBHW060743100426
42813CB00032B/3385/J